Passport
for a
Reformation

A history of the
Church of God reformation movement's
missionary endeavors outside North America

by
Lester A. Crose

Published by
Warner Press, Inc.
Anderson, Indiana
Arlo F. Newell, Editor in Chief

Copyright © 1981 by Warner Press, Inc.
ISBN: 0-87162-242-4
All Rights Reserved
Printed in the United States of America

This book is dedicated
with sincere love and high esteem
to all the missionaries who have so well
represented the Church of God
reformation movement

Contents

Foreword 7

Preface 9

Introduction 11

1. Pioneers in Mission 13

2. Toward a United Outreach 22

3. Moving Out between the Wars 49

4. Regaining Momentum 92

5. Churches Emerge from Missions 129

6. The Third World Church in Developing Nations . . .190

7. Partnership in World Missions 241

Appendix A 258

Appendix B 268

Foreword

This book was written in response to the need for an overall history of the worldwide missionary work of the Church of God reformation movement. Its publication date is announced during the 1980-81 year of centennial celebration now in progress in all of our churches in many countries around the world.

The purpose of this book is to present an authentic and well-documented account of the beginnings and development of our missionary outreach in area after area and country after country.

Through the years many small books and booklets have appeared giving brief accounts of the history and expansion of our missionary outreach in a number of areas of the world. Those publications, along with reports and extended articles in our church periodicals, have kept the church in America and abroad both informed and challenged.

The author, Dr. Lester A. Crose, gives us an up-to-date and authentic account covering a period of ninety years since our first missionary crossed the boundary into another country to share the message of salvation through Jesus Christ.

For that task, and task it was, he was well prepared, having served as missionary in several fields, and having been chosen to carry the heavy responsibility of executive secretary of the Missionary Board for twenty-one years. During those years in office he periodically visited all of our mission fields for consultation with both missionaries and church leaders on continuing outreach and development. On such visits he kept careful notes and obtained statistical information that have been a most valuable source for the preparation of this volume.

The church is indebted to this dedicated missionary and Board executive for the careful and painstaking research he did in preparing this latest piece of literature dealing with the history and development of the Church of God reformation movement. It will be a source of information for years to come.

Adam W. Miller
Dean Emeritus
Anderson School of Theology

Preface

The Missionary Board of the Church of God is the vehicle for thoughtful and concerned efforts in world mission on the part of Church of God Christians in the United States and Canada. This Board functions under the General Assembly of the Church and is founded and maintained under the assumption that all Christians are called to world mission and some are particularly gifted for special assignment in the mission task. Throughout the history of this Reformation Movement the focus has often been on those who have been called in particular, but the real responsibility for mission has rested on the total church.

It is significant that this book is being published during the centennial year of the Church of God in the seventy-second year of the Missionary Board. The organized work of missions has been important to the life of the movement, and even before the Missionary Board was formulated in 1909, missionary activity was already being undertaken. Ninety out of our one hundred years have witnessed active involvement in world missions.

Response to human need has always motivated Church of God people, but I am impressed that efforts to respond to that need through the Missionary Board have always been based on a biblically sound theology of mission and on the best in mission philosophy. As you will see as you read *Passport for a Reformation,* method and practice have not always reflected intent and knowledge.

In an effort to chronicle this tremendous story, the Missionary Board approached a forty-four-year veteran of both field and administrative experience. Dr. Lester A. Crose was asked to "share out of his knowledge and experience" the missionary story of the Reformation. We are all indebted to Lester for this remarkable effort.

I suppose one always reads a book about a subject in which one has had special interest to determine whether the author has been successful in noting one's own preconceived ideas on the subject. I fell victim to this temptation. What I found was encouraging to me as I know it will be to you. (1) Early in the Movement, missionary motivation, zeal, and response to human need were strikingly evident. (2) There has always been a keen openness to what is best for the church abroad as opposed to the structure of programs suited to what the church may desire in North America. (3) National people were sought and recruited from the beginning and they figured significantly in the development of many new works. (4) The Missionary Board, often through the leadership of the author of this book, has positioned itself in the vanguard of education for mission at home and structure for mission abroad. (5) The quality of missionary leadership and dedication has been superb.

If you are looking for missionary stories only, you may be disappointed. If you are hoping for a challenge, you will find it in the lives of hundreds of dedicated servants who carried the passports of several nations, but who also carried the passport for a Reformation.

Donald D. Johnson
Executive Secretary-Treasurer
Missionary Board of the Church of God

Introduction

The writing of this book has filled the need to present in narrative style a historical record of the cross-cultural missionary enterprise of the Church of God reformation movement. It is restricted to those missionary activities that have taken place outside the United States of America and Canada. To cover ninety years of effort on the part of scores of missionaries has required an arbitrary determination on my part as to what to include. Numerous outstanding events had to be omitted due to lack of space.

Therefore, I opted to write from my own perspective — that of a missionary kid, missionary, and mission administrator. In many respects the story represents the pilgrimage of my own relationship to the missionary movement of the Reformation Movement. I wish I could have written about the significant contribution of every missionary, but that could not be. I am leaving to others the opportunity to write in detail about what took place in each country where North American missionaries served.

Throughout the book I have used some vocabulary reflecting usage of words during certain periods of time. The word *saints* denoted believers who were saved from their sins and living a holy life. *The truth* meant that body of beliefs from the Word of God generally held by the Reformation Movement. *The Church of God reformation movement* or *the Reformation Movement* or *the Move-*

ment all indicate the group called out of denominationalism by Daniel Sidney Warner, beginning in 1881, which now has its general offices in Anderson, Indiana. In the first two chapters I used the word *native* in its correct and highest meaning. Subsequently, *national* is employed due to the connotation later surrounding *native*. Instead of *United States of America* I have chosen to use the commonly accepted word *America*. There are other words that are strictly missionary lingo, but the context in which you discover them will no doubt reveal their meaning.

Thanks to the Missionary Board of the Church of God for granting me this opportunity to describe the development of concepts, methodologies, and approaches in world evangelization over the ninety years covered. The basic philosophy and theology of missions remained constant, as I have endeavored to show. Special thanks to Adam W. Miller and to Donald D. Johnson for taking time to read the manuscript, making valuable suggestions. I have appreciated the extra work generously given by Patti Reed and Rosetta Means, and especially Shirley Dickinson, who did the typing. A number of my students at Anderson School of Theology deserve mention, as they elected to do research for me instead of writing semester papers. And Ruthe, my understanding wife, deserves my sincere thanks for her patience during the time of preparation and writing. So many times the normal routine of our home life was interrupted.

I stand in debt for having been a part of the modern missionary movement. A small payment has been made, as I have enjoyed making this contribution, a part of the total volume of material prepared for the observance of the centennial of the Church of God reformation movement.

Chapter 1

Pioneers in Mission

(1880-1900)

IMMEDIATELY following its inception in 1881 the Church of God reformation movement rode on the wave of a *flying ministry*. Groups of itinerant evangelists crisscrossed the Midwest of America by horseback, buggy, and train. These pioneer evangelists stopped wherever opportunity made it possible, preaching, singing, and distributing literature. They called people out of the current confusion of denominationalism into the light of the New Testament church. They preached salvation from sin, calling people into the fellowship of the saints. Walking in the "evening light" (Zech. 14:7—one of the graces of the coming kingdom of Christ), they put forth every effort to spread the truth about holiness and unity.

These youthful, energetic, and dedicated evangels went where the Holy Spirit led them. They ventured forth with faith that God would support them and the cause they represented. When in one place a few believers were established they would move on. There was little, if any, organization. Pastoral leadership rarely emerged for groups of believers. A New Testament pattern in proclaiming the Good News was sought and followed. Being nonsectarian, these preachers of the gospel were against denominationalism, and they sought and practiced Christian unity. Going a step further, these men and women claimed belief in the universality of the Church, and that the entire world was the field to harvest.

By 1882 the *Gospel Trumpet,* edited by D. S. Warner, founder of the Movement, was being read in Canada. By 1888 Warner and his evangelistic company were in Ontario, Canada, for a series of meetings. Within a year a group in Welland, Ontario, had left denominationalism, and a pastor was ordained for the flock.

During the first decade of the Movement the emphasis was mainly on reformation in North America, but early in 1890 a call went out in the *Gospel Trumpet* to send literature even to overseas countries of the world. That call apparently created interest in "the old country"—Europe. In 1892 W. J. Henry and J. H. Rupert were working in England preaching the truth. Dr. G. R. Achor gave up his practice as a physician and sailed for England in 1893, taking with him over ten thousand tracts and books. A horse-drawn "gospel van" was built and used in evangelistic work throughout England, Ireland, Scotland, and Wales. Other evangelists such as J. W. Daugherty, W. W. Titley, and Lena Shoffner joined the group. In this same year one of the pioneers wrote, "A new epoch has come in this last reformation." The good news was to go to every nation. Actually, in 1894 D. S. Warner was making plans to go on a preaching tour around the world, but his health was failing. He died in December of 1895, and E. E. Byrum became the editor of the *Gospel Trumpet.*

Many of the saints in the North Central states were of German background and knew the German language. By 1895 a printing press in Milwaukee, Wisconsin, was publishing a semimonthly paper called the *Evangeliums Posaune* (German *Gospel Trumpet*). In 1894 J. H. Rupert had gone to Germany from England and was locating many persons who were friends and relatives of saints in America. J. H. Rupert and his wife worked in Hamburg, and soon other leaders such as George Vielguth and Karl Arbeiter were to go to Germany. Very quickly the Reformation Movement became established in Germany.

The work in Scandanavia had its beginning in 1895 through the efforts of the saints in America who had originally come from that part of Europe. Now they wanted to return to carry the good news of the gospel—the truth. Thomas Nelson and O. T. Ring were among the first to go, followed by S. O. Susag to Norway, Nels Renbeck to Denmark, and C. J. Forsberg to Sweden. This expansion, as well as that in the British Isles, developed less rapidly than that which was started in Germany during the last decade of the nineteenth century. Furthermore, all these efforts in Europe were primarily extended evangelism out of America, a part of the *flying ministry* of the first decade of the Reformation. Those efforts fell short of what is generally considered today as cross-cultural missionary endeavor.

Missionary Work Defined

First, who is a missionary? In simplest terms, a missionary is a person called by God and sent by God's Church to proclaim the gospel to people of another culture. A missionary is one who assists those who have accepted Jesus Christ in other nations to fellowship one another in congregations. To complete the cycle, those new congregations of believers will send out missionaries into other nations. This follows the example of the Apostle Paul in the early church.

Is every Christian a missionary? Yes and no. If we embrace the concept of the *lay apostolate*, we must accept the idea that every Christian should be a *flaming evangel*, a person who is sent to minister to those in need. But where the gifts of the Spirit are revealed in the New Testament, apostleship is one of those gifts. The words *apostle* and *missionary* have the same meaning, the first being

15

of Greek derivation and the other of Latin derivation. So even though every Christian should be on some form of mission, there is a sense in which certain persons, as God wills, receive the spiritual gift to be cross-cultural missionaries. This means that missionaries are those who introduce the Good News to persons having behavioral patterns and traditional ways of life different from their own.

And so, from this point on, this book is about the acts of Church of God apostles, or missionaries. In the beginning of the Reformation Movement our pioneers apparently and understandably did not comprehend totally what missionary work really was. They simply followed the Lord as they felt impressed to serve him. But that indeed led quickly into cross-cultural experiences, as we shall now see.

Into Mexico

Even though as early as 1891 J. W. Byers, one of our earliest pioneers in California, began to study the Chinese language to work among Chinese in California, his real interest centered in learning Spanish in order to do work among the Mexicans during the grape harvest at Boston Rancho. During that same year, the Spirit impressed B. F. Elliot while he was preaching on a street in Santa Barbara, California, to carry the Good News to the Spanish-speaking people. He decided to obey God, just as Paul did, and "go unto the Gentiles." Someone loaned Elliot a Spanish grammar book and a Spanish New Testament. With these he learned the Spanish language and was ready to go into Baja California, Mexico. In San Diego, where Elliot was to take the boat for Ensenada, D. S. Warner pressed two dollars into his hand. It was exactly the amount needed to make up the boat fare. With B. F. Elliot on his first trip was S. C. Shaw and Elliot's five-year-old son.

In Ensenada, the three rented an upstairs room for a dollar a week. The law prohibited street preaching, but Elliot and Shaw did door-to-door evangelism, talking with and praying for the people. Then they pushed southward. A good-natured Swiss man loaned them a donkey, which was a desirable means of transportation in those days. The donkey was loaded down with equipment and food, but there was room for the boy to ride and also for a good supply of Testaments and Gospels. This was indeed the first cross-cultural missionary endeavor of the Reformation Movement, and it was into an area occupied by people then known as Indians and Spaniards. God blessed Elliot with a degree of success. He developed a permanent mission in Ensenada and did evangelistic work as far south as La Paz and across the Gulf of California to Mazatlán and on into the interior. During the following eight years Elliot made at least four trips into Mexico. He recounts his ventures of faith in a book published in La Paz in 1906 entitled *Experiences in the Gospel Work in Lower California, Mexico.* By 1897 Elliot wanted to start a Spanish *Gospel Trumpet,* but E. E. Byrum discouraged him, saying there were too many problems to begin such a venture.

Confluent Forces in India

A young Indian man by the name of A. D. (Alla-ud-Din) Khan in East Bengal Province of India was reared a strict Muslim, but early in life he came under the influence of some Australian Baptist missionaries. In December 1893, while still in secondary school, he was converted to the Christian faith, and six months afterward he was baptized. That brought on several months of severe persecution by Khan's family and friends. First they appealed to his feelings. Then some resorted to sorcery and witchcraft. Finally his food was poisoned, but he survived, maintained his faith, and was finally given his liberty by the family.

In 1895, when A. D. Khan was seventeen years of age,

he began studies in the London Mission College of Calcutta in the big city. He observed churches of many denominations, and he was uncertain which one to attend. On his own he began a serious study of the New Testament. Following are some of his conclusions:

(1) God has but one church.
(2) God's church is named by God.
(3) Christ is the head of the church.
(4) The Holy Ghost is the administrator of the church.
(5) God organizes the church and appoints ministers.
(6) There must be unity in the church in all matters of doctrine and practice pertaining unto life and godliness.
(7) There are no sinners in the church of God.
(8) A hireling ministry and program worship is foreign to the church of God.
(9) The love of God is the only tie that binds believers together.
(10) The Word of God is the only guide in all matters, doctrinal and spiritual.

About this time A. D. Khan read an advertisement by a man in Texas promising religious literature samples. The requested dime was sent and several religious papers received. Among them was the *Gospel Trumpet,* which immediately caught his attention. He agreed with the articles on sanctification, holiness, unity, and divine healing; so he wrote for several books and other literature. This began regular correspondence with E. E. Byrum. Clearer light on the truth flooded his soul. By 1896 Khan committed himself to the truths of the Church of God reformation movement, and he started Saturday night meetings in a Calcutta shop. He also began publishing in both English and Bengali a paper called the *Fire Brand, an anti-sectarian holiness monthly journal.*

Several young men, three of whom were destined to become leaders in the Church of God in India, joined A. D. Khan in his efforts. R. N. Mundul, a convert from Hinduism, was one of these. Khan married one of his daughters, and two other daughters, Sonat and Nalini, spent their entire lives as leaders at the Shelter in Cuttack, a home for unprotected minor girls that was started within a year or two. Mosir Moses, a convert from Islam, was to become the main leader in Calcutta for the duration of his life. And J.J.M. Roy from the state of Assam, also studying in a college in Calcutta, felt the call to full-time service before returning to his home in Shillong where he devoted the rest of his life to the ministry.

Early in 1897 the Gospel Trumpet Company sent a half-ton shipment of books and tracts plus two small hand-operated presses to A. D. Khan. But something even more dramatic was happening which aroused the compassion of the saints in America. What became known as the Great Famine struck India, with more than twenty thousand deaths daily. An appeal was made through the *Gospel Trumpet,* and twenty-one hundred dollars was raised immediately. Gorham Tufts, Jr. of the Open Door Mission in Chicago was chosen to take the gift to India. He contacted Robert and Laura Jarvis, who had established the Faith Orphanage in Lahore. They had approximately two hundred children whose parents had died as a result of the famine. The Jarvises began reading the *Gospel Trumpet* and rejoiced in it. Within two years A. D. Khan had made contact with them and established relationships.

Gorham Tufts remained in India a little over a month. On his return to America he stopped in Port Said, Egypt, to distribute literature. Port Said was the largest coaling station in the world, and ships from all over the world took on fuel at this port at the north end of the Suez Canal.

By 1898 A. D. Khan completed his work at the college in Calcutta and devoted his whole time to the Lord's work. He had read about missionary homes in America and had started one in Calcutta known as the Church of God Missionary Home, an Apostolic Bible Institute and Publishing House. Khan made an evangelistic tour into the southern state of Kerala. This was really the beginning of the work of the Church of God in South India. He also made a tour into the state of East Bengal where his original home was located, but his efforts in the town of Bogra were not too successful.

Early in 1899 Mosir Moses made an attempt to enter Tibet, reaching only the boundary. He remained in a border town for one year, trying again and again to gain permission to enter Tibet, but failing. He studied the Tibetan language, distributed Gospels, and witnessed to many Tibetans on the Indian side of the border. This illustrates the missionary zeal of a young church. It should be noted here that the work of the Church of God in India was started by Indians and not by American missionaries.

By this time the brethren in India were requesting missionaries from America, and you will read about that in subsequent chapters. Two events gave motivation to our missionary outreach in India: A. D. Khan's experiences, including contacts with E. E. Byrum, and relief work among the starving people of India. The church in America responded with love and service. This became the second missionary outreach by the Church of God in America.

A Way Is Being Prepared

An interesting story surrounds the life of a young man named William J. Hunnex, a Britisher who lived in London in the year 1880. He attended a missionary rally in Albert Hall where he heard a young woman speak who had been serving in China as a missionary with the China Inland Mission. They fell in love, were married, and both went out to China with this same Board, which had been founded by James Hudson Taylor in 1866. They had two sons, William A. and Charles E., who grew up in China. In 1900 the Boxer Rebellion broke out against all foreigners. Many hundreds of missionaries were killed, but the Hunnexes were spared. In the next chapter you will learn what happened to these two sons, who were by that time young men.

A second development was taking place in East Africa. During the last decade of the nineteenth century the British felt forced to annex certain areas. The slave trade of Africans being sold needed to be stopped. There was rivalry with the French for control of the Indian Ocean. Egypt was expanding deeper into Africa. Consequently, Britain invaded Egypt in 1882 to protect its vested interests in the recently completed Suez Canal. German expansionism had absorbed Tanganyika, now known as Tanzania. Missionaries and explorers entered Kenya, with missionary Krapf being among the first. Then those like David Livingston fired British interests. In 1895 Kenya became a British East Africa Protectorate, and in 1900 Kenya was formally annexed by Great Britain. To further aid in the development of the interior of Kenya, work began in 1896 on the Mombasa-Kisumu railroad. It required five years to complete. Gradually Britain gained full control, using force when necessary. Tribal authority came to an end. Taxes were levied, and white settlers, or farmers, moved into the highlands of Kenya. Missionaries also pressed into the interior. The stage was set for the beginning of what is now the Church of God in Kenya.

We are ready to see how multiple spontaneous and independent missionary efforts on the part of Church of God persons brought about the formation of the Missionary Board of the Church of God. We enter two decades of emerging interest and involvement in world missions.

Chapter 2

Toward a United Outreach
(1900-1918)

WITH THE TURN of the century there materialized very
rapidly within the movement a diversity of independent
expressions of concern for those who had never heard
about salvation through Jesus Christ. An explosion of
Spirit-led events challenged individuals to dedicate themselves to go into foreign countries where Christ was almost
unknown and to endure the hardships and uncertainties of
living in unfamiliar cultures. Most of the time they struggled by faith with inadequate finances. In many countries
fatal diseases were prevalent. It required tremendous
courage, especially for families, to answer the call to missionary service.

Expansion and growth of the work continued during the
first decade of the new century in spite of a lack of coordination. From the beginning the movement frowned on
organization. In fact, there was teaching against organizing
the work of the church, for it was believed that humanly
inspired direction would hamper the leading of the Holy
Spirit. Therefore, those who felt called to go, went on their
way with zealous commitment but with no official sanction
or recognition by the church. They were inspired to reach

"all the inhabited countries of the world." What a challenge for such a small group of people! To take the gospel into all the world was a command they well recognized from the Word of God. Therefore, these early missionaries were constrained to convert those of the non-Christian world. They proclaimed the good news that Jesus Christ is the Savior from sin and that through repentance and belief in Christ anyone from any nation could enter the kingdom of God. This was done primarily through evangelistic preaching. Literature was used extensively. Copies of the *Gospel Trumpet,* books, and tracts were distributed on trains and ships, along roads, in the cities, and at the doors of homes. By 1906 over thirty thousand dollars worth of literature had been sent into other countries of the world by the Gospel Trumpet Company.

It should be noted, however, that early in this Reformation's world outreach, forms of ministry other than evangelism quickly developed. The evangelistic approach always remained paramount, however, even to the present day. But sometimes famine occurred where the missionary resided. Orphans were left homeless. Or thousands of refugees came flooding in. This required relief work on the part of the missionary. Compassion was expressed in yet other ways. Where there was mass illiteracy, even among children, education in one form or another appeared necessary. Where disease and unsanitary conditions prevailed, some form of medical assistance was required. Strong campaigns were launched against prostitution. At times agricultural and vocational projects were initiated. All these forms of service were employed at one time or another to meet the needs of persons in countries where our early missionaries went. As a result groups of converts to Christ began to appear in the islands of the West Indies, in Central America, in several countries of Europe, in Egypt and Syria (now known as Lebanon), in Kenya (later to be with the Church of God), in India, Japan, China, and Australia. Thus the Church of God reformation movement began around the world.

Those were the days when a passport could be secured for a fee of only one dollar. It was simply a large certificate from the secretary of state, folded neatly to pocketsize, giving a description of the bearer to aid in identification and requesting proper recognition and protection if necessary for the person or persons identified therein. A picture was also affixed. As a boy my first appearance on a United States passport was on one of those certificates.

As early as 1897 when Gorham Tufts was sent to India with relief funds some organization took place, though probably not recognized as such. *The Gospel Trumpet* requested that money be sent to the editor for distribution. In 1905 a "Home and Foreign Missions Fund" was established under the care of the editor of the *Gospel Trumpet*. The editor, E. E. Byrum, decided when, where, and how funds were to be sent or used in the cause of missions. Also a "Missionary Box Fund" was created to assist in raising funds for the support of missionaries. This was to subsidize a missionary's income beyond what she or he had received directly from the saints. In reality, these simple forms of organization were very successful.

The first decade of this century was characterized by a type of unorganized, spasmodic, free-lance missionary service. Some attempts were more successful than others. This is not to suggest that God was not at work through all of them, because sincere men and women of God did the best they could under varying circumstances. Some individuals who went were more able and gifted than others. Furthermore, during this decade these highly dedicated persons went forth with practically no briefing and no recourse to knowledgeable persons when they were faced with problems and difficulties on the field.

To the Islands of the West Indies

Several early attempts were made to evangelize the islands. Unfortunately, little follow-up materialized; so in most places it was several years later when the work actually began. In 1901 James S. McCreary went to **Cuba.** In Havana he did evangelistic work among the soldiers and natives who knew English. Also in 1901 evangelism was carried on in **St. Kitts** by Fred. A. Dunnell. Outdoor meetings were conducted by J. E. and Martha Wilson in 1909 on the **Bahama Islands.** And in 1905 Edward B. Grant felt called of God to go to **Bermuda** to start the work there.

It was in **Jamaica** where the movement's pioneer missionary efforts were very successful from the beginning. In January of 1907 a great earthquake practically destroyed the city of Kingston, the capital of Jamaica, taking over one thousand lives. In April a letter from Isaac DeLevante appeared in the *Gospel Trumpet* telling of the earthquake in Jamaica and appealing for missionaries to come. DeLevante was a Jamaican Christian who had read the *Gospel Trumpet* and felt constrained to write to the Church of God in Anderson for assistance. Earlier in 1906 George H. Pye had stopped in Kingston on his way to Trinidad and had written back home that he had discovered a group of people in that city who were willing to accept the pure gospel. In Anderson a young couple, George and Nellie Olson, who were workers in the Gospel Trumpet Home, were feeling directed into missionary work. When this call came from Jamaica they were convinced, after much prayer, that they should accept and began immediately to make preparation to go to Jamaica where the needs were so great. That call was confirmed in June during the first camp meeting held in Anderson when a young Jamaican, A. S. McNeil, who had come under the influence of H.M. Riggle in Pennsylvania and was also attending the camp meeting, urged the Olsons to go.

E. E. Byrum gave the Olsons $150 from the Missionary Fund, and many of the saints attending the camp meeting pressed money into their hands and pockets. When they landed at Port Antonio on the north shore of Jamaica they had only $87.25. They changed boats and the next morning landed at Kingston where they found the city still in ruins. George Olson went in search of Isaac DeLevante while Nellie waited in a park with their baby boy. The first meeting was held in the open air the following day, and a woman was converted. Almost no funds came from America, but in a way that was good, for it placed the financial responsibility for the work on the shoulders of the Jamaican converts from the very beginning. The work grew so rapidly that the first Assembly was held the following year. In that same year expansion into the country areas was started. Those were difficult days, however. The Olsons lived by faith, and God supplied their needs.

Early in 1906 George Pye and his wife felt called of God to sail for **Trinidad.** They rented a hall in Port of Spain and conducted evangelistic meetings. N.S. Duncan arrived that same year but remained only a short time. The work seemed to grow rapidly, but financial difficulties plagued the missionaries. By 1908 there was mention of a Trinidadian named Edward Cumberbatch, who was the first native minister of the Church of God on that island. I had the privilege of working with Cumberbatch in Trinidad and Tobago while serving as a missionary there during World War II. His son Carlton has been president of the West Indies Bible Institute (now West Indies Theological College) for many years.

C. E. Orr was in Trinidad for a brief evangelistic tour. But there was apparently no understanding about establishing congregations, thereby maintaining continuity. This was in contrast to the beginning of the work in Jamaica. Within two years George Pye returned to America. This form of independent and short-term missionary service was not establishing a strong national church, and it required many years to rectify this error in missionary strategy.

On his way home from Trinidad, N.S. Duncan stopped in Barbados and reported opportunities there, but nothing was done on that island for several years.

Happenings in Europe

A continuation of independent activities persisted. William and Anna Cheatham in 1907 were working in **England** to secure five hundred subscriptions to the *Gospel Trumpet*. They were using a "tabernacle tent" in rural areas. That same year, the Cheathams and the Titleys went to Belfast, **Ireland,** where they conducted open-air meetings and rented a hall. By the following year there was a small congregation in Belfast and the Cheathams were holding meetings in the "tabernacle tent" shipped from England. In 1904 a Brother Springer went to **Switzerland** and distributed literature. The following year George Vielguth made his first visit to Switzerland and in 1907 began holding regular meetings. By 1908 there were a few scattered saints being visited by Karl Arbeiter and George Vielguth. This appeared to be an extension of the work out of Germany. The year 1907 marks the beginning of the work in Budapest, **Hungary**, with contacts being made from Germany. As early as 1902 German workers established a work in **Russia,** with Ferdinand Schwieger going there in 1907. And in 1909 Rudolph Malzon and the Doeberts experienced considerable success in evangelizing German villages in eastern Poland, the Ukraine, and the Caucasus—all parts of Russia. Finally, in 1909 Adam and Mary Allan, both natives of Scotland, and their daughter Naomi left Portland, Oregon, and sailed for **Scotland** where they started a work in Aberdeen mostly through the distribution of literature. Naomi Allan still lives in Belfast, North Ireland.

The most flourishing work of the Church of God in Europe was emerging in **Germany.** At the turn of the century George Vielguth (from a German family in the Church of God in America) sailed for Hamburg and began a congregation. He went on to Essen. Through a second trip two years later the congregation in Essen was established. Karl Arbeiter also came to Germany the next year. Vielguth made his third trip to Germany in 1906, taking the

27

Doeberts with him. It was at this time that the first conference of the Church of God in Germany was conducted. The Reformation Movement was spreading in Germany, with the center being established in Essen. A weekly publication of a German *Gospel Trumpet* was started. A missionary home was built in Essen, with Otto Doebert and his wife as managers. It was said that gospel literature was being distributed throughout Russia! In the second Assembly held in 1909 there were saints from Russia, Poland, and all parts of Germany. It should be noted that, in order to encourage the work in Germany, E. A. Reardon visited the saints there on his way home from his one-year stay in Egypt.

Two Important Visits from India

Major focus again centered on **India.** At the turn of the century another famine brought suffering and death to thousands. Again the saints in America responded and Gorham Tufts sailed the second time to India with seventeen hundred dollars. Not only were people starving to death, but the plague was killing more. Tufts also carried a large amount of literature with him, valued at more than one thousand dollars. It was on this trip that Gorham Tufts met A. D. Khan. Both of them were vitally interested in the support of the Faith Orphanage in Lahore operated by the Jarvises. In fact, Brother and Sister Jarvis had now taken their stand with the Church of God reformation movement, and they felt the need for more missionaries to assist them in caring for the orphans.

By this time J.J.M. Roy had completed a graduate degree in Calcutta and returned to his home situated in the Khasi Hills in the state of Assam, northeast India. His call from God was to spread the Good News among the tribal people of that mountainous area. He began to write E.E. Byrum requesting that missionaries be sent to assist in that large undertaking. By 1901 the Jarvises needed a furlough, and so they spent a number of months in America visiting over one hundred congregations and traveling some thirty thousand miles. Returning to India after having generated considerable interest in the work of the orphanage, they took with them Andrew Shiffler from Denver, Colorado, and Mrs. Jarvis's sister Marie. All four missionaries devoted themselves steadfastly to caring for and training the orphans.

Progress was being made in Calcutta. The name of the paper published by A. D. Khan was changed from *Fire Brand* to *Victory*. Brothers Moses, Biswas, and Holdar were reaching out to Bogra, East Bengal state. A. D. Khan was visiting the work at the orphanage in Lahore. The first camp meeting of the Church of God was held in Calcutta. There was, however, one setback. E. E. Byrum began receiving letters from the brethren in Calcutta saying they could no longer have any connection with Gorham Tufts. The break finally came as he became superintendent of the Apostolic Bible School in Calcutta.

E. E. Byrum felt impressed in 1903 to invite A. D. Khan to America to have wider contact with the church. A favorable response was received, and A. D. Khan arrived in the United States in time to attend the camp meeting in Moundsville, West Virginia. Khan observed that this visit "brought East and West in closer touch with one another." He traveled extensively throughout the churches creating great enthusiasm for the missionary cause. While in America he wrote a book entitled *India's Millions*, which influenced many of the saints to consider seriously some form of missionary service. This was really the first major promotion of missions in the Movement. What soon happened in India was the harvest of Khan's seed planting while in America.

For some months E. E. Byrum had been giving serious thought to making a world tour. An increasing number of people in the movement were feeling led to foreign fields as missionaries, and they were writing the editor of the

Gospel Trumpet for information and advice. Also, letters were coming in from other countries where the Movement's literature had been received and read. Many of these readers were seeking spiritual advice and more information about the Church of God; so E. E. Byrum felt it would be good if he were more familiar with the world situation. To assist further in his editorial work he wanted to observe a number of original manuscripts of the Bible so that he could see certain passages of Scripture that the "higher critics" were saying were not in the original manuscripts. And finally, Byrum wanted very much to visit India, going with A. D. Khan as Khan returned so that he could see what was developing in the Church of God there.

In January 1904 they sailed from New York. With them were the first missionaries of the Church of God going to India: George and Mary Bailey with their one-year-old boy, and Evalyn Nichols, all from the Northwest. They visited museums and libraries in Oxford, London, Paris, Venice, and Rome, and they observed the Muslim world in Tangiers, Morocco. In Port Said and Cairo, Egypt, the missionaries distributed literature. And they included in their trip a pilgrimage to the Holy Land. Their arrival in Calcutta was in time for the annual camp meeting. By then there were thirty saints in the missionary home in Calcutta, and the Movement was progressing. E. E. Byrum visited Shillong, Bogra, and Lahore. Robert Jarvis had started the Faith Missionary Home in Lahore, as well as having carried on the orphanage. There is a note that says twenty dollars per year per child was required to keep orphans. Evalyn Nichols took an interest in the work in Assam and began immediately to learn the Khasi language. Upon completion of his visit in India, E. E. Byrum returned home by way of Japan and China. Later that year the Church of God Association of India was formed as a legal entity. Also, two more missionaries arrived from America: Josephine McCrie for Calcutta and Edith Ashenfelter for Lahore.

The following year George and Mary Bailey felt the climate of India too severe for the family; so they returned to the United States, saying they would encourage younger persons to volunteer for missionary service. A. D. Khan's wife died from cholera. Amos Abernathy arrived in Lahore from America to be in charge of gardening at the orphanage. It was not long until he was married to Edith Ashenfelter. A major move took place that had a significant effect on the work for many years. A. D. Khan felt impressed to move to Cuttack, the capital of the state of Orissa, several hundred miles south of Calcutta. The Calcutta Missionary Home and the publishing work found a new home, and this became the main center for the Movement in India. Revival broke out among the people and a great spiritual awakening took place. Persecution was experienced. The first annual camp meeting was held, bringing people from many parts of India. Josephine McCrie moved to Cuttack from Calcutta. In the north, Brother Roy started a paper in the Khasi language called *Ka Jingshai Ka Gospel,* meaning "The Light of the Gospel." The group of saints in Calcutta continued meeting in homes under the leadership of Mosir Moses.

During the next few months tragedy struck. In Lahore the orphanage was destroyed by fire. Maria Jarvis died from a severe fever. In the Khasi Hills Victor and Florence Maiden and their four children, along with Ira Zaugg, arrived to establish the Industrial Missionary Home about ten miles outside of Shillong. Soon afterward James Strawn joined the industrial project. The concept of an industrial farm was believed necessary to give employment to new converts who were being persecuted. But this location proved to be fatal to the project, for malignant malaria was prevalent. After only six months in Shillong death came to Jesse Earl and Laura Grace, the two oldest Maiden children. In three days, three-year-old James Ray died. Within the next three weeks Florence, Victor's wife, died, and after five days Glenn, the five-year-old, succumbed. James Strawn, who had arrived only three months before, also died. All these deaths were from what was commonly called "black water fever," or malignant malaria. What a blow this was to the group of believers in the Khasi Hills. Still today their tombstones are easily seen in a cemetery just outside Shillong. I have been there several times and have felt the sacredness of the spot where faithful missionaries are buried.

Grief-stricken, Victor Maiden gave up the Industrial Missionary Home and went to Lahore to assist at the orphanage. But a year later he, too, died from malaria. Two bright spots during this time were the marriage of A. D. Khan to Naline lata Patia of Cuttack and the securing of a missionary home in Lahore. Thaddeus Neff and Alice Hale arrived from America to assist at the orphanage in Lahore and to do evangelistic work. Lottie Theobold came to Cuttack. Laura Jarvis died after seventeen years in India, and after two years Robert Jarvis married Lottie Theobold, who had come from Cuttack to Lahore to help in the work among the orphans. Andrew Shiffler left Lahore for Darjeeling, an important town in the foothills of the Himalaya Mountains, where he opened a colporteur supply depot to provide literature, including Bibles, for distribution among the tribal people of that area.

In 1908 the second important visit of A. D. Khan to the United States began. George P. Tasker and Hiram A. Brooks were chosen in America as a delegation to foreign lands in the interest of missions. On their way to India they stopped in Egypt for a few days, and we shall see later the result of that visit. Tasker, Brooks, and Khan visited the saints in Shillong, Lahore, Calcutta, Cuttack, and in the newly opened field in Cannanore, South India, where J. N. Spadigam was in charge. Illness prevented Tasker and Brooks from going on to Japan and China. Instead they decided to return to America by way of Egypt, and A. D. Khan went with them. On this second trip Khan was absent from India for almost two years. He traveled throughout America speaking to large crowds at camp meetings. He made a trip with E. E. Byrum to the British

West Indies and Central America, meeting early missionaries there. As during the first visit, A. D. Khan generated significant interest in taking the gospel to all peoples of the world. And he played an important role in the formation of the Missionary Board when it was organized in 1909.

For the First Time in the Near East

When E. E. Byrum and company were on their way to India in 1904 they stopped for several days in **Egypt,** visiting both Alexandria and Cairo. They went on the streets distributing literature but had no particular results. But through reading his Bible, an Armenian medical doctor named G. K. Ouzounian, in Alexandria, received the light the following year calling him out of Babylon (denominations) into the unity of the people of God. Two years later, at the invitation of Hanna Arsanious, an Egyptian Christian who had read some Church of God literature and had written to America for someone to come to Egypt to help, George P. Tasker and Hiram A. Brooks stopped in Egypt for an extended visit on their way to India. This was a good opening. They were permitted to distribute literature and to conduct evangelistic services. Meetings were conducted primarily in Alexandria and Assiut in Upper Egypt. There appeared to be real potential, but both the visitors, and the few Egyptians felt the need for a missionary to come immediately. E. A. Reardon left the missionary home in Chicago at once and arrived in Egypt before Tasker and Brooks went on to India. Reardon remained in Egypt for only seven months, living in Assiut, but he helped build a foundation for the work in Assiut under the leadership of Mossad Armanious and in Alexandria under G. K. Ouzounian. The seed had been planted and was beginning to bear fruit, but after Reardon returned to America no resident missionaries of the Church of God were sent to Egypt until 1923, even though a request for missionaries from the saints in Egypt was frequent. Contacts were maintained through correspondence and occasional visits by missionaries passing through Egypt.

A kind of historical accident occurred one day in 1907 on a street in downtown Cairo. Tasker, Brooks, and Reardon met Vartan Atchinak and his wife who, along with her sister Asma Trad, had started the Bible Lands Gospel Mission in Schweifat, a village on the Lebanese hillside just out of Beirut. The Atchinaks were on their way to America to find teachers for the school. They would prefer Church of God teachers. Even though the response was not immediate, Church of God missionary teachers did arrive later in Syria.

Into Japan and China

Crossing the bay between San Francisco and Oakland on a train ferry, A. U. Yajima, a young Japanese Presbyterian minister from Hawaii, picked up and read a copy of the *Gospel Trumpet*. His heart was touched with the truth contained therein. Later, in response to a letter he wrote to E. E. Byrum, Yajima was told to contact J. D. Hatch in Los Angeles. Hatch took Yajima to the Lodi Camp Meeting in central California, which was the main camp meeting in California at the time. During that meeting Yajima was impressed to seek conversion, which he had never experienced, and to ask for more light on the truth of God's Word. My father, John D. Crose, then a young minister, gathered along with others around A. U. Yajima as he knelt at the altar.

After working briefly in the Gospel Trumpet office in Moundsville, West Virginia, Yajima felt called of God to return to his homeland, **Japan,** and take the Good News to his own people. Arriving in Tokyo in 1908, he started a work of the Church of God by doing personal visitation, conducting meetings, and having a paper printed called *Pure Gospel*. He felt the need for assistance, and so he wrote to America for missionaries. The response was almost immediate. J. D. Hatch and W. G. and Josie Alexander, along with their daughter Grace, sailed for Japan in 1909. The Alexanders had been impressed by Yajima at the Lodi Camp Meeting and had felt the call to Japan at that time.

In chapter 1 mention was made that William J. Hunnex, his wife, and their two sons survived the Boxer Rebellion in China. During 1904 the parents sent William and Charles to America for higher education. Soon after their arrival both came into contact with the movement, but in different places. By 1905 both young men were at Moundsville working in the Gospel Trumpet office, and they generated considerable enthusiasm regarding missionary work in China. Both of them wanted to be missionaries to China. Having grown up there, they knew the language and the culture. William A. Hunnex married Gloria Hale, sister-in-law of Mabel Hale, from Kansas, and they sailed for **China** in 1909 to begin a work in Chinkiang. Charles waited another year before he was ready to go.

A Second National Agency Is Born

The need for some form of organization to bring together and coordinate the missionary outreach of the Church of God reformation movement became evident by 1909. Twenty years of voluntary and independent expressions of missionary endeavor were now culminating in the formation of a Missionary Board. During the next fifty years the church looked to the Board to lead in giving expression and direction to the church's missionary interests.

The Missionary Board became the second Church of God agency to organize on a national level. Harold Phillips writes in his book *Miracle of Survival,* ''The Gospel Trumpet Company was the first organized institution of the Church of God movement—the first such organization to be incorporated, and thus the first to be governed by legally registered bylaws.'' That was in 1904.

Good as these early missionaries were who went out on their own under God, problems began to arise and multiply. This gave the church at home a growing concern for the well-being and future of its missionary expansion into new fields and the growth of work already existing. Many of these pioneer missionaries felt responsible to no one but to God. Therefore, each one did what he or she felt should be done, seeking always the guidance of the Holy Spirit. But strained situations began to develop where there were more than one or two missionaries. Living in a new culture, many were unable to cope with new and strange situations arising. This caused differences among missionaries and sometimes between missionaries and native workers. No one was available to give advice. A few began to write home to E. E. Byrum, but he was already overloaded with correspondence and therefore was unable to devote the time and energy necessary to care for these important matters.

Financial support also was creating some misunderstandings. Missionaries went to the field on faith—faith that God would supply their needs. But some could tell the story of their work better than others, by letter or when they were home on furlough and, therefore, they got more support. Churches became aware of these developing inequities, and pastors were asking questions and suggesting there might be a better way. Also, new missionaries going out on their own were most of the time ill-equipped, not knowing how to care for themselves, how to live in another country so different from their own, or how to learn a language. Consequently, the inevitable happened.

Following is a quotation from George P. Tasker's diary dated June 12, 1909:

On June 12, 1909, after an address on Government in the Church, H. M. Riggle, after presenting our plans for a missionary paper, to be called the Missionary Herald, recommended that, "certain brethren should be recognized amongst us, by common consent, as having and exercising in behalf of the Church, the responsibility and care of the foreign missionary work. They should be capable of advising, instructing, encouraging and restraining." The names here presented, and that were acknowledged by the immediate rising to their feet of the entire assembly of ministers, were D. O. Teasley, J. W. Byers, E. E. Byrum, E. A. Reardon, G. P. Tasker, H. A. Brooks and D. F. Oden. Brother Riggle then said, "it is intended that the entire ministry should cooperate with these brethren," to which all said, "Amen."

This was a bold step forward for a church that did not believe in organization. It was to provide purpose, meaning, and coordination to former independency. It was to make possible more systematic giving so that missionaries would receive more equitable remuneration for their services. It should be noted that all these brethren had been abroad except one. It was assumed that their observations and experiences would enable them to know better how to look after missionary funds and personnel.

The official minutes record, "The first formal meeting of the Missionary Board of the Church of God, chosen and appointed by common consent of the ministers present at the annual camp meeting held at Anderson, Indiana, June 1909, was held in Room E34 of the Gospel Trumpet Home, June 8, 1910." Decisions of great importance were made. Bylaws were adopted to govern the society. Following are the first officers elected who became the first board of directors: D. O. Teasley, chairman of the Board; E. E. Byrum, vice-chairman; and G. P. Tasker, secretary-treasurer. Teasley remained chairman until F. G. Smith was named president in 1912, and Tasker remained secretary-treasurer until he went to India the same year and was succeeded by J. W. Phelps. A letter was sent to the Gospel Trumpet Company describing the organization of the Missionary Board and giving authorization to turn over, on request, to the secretary-treasurer all funds collected for missionary work by the Gospel Trumpet Company. The letter also outlined the principle business of the seven men as follows: (1) to act as an advisory board in the matter of missionaries going to foreign fields; (2) to have charge of all collections and disbursements of missionary funds; and (3) to take a general interest in the dissemination of missionary information.

A "Home and Foreign Missionary Fund" was established. The treasurer was authorized to keep the funds of the Missionary Board with the Gospel Trumpet Company until further action was taken. Church people were already beginning to send in money on a regular basis to support missionaries. The idea of sending and supporting missionaries was in the process of being firmly established.

Three goals were set by the Board for itself:

1. More correspondence with the missionaries,
2. To develop a world-wide vision and to become acquainted with and interested in the world-wide field, and
3. To make a more systematic effort towards more systematic giving.

The Board also decided to encourage missionaries to "undertake only as much work as can be perpetuated by the means regularly supplied." Preparatory instructions were framed for "intending missionaries":

1. A thorough working knowledge of the Bible and its fundamental doctrines,
2. An acquaintance of history and principle doctrines of various non-Christian world religions,
3. An intelligent understanding with the evidences of Christianity and the origin of the Scriptures, and
4. A knowledge of religious geography and history of other countries, especially where he is to work, and the situation of Christianity in that country.

In that first annual meeting twenty-seven missionaries were recognized: British Isles—4, China—2, Japan—4, British West Indies—2, Germany—4, and India—11. There were actually only nineteen missionaries because eight of those listed were evangelists. The first missionaries appointed by the Board during that meeting were N. S. Duncan and his wife, who were to go to Barbados.

Duncan had been in Trinidad before. In order to have the necessary funds to go, he was selling his property in the United States. The Board also approved Charles E. Hunnex for service in China. The missionary family grew rapidly, and eight new missionaries were sent out during the next year. Within two years sixty-five regular missionaries were on the field: India — 20, British West Indies — 18, Denmark — 2, Germany — 6, Russia — 5, Ireland — 1, China — 5, Japan — 4, and Egypt — 4. Actually, seventeen of those listed were evangelists or pastors, not missionaries in the strictest sense. Six new missionary homes were built and properties purchased.

Certain policies were being formulated for the benefit of the work. It was thought caution should be exercised "in the immediate establishing of orphanages." There was reason for this because so many wanted to start orphanages and the Board considered such an objective not to be the prime purpose of missions. Encouragement was given to those preparing for missionary service to take correspondence courses being offered by the Church of God Missionary Home in New York City. An early attempt was made to regularize the disposition of funds raised by missionaries home on furlough. The Board had to deal with the necessity of making a 50 percent cut in missionary allowances when the bottom dropped out from under missionary income early on. And it was thought best that "the native church should support its own native ministers in a native style." To be sure only true missionaries were sent to the field, a motion was adopted that only "apostles" should be sent.

In 1912 the Missionary Board moved all missionary correspondence from the general files of the Gospel Trumpet Company to missionary files in the Board's office. By 1914 the Missionary Board was in need of holding property and carrying on legal business. Therefore, it became incorporated under the laws of the state of Indiana, adopting a new constitution to conform to those laws related to the incorporation of a not-for-profit organization. It was necessary to add four members, making a membership of eleven. From then on the Missionary Board could register in other countries as an alien corporation in order to hold properties and do business.

From the very beginning it was considered imperative to have a missionary publication. D. O. Teasley was selected as editor of the *Missionary Herald,* which was a paper for missionary activities only. It drew together and united all efforts. It kept the church informed. In the opinion of some it helped to develop for the Church of God a modern missionary movement. Unfortunately, it existed for only three years, and in 1913 the *Gospel Trumpet* made an announcement that it would devote one issue per month to missionary emphasis.

Missionary Board Has Positive Effects

Following the formation of the Missionary Board all signs pointed toward a more united outreach. Coordination, however, did not always come easily. Most missionaries gladly accepted the Missionary Board as a point of reference for helpful advice and positive direction. Churches at home appeared pleased with the decision of the ministers to appoint the Board and responded in such a manner as to prove they could do better together through the Missionary Board what would be impossible for them to accomplish individually.

This had an immediate effect on the mission field where growth and expansion took place, hindered only by the ominous clouds of World War I. Properties for churches were being purchased in **Jamaica,** and George Olson was making visits to the **Cayman Islands, Panama,** the **Canal Zone,** and the **San Blas Islands** to carry the truth there. After nine years of work in Jamaica George Olson reported in 1916 that there were twenty-six congregations, and the church properties were being held by local boards of trustees whose members must be confirmed by the

American board. L. Y. Janes was in Jamaica to help for a while and hoped to go into Spanish-speaking work in Central America. When E. E. Byrum and A. D. Khan made their stop in Jamaica in 1910, Khan offered his pocket watch as a gift to George Olson. Olson accepted it graciously. Shortly afterward Nellie Olson was permitted to buy a horse so that she or her husband could visit members of their congregation in Kingston. A gift of dried fruit, a kind of trial shipment that the Olsons greatly appreciated, was received from J. W. Byers. Later a committee was appointed by the Missionary Board with Jennie Byers responsible for the collection and distribution of missionary fruit (dried peaches, apples, apricots, and prunes). This project was promoted all over America. Unfortunately it died out during the war, primarily because the dried fruit would spoil before reaching the missionaries.

When N. S. Duncan and his family arrived in **Trinidad,** having been appointed by the Missionary Board to revive and establish the work, he did just that. E. N. Reedy and Archie Rather soon came, and then George Coplin and Frank Shaw, who went later to Barbados. Thaddeus and Katrina Neff followed and started a work in Princes Town among the East Indians. During World War I Neff had some difficulty in persuading authorities that he was not a German spy. Early ministers in Trinidad, working with the missionaries, established groups of saints in a number of towns on the island.

When George Coplin and J. Frank Shaw sailed to **Barbados** from Trinidad they found four persons professing to be saints, and so a congregation was started at Mile and a Quarter. Coplin built the large church building in Bridgetown, and for a while he had the oversight of the work in both Barbados and Trinidad. Shaw purchased The Grange, a missionary residence in Bridgetown that had been the home of a former postmaster general. My wife and I lived in it during World War II, and that is where our son John was born. Shaw helped build many of the small country churches. L. W. and Opal Brookover arrived during this period of time, remaining for many years. In 1915 Coplin and Shaw visited **British Guiana,** now known as Guyana, and became acquainted with George L. Jeffrey. After embracing the truth, Jeffrey and his one congregation came with the Church of God. In **Panama** and the **Canal Zone** the efforts of George Olson were effective in establishing small congregations among West Indians who had come from Trinidad and Jamaica to work on the digging of the Panama Canal. Further north in **Mexico** Dave and Mae Patterson were assisting B. F. Elliot.

In **Germany** the saints were continuing to raise money to support their missionaries as they went to German colonies in Russia. A new group was started in Budapest, **Hungary.** William Hopwood became pastor of the congregation in Birkenhead, **England,** where he remained until his death in 1936. The work in **Switzerland** centered in Zurich, with Gottfried Zuber as leader. Adam Allan moved from Scotland to **Ireland** where he remained until his death years later. But the chief progress in Europe during this period was in **Denmark.** A great revival broke out in 1912 and 1913. Converts were found in several towns and cities. Evangelists came and went. Congregations were established, and by 1915 there were thirteen. During those early years, the congregations felt considerable opposition from the state church. The big question always asked was, "Have you seen the church?" And that's how the Church of God saints greeted each other.

During its annual meeting in 1912 the Missionary Board had conversation with Vartan Atchinak and Asma Trad from **Syria,** now known as **Lebanon,** about the possibility of sending a missionary teacher to their school in Schweifat. That summer Bessie Hittle (later Russell Byrum's wife), Minnie Tasker (George's wife), and Josephine McCrie arrived in Beirut and went on to Schweifat, a village just outside Beirut. Later that year F. G. Smith and his wife, with Nellie Laughlin, a public school teacher from Vermont, and George Tasker arrived.

George and Minnie Tasker and Josephine McCrie went on to India, leaving Bessie Hittle, Nellie Laughlin, and the Smiths in Syria. House meetings were conducted. Bessie and Nellie gave less time to the school and more time to evangelism. Converts, especially among young women, came from among the better families of the village. Feeling the need for a manual to teach new converts the truths of the Bible, F. G. Smith wrote *What the Bible Teaches*, and as he wrote it, it was translated into the Arabic language. As World War I began, Americans were advised to leave the eastern Mediterranean because it was ruled by Turkey, an ally of Germany. The Smiths left Syria and shortly afterward Bessie Hittle also left, leaving behind a happy, earnest company of saints. Nellie Laughlin elected to remain, not knowing what the future would bring but feeling she could be of help to the people. All contact with her was cut by 1917. But she was able to find food to keep the small community of believers alive, and she spent her time indoctrinating these young converts in biblical truth. Nellie had become a full-time missionary and was the only missionary of the Church of God in that entire area. The few saints in Egypt had their own leadership and an occasional American visitor before the war.

The orphanage at Lahore, **India,** was discontinued due to the general feeling that the need was no longer present. Those missionaries directly connected with the operation of the orphanage, such as Abernathy, Zaugg, Neff, and Hale, returned to America. In Shillong Indian leader J. J. M. Roy married missionary Evalyn Nichols, and they took the family name of Nichols-Roy. Their productive labors together spread over six decades. Soon after A. D. Khan returned to India from his second visit to America, seven and a half acres of property was purchased in Cuttack. The deed for it was held in the name of "Church of God Association of India." This holding became known as Mount House, which consisted of a missionary home and ultimately a chapel. The congregation that emerged was self-supporting and self-propagating, and they conducted meetings in nearby villages. A. D. Khan managed the United Printing Works. George and Minnie Tasker arrived in India in 1912 and had been sent by the Missionary Board to be a "directing force" for the significant work emerging in that country. Tasker took up headquarters in Lahore, remaining there until the work at Lahore closed down in 1921. The Shelter was started in Cuttack in 1914 by A. D. Khan and was operated by E. Faith Stewart, a new missionary, plus Sonat and Nolini Mundal, Khan's sisters-in-law. The home was for the protection of minor children and was greatly needed. Three years later seven acres of land was purchased in Cuttack for the Shelter, and within two more years the main building, which is still being used, was erected. At that time a child could be supported by a sponsor for five dollars a year. An elementary school for girls was soon started for these girls.

Some progress was being made in **Japan,** although it was considerably slower than in India. In 1911 W. G. Alexander purchased two acres of land in what was then a suburb of Tokyo called Musashi Sakai. He built there a missionary residence, quarters for Japanese leaders, and a chapel. A printing press was used for turning out six thousand copies each month of the *Pure Gospel* in the Japanese language, as well as other pieces of Christian literature. J. D. Hatch remained in Tokyo where he worked with Brother and Sister Maekawa. They held street meetings and distributed tracts, even on something new—"electric cars." Hymns were translated into Japanese. J. D. Hatch became seriously ill after a few years of service and returned to America in 1916 where he died soon after. Zuda Lee Chambers went to Japan the following year and began her work in Tokyo, first of all by studying the difficult language. Shortly after the close of World War I an excellent piece of property was purchased in the Hongo district of Tokyo. This soon became the headquarters of the work of the Church of God in Japan.

Across the East China Sea from Japan things were happening in **China.** William and Gloria Hunnex were already there starting a work in Chinkiang, some 150 miles up the Yangtze River from Shanghai. Individual saints in America had been giving to a "China Fund" sponsored by the *Gospel Trumpet*. A missionary home was erected on one acre of land purchased just outside Chinkiang. It provided living quarters for missionaries, a chapel, classrooms, and later a small orphanage. The main street in Chinkiang soon had a rented hall where services were conducted. Charles Hunnex was appointed by the Missionary Board in 1910 as a missionary to China, but was advised by the Board to wait until some rioting calmed down before departing from America. Pina Winters was also sent to do general missionary work with the Hunnexes. Charles soon opened a new work in Yangchow from which emerged Chinese leadership. In 1912 a revolution changed the monarch into a republic, which gave hope for more freedom. Tracts and a paper in Chinese gave evidence of a strong literature emphasis. Because of a serious illness Charles returned to America. While recuperating in the Church of God Missionary Home in Oakland, California, he met and married Annabel Lee from Nebraska. Before returning to China, Charles brought to the attention of the Missionary Board a serious problem for the Chinese Christians. In America the saints greeted each other with a holy kiss, and they were not given to drinking tea or coffee. But in China, as Charles pointed out, tea was the common drink and the practice of the holy kiss did not seem to fit at all into the culture. The Board suggested that in China they make whatever adjustments were necessary on these matters. In 1916 Daisy Maiden and Belle M. Watson were appointed as missionaries to China, and they went out with William and Gloria Hunnex, who were returning to China following their first furlough. Daisy and Belle first of all took up the study of the Chinese language in the Nanking Language School only fifty miles away from Chinkiang. At the writing of this book, Daisy Maiden Boone is still living in Santa Cruz, California, and is ninety-eight years of age.

An **Australian** by the name of E. P. May came into contact with the Church of God in America as a young man. For several years he was a worker in the Gospel Trumpet Home in Anderson. In 1917 he went back to his homeland to establish the truth first of all in Sydney. He rented a hall and called it the Unity Mission. It could accommodate 150 persons. He started publishing the *Australian Gospel Trumpet* and carried on considerable correspondence with interested people. Unfortunately, after seven years he ran into financial difficulties and a fire destroyed the printing equipment and supplies. Also, differences arose between him and church leaders in America. Relationships broke off, and there was no more contact with E. P. May until 1963.

In **Kenya,** East Africa, there was further preparation for Church of God entry into that country. By 1901 the railroad from Mombasa and Nairobi had reached Kisumu on Lake Victoria. This opened up the Western Province. American Quakers from Richmond, Indiana, settled at Kaimosi in 1902 and the Church Missionary Society of the Church of England, at Maseno in 1908. A. W. Baker, a Christian British attorney in Johannesburg, South Africa, and founder of the South African Compounds and Interior Mission, sent Robert Wilson north to Kenya to establish a mission in the interior among primitive African tribes. Following some exploration Wilson decided on a large piece of land given by Chief Otieno in Bunyore, situated between Kaimosi and Maseno. In 1905 this new mission was started and named Kima, Wilson's nickname for his wife. In the local vernacular "Kima" meant "anything with life having a healthy condition." How appropriate for what Kima was destined to become in terms of Christian life and witness.

The first few years were difficult. Wilson built a house and small church building. Even though the singing of Christian hymns by the missionaries, with Mrs. Wilson playing the small harmonium, attracted curious individuals, the Africans were shy and hesitant. In the beginning the girls and women would "fly away." After two years A. W. Baker sent an African Christian evangelist, Johana Bila, from the Zulu tribe to assist in the work. That was also the year of the Great Famine. Bila was successful in that a number of Africans were converted. Unfortunately, Bila's ministry lasted only three years, for he died from fever and was buried in Kima. About the time of his death the first baptismal service was conducted and two Bunyore people were baptized. It took two more years before thirteen more were baptized.

At the beginning of World War I, H. C. Kramer and his wife arrived to replace the Richardsons (he died of malaria), who had replaced the Wilsons (he had suffered a sun stroke). A. W. Baker, accompanied by his daughter Mabel, came with the Kramers to inspect the mission. When her father returned to South Africa, Mabel elected to remain in Kenya to devote her entire life to missionary service there. At the time of this writing she is still living in Johannesburg. Mrs. Kramer and Mabel Baker began the long and arduous task of learning the language, reducing the language to writing, and then translating portions of the Bible. That tremendous and difficult job extended over many years. First the Gospel of Mark and then John were translated. Then came a translation of the entire New Testament, which was published by the American Bible Society. During the war years famine and smallpox, flu and the plague, were always present. But progress was made. A school for children was conducted in the afternoons with the use of wall charts and a few slates. Sewing classes were started for girls. The women were superstitious about eating chicken. Chairs were for men only. Gradually, Christian concepts changed some of these cultural patterns. Over in America, not knowing anything about what was developing in Kenya, Samuel Joiner and his wife, along with William J. Bailey and his wife, were becoming burdened for the lost in Africa. In 1917 the Missionary Board of the Church of God gave approval for these persons to go as missionaries to Africa when the way should open. That took place, as we shall see, within five years.

World War I spanned the years 1914-18. Missionary outreach was limited. No new areas were entered in so-called non-Christian lands. The work in Europe was greatly curtailed and missionaries were forced to leave. The one exception was Denmark where the war seemed to have little effect on the growth of the church. In Germany, Poland, Russia, and Latvia the indigenous movement of the Church of God struggled on, even though separated from the church in America. There was considerable loss in church property, some displacement of individuals, and the occasional falling away from the truth. In America the constant shortage of funds hindered growth in the British West Indies. Any income increases were offset by inflation. There was little left over for new outreach. Syria was cut off from America by a blockade set up by the Allies in the Mediterranean to seal off Turkey, an ally of Germany and ruler of all the eastern Mediterranean. Half of the people of Lebanon, then a part of Syria, died of starvation during the war. By the time the Missionary Board met in mid-1917, however, they foresaw the overthrow of Turkey as opening fields to the Muslim world. Board members also saw the revolution in Russia as a hope for democracy in that country. Plans, they said, should be made in advance to take advantage of approaching opportunities. And the record of the Board meeting in 1918 just before the war ended states that, in spite of war in some parts of the world, other places were open and "white unto harvest." Opportunities in the West Indies, South America, Australia, Japan, China, and India were cited. The stage was set for something great to happen when missionaries would be free again to go into all the world, and the Missionary Board had behind it ten years of valuable experience.

Chapter 3

Moving Out between the Wars
(1918-1945)

THE WAR to end all wars had been fought and won by the Western Allies. World War I came to an end on November 11, 1918, and the world was to be safe for democracy, assisted by a new world body called the League of Nations. A redistribution of colonies emerged, mainly in the Middle East and Africa. Germany and Turkey lost everything, and Great Britain, France, and Belgium profited greatly. With the exception of a few skirmishes here and there, peace had come again to the world and people once more could move about freely. All of this was immediately reflected in missionary movement out of America.

During its first meeting following the war, the Missionary Board felt the need to discover the exact nature of the situation around the world, especially in countries where missions of the Church of God existed. F. G. Smith, then president of the Missionary Board, and E. A. Reardon, valued Board member, were chosen to go on a "missionary inspection tour." This was because both had experienced brief missionary service in the eastern Mediterranean. They proceeded westward, visiting Japan, China, the Philippines, Australia, India, Egypt, Syria, Palestine,

France, and the British Isles—a journey covering forty-six thousand miles and requiring eleven months. They observed various missionary methods being used not only by Church of God missionaries but by other Protestant agencies. They made note of the condition of the Church of God mission stations and missionaries and of the prospects for expansion following the war. Their report to the church in America is found in a booklet published by the Missionary Board in 1920 entitled *Look on the Fields,* which also included reports and information on missions in Europe, the British West Indies Islands, the Canal Zone, and South America, which had not been included in the tour by Smith and Reardon. This booklet did much to enlighten the saints in America about what was going on in their mission and what needed to be done. A fresh wave of enthusiasm and a renewed dedication to the task ahead were generated.

Near the back of *Look on the Fields* E. E. Byrum, then vice-president of the Missionary Board, wrote a few pages about "the urgency of missionary action." It was straightforward promotion asking for donations for the support of present missionaries, for making possible the sending of new missionaries where urgently needed, for partial support of native workers, and for badly needed church buildings. Byrum suggested making out a will and printed a sample document. He also asked for gifts from Sunday schools.

Smith's and Reardon's report to the Missionary Board was much more detailed. They endeavored to interpret the situation accurately on each field and the valid needs as they observed them. Smith and Reardon then hoped to establish priorities that the Board could consider. They presented new opportunities and felt this called for planned expansion. A suggestion was made to update some methods they felt required change. All of this only confirmed the following paragraph which is found in F. G. Smith's Report of the President to the Missionary Board on June 9, 1919:

The one thing that towers above local interests, sectional interests and national interests—the work that knows no distinctions of race, color or speech; the work that can therefore legitimately command and merit universally the support of every child of God, is MISSIONS. Church institutional work of every kind and description is simply auxiliary; whereas the work of missions is not auxiliary to anything and cannot be subjected without destroying its life and character, for it is *church work itself*. It is not a mere business enterprise to be measured in terms of dollars and cents, but a direct soul-saving work. It does not differ in fundamental character from the church work in our own local congregations in this country.

Time was taken in the 1920 Missionary Board Annual Meeting to outline some "plans for organization and conduct of our missionary work." Some goals for expansion were considered. There was observed a "development of new internationalism." Individuals throughout the church were beginning to break through the barriers of isolationalism and to look on the fields, which were ripe and ready for harvest. To gain a broader perspective on what was happening in the world of missions, Missionary Board President F. G. Smith encouraged the Board to join the Foreign Missions Conference of North America, the interdenominational gathering of those bodies devoted to missionary work. Copies of the International Missionary Cable Code Book were ordered to be distributed to all our missionaries so that cables could be sent to and received from the Board by means of a few code words instead of several sentences. That saved a great deal of money as well as making possible more frequent and quicker communication between the Missionary Board and missionaries, and between missionaries located in different countries. That was important at this time of a fresh moving out because correspondence both ways was by boat mail, which sometimes required months before a missionary could receive a reply to a very important question.

That same year the Missionary Board opened its own account with Anderson Banking Company, no longer to

51

carry on its financial business through Gospel Trumpet Company. Discussion took place about the relationship of a mission to the native church that was developing. In retrospect it is not too difficult for us today to know what position the Board should have taken on that subject, for that was an era of political colonialism, and the concept of colonialism easily rubbed off on missionaries and Board members. Financial matters were cared for on a more businesslike basis. Field budgets were developed and were submitted to the Missionary Board for consideration and adoption, usually after reducing the asking considerably. Furlough allowances were now granted to missionaries on furlough in America. Before, they had lived on the freewill offerings received from the churches visited. There was one decision, however, that was destined to cause many problems in relationship with the young churches developing in each of the countries where we had missionaries.

Following a method commonly practiced by most Protestant missions, the Missionary Board created the office of field secretary, which was held by a missionary at each mission. This person became the representative of the Board. This was initiated when Floyd W. Heinly and his family were sent to India as missionaries to assume control over our missionary endeavors there. The Board took considerable time and several pages in the minutes of the meeting to detail the responsibilities of the field secretary. For a time the results were almost disastrous in India. In retrospect we can say that this was a major error committed by the young Board relative to the work in India. Recall for a moment the high quality of able leadership in the Indian church. Strong letters of protest from these leaders were received by the Board. They objected to having a missionary appointed by the Missionary Board in America to manage the work of the Church of God in India. After all, the movement in India had its own missionary board, and the brethren felt they were capable under God to give guidance to the work in their own country. But this pattern of organization of a mission followed exactly the colonial system of control and administration. The common saying was "He who pays the piper calls the tune." The American church by that time was supporting the missionaries and much of the work in India. And so the decision stood. The attitudes of colonialism prevailed. We cannot be overly critical of those on the Board at that time, for this was the manner in which most missionary endeavors around the world were organized. However, the decision did create serious problems during the following years in India, and it set back the clock of time that should have led rapidly to self-reliant churches. Instead, the young churches became mission oriented and ultimately developed a mission complex. They became known as mission churches without self-identity and the ability to stand alone as viable churches.

During the early to mid-twenties other innovations materialized. The Missionary Board voted to buy a camera and an adding machine. In one meeting considerable concern was expressed as to whether or not a self-starter should be purchased as special equipment for the automobile to be sent to Jamaica. There were more important items of business. Missionary salaries were reviewed to make certain that a degree of equality was maintained in what was being received by all missionaries. A Grant-in-Aid plan was worked out for the support of native workers and it was tried as an experiment in Jamaica and Syria. Report blanks that were to be filled out daily were devised for missionaries and then for national workers by which monthly information would be received by the Missionary Board from each missionary and worker on how many sermons were preached, how many homes were visited, how many sick were prayed for, how many baptisms were done, how much time was spent in study and preparation, how many personal interviews were done, and on and on. Believe me, that system did not last very long! Systematized budget askings from the missions assisted the Board during its annual meetings to give intelligent consideration to each field and arrive at a responsible operating

53

budget for the next year. At first some missionaries had difficulty with the process. Even such a person as H.M. Riggle, who was at the time a missionary in Syria, had some serious misunderstandings with the Board over this, and the minutes record a temporary "disaffection" on the part of Riggle. For the first time in its history the Missionary Board began the practice at the beginning of each of its annual meetings to appoint a resolution committee to facilitate its work.

When the Missionary Board was first incorporated in 1914 there were eleven members elected to comply with the requirements of the state of Indiana. By 1921 a larger representation was felt necessary. Consequently, the Board revised its Articles of Incorporation to allow for fifteen members to be in lots of three for five-year terms. This allowed for continuity in the work of the Board. Members were selected through nomination by the Board and then accepted or rejected by the Ministerial Assembly meeting each June in Anderson, Indiana. Later on, nominees were presented by the Missionary Board in pairs for each of the three expiring terms each year, and the General Ministerial Assembly would vote by ballot. Down through the years there was no major change until Articles of Reorganization were adopted by the Board in 1970, and then in 1980 its membership was enlarged from fifteen to twenty persons. From the beginning of its existence the Board had been charged with the responsibility of carrying on missionary work among minority groups in America.

After ten years it was felt impossible for the Board to be responsible for both home and foreign missionary work; so it requested that another Board be formed to assume the responsibility of home missionary endeavor. In 1921 such a Board was brought into being by the General Ministerial Assembly and named the Board of Church Extension and Home Missions. One final item should be mentioned related to the Missionary Board. In 1923 it produced the first Missionary Manual for missionaries, presenting relationships of the missionary as well as rules and regulations governing his or her activities. As would be expected, that manual reflected the thinking and attitudes of colonial days. How well I recall as an eleven-year-old boy my first compliance with the manual. When my parents and the two of us boys landed in Port Said, Egypt, on our way to Syria in 1923, the first thing we did was to proceed to a store and purchase white pith helmets for each of us, for that was what was recommended in the manual to prevent sun stroke. All four of us came out of the store wearing those white sun helmets, identifying us with the colonial world!

In 1923 a great earthquake rocked Japan, causing much destruction and suffering in Tokyo. Although our missionaries and the Japanese Christians of our fellowship were unharmed, the Christian community in America sent relief to Japan to help rebuild homes. Recovery was slow but was assisted greatly by these expressions of love and concern. Another tragedy had taken place in Turkey where tens of thousands of Armenians were massacred. Refugees poured down from Turkey into Syria, settling for the most part in large camps in Aleppo, Damascus, and Beirut. My father became much involved in refugee work through the Near East Relief soon after arriving in Syria. As a boy scout I helped in collecting blankets and empty five-gallon kerosene tins for use by the refugees. Throughout the history of our missionary movement our missionaries have demonstrated Christian love and compassion when famine, earthquake, flood, war, or any other calamity resulted in human suffering. In 1926 the Missionary Board sent thirteen hundred dollars to the Near East Relief to be used for the Armenian refugees in the Beirut area. And for several years the Church of God Mission in Syria conducted a medical clinic and held meetings and a Sunday school in that same refugee camp.

Within the framework of the Church of God reformation movement's polity there is no stated creed to which all must conform. On a very few occasions this has provided the basis for problems arising with missionaries. The Missionary Board in its Missionary Manual has never presented a statement of faith to which missionaries must subscribe before going to the field. Little wonder, therefore, that infrequently a missionary might disagree with the Board and terminate services or go independent. George and Minnie Tasker, after being with the Movement for twenty-five years, left the services of the Board and separated themselves for some years from the Church of God. "G.P.'s" views on the church and sanctification were considered on the liberal side, and there was disagreement on methodology used in approaching Muslims. In retrospect it could be said that George was a man ahead of his time. The Taskers continued missionary service independently and later renewed fellowship with the Reformation Movement.

One other example was E. Faith Stewart, a missionary for many years in India who served primarily at the Shelter. Her problem was basically administrative in nature, and she had difficulty in cooperating with other missionaries on the field. Her services with the Missionary Board terminated in 1929, and a year later she went to Cuba as an independent missionary. The Board has never desired to legislate arbitrarily or to force an issue when coming into disagreement with a missionary under its appointment. Usually through negotiation and the desire to keep the unity of believers, a solution can be found to the satisfaction of all. However, if an impasse ultimately develops, the Board will present to the missionary the concept that if he or she cannot agree with the teachings and practices generally held by the Church of God reformation movement, then the honorable thing is for the missionary to withdraw gracefully, thereby causing no disruption in the work.

One of the earliest attempts to withdraw a mission in favor of the national church took place when Adam and Grace Miller returned from Japan in 1927 after a five-year term of service there. The Millers were not to return to Japan and it was recommended that since the Church of

God in Japan was strong enough and had capable leadership no more missionaries should be sent. Frequent contacts were maintained with the Japanese church until all communication was severed during World War II. But the experiment in establishing a self-reliant church in a mission field had been for the most part successful. It should be observed that all during the twenties there was continued talk by missionaries about the churches in mission lands becoming self-supporting. Perhaps too much emphasis was placed on the financial aspect of the indigenous church and not enough on self-governing and self-propagating. In 1925 J.W. Blewitt, a highly honored member of the Missionary Board and head of the Church of God Missionary Home in New York City, made a trip around the world to see what could be done to encourage missionaries to lead the churches more rapidly into being the church and not responsible to a mission. As an MK (missionary kid) I remember our family's taking Blewitt to Palestine in the new Model T Ford that the Board had provided and narrowly escaping being robbed by bandits just before reaching Haifa.

A major financial situation that brought on the Great Depression began to develop in America. In 1926 there were 10 percent cuts in remittances to the fields. That was hard enough, but by 1928, 15 percent cuts were levied. In the course of those two years something happened in the American church that must have reflected the need for more adequate financial support for the few general agencies of the movement. What became known as Associated Budgets was proposed, and after much deliberation the Missionary Board finally agreed to participate. This united form of fund raising among the churches by the national agencies of the church was the forerunner of World Service. The financial crash came on October 24, 1929, when the stock market on Wall Street collapsed. That marked the real beginning of the Great Depression. Millions lost their jobs; thousands, their homes. Payrolls declined, savings were used up, and banks closed their doors. There were soup kitchens and breadlines in every major city. Farmers were hard hit. The deepest years of the depression were 1931 and 1932.

This development in America caused a world economic collapse. Obviously, missionary contribution in America fell off rapidly. But hardships that missionaries experienced were only a reflection of the situation in the home church in America. Even though there were severe cuts of 50 percent and on occasion 75 percent in remittances, missionaries remained at their posts of duty. Little if any expansion took place, and the work took on a holding pattern. You could count on the fingers of one hand the number of new missionaires sent out by the movement during those difficult years. My wife, Ruthe, and I were among those few. I was appointed by the Missionary Board in 1933 and my annual allowance was $480. The following year Ruthe was appointed, and I made the trip by boat from Beirut to New York for a hundred dollars. We were married in Oklahoma where scars of the depression were glaringly evident. A number of young people's groups in churches in the Tri-State area raised the amount for our fares for the journey to Beirut. On the field, native workers who had been receiving financial assistance from the Board found it necessary to take on other employment to keep bread on the table. Instead of continuing to rent residences, many missionaries conserved budget by living in homes of other Christian workers who were home on furlough. Yet with all these seemingly adverse circumstances there was scarcely any complaining. Everyone was in the same boat. Missionaries held on in faith, believing that God would provide the basic needs. And God did just that through a dedicated and influential woman in the church.

At the turn of the decade Nora Hunter, a minister of long standing in the Church of God, made a trip to the eastern Mediterranean, visiting the missions in Egypt and Lebanon. Her heart was touched when she observed the effect of the Great Depression not only on the missionaries but also on the work, which was being severely curtailed. Her concern did not diminish upon return to America, but she began to visualize what the women of the church could do once they were mobilized. This was in spite of recognizing the reality of the depression. During the Anderson Camp Meeting in 1931 Nora Hunter gathered around her several capable women and they began to work on the possibility of organizing women of the church to raise the necessary funds to keep missionaries on the field. The records of the Missionary Board indicate the depression had really settled in by that time, and that year ten missionaries on furlough were waiting to be sent out again. The group of women headed by Nora Hunter came before the Board to seek its blessing and to discover how best to go about meeting their objectives.

In mid-1932 the National Woman's Home and Foreign Missionary Society was organized and a constitution and bylaws adopted. Nora Hunter began her travels throughout America, challenging the women of the church to raise money by making things and selling them. Women of the church all across the country caught the vision, put on their aprons and baked, and made all kinds of things to sell. As a result, funds began to be made available for assisting the missionary work of the church. Because of aid received, not one missionary left the field due to the depression. Every missionary recognized the tremendous effort and what it meant to the cause of missions. In 1934 the Board records read, "The National Woman's Home and Foreign Missionary Society is doing a superb job, keeping missionaries on the field." The missionary outreach of the Movement had been saved, thanks to the women of the Church of God! By the following year it appeared that America was slowly coming out of the depression, and hope was being expressed for the future. Later on, in 1946, the society's name was changed to the National Woman's Missionary Society, and in the seventies it was changed again to Women of the Church of God.

It should not be overlooked, however, that the financial effects of the depression were felt on mission fields right up to the beginning of World War II, which began in September 1939 when Germany invaded Poland. In fact, the first time during that decade when our missionaries received 100 percent of their budgeted allowances was in the November 1939 remittance. The genius on the field was the ability achieved by both missionaries and national church leaders to make maximum use of the limited funds available. Priorities emerged with major emphasis placed on direct evangelism and away from costly institutions.

The Beginning of the End

There were other more important issues that were beginning to capture the thinking and imagination of missionary leaders around the world. First of all, there was a growing unrest throughout the colonial system. During the late twenties and throughout the thirties there were forces at work that would ultimately bring an end to imperialism and colonialism. This development was destined to have a major impact upon the missionary movement, especially as related to the emerging churches in mission lands.

First of all, more and more uprisings and revolts occurred throughout the colonial world, but especially in the Middle East, Africa, and India. Western-educated national leaders began to demand freedom and to organize resistance movements. Also, the masses came to realize they were living in a situation geared to profit imperialistic powers. An awakening, or a kind of renaissance, took place among ordinary men and women. Political revolutions occurred more frequently and with increasing violence, all of which generated bitter antipathy and hatred toward Westerners. These revolts were fueled by a rising xenophobic nationalism. The love of their own country caused people to hate Western imperialism. They wanted freedom for their country wherein they could enjoy all the blessings of political independence. A national consciousness with definite aspirations emerged. And so tensions developed as people began and continued the struggle for political independence.

That period of time was charged with the words *freedom* and *human rights*. Many a young national leader was graduated from some mission school after being taught the following basic Christian concepts, which he readily transferred into his own national political arena: "You will know the truth, and the truth will make you free. . . . If the Son makes you free, you will be free indeed" (John 8:32, 36). "There is neither Jew nor Greek . . . slave nor free . . . , for you are all one in Christ Jesus" (Gal. 3:28). American missionaries also conveyed the spirit of a bold statement in our nation's Declaration of Independence that reads, "We hold these truths to be self-evident, that all men are created equal, and are endowed by their Creator with certain inalienable rights." Consequently, the struggle for freedom and human rights emerged not only from education and the abuses of colonialism but also from the spirit and teachings of missionaries over a period of several decades.

Because the people of the colonies thought the colonial powers came from Christian nations, a revival developed among some of the major world religions such as Islam, Hinduism, and Buddhism. People began to take pride in their history and the ancient civilizations they had earlier enjoyed, including the beauties of their ancient religions. With this in mind they thought they could offset the inroads being made by colonial missionaries from the West. Anti-foreign nationalism coupled with religious fanaticism was a force difficult to combat. These combined forces gave anti-colonial people great power as they struggled for political freedom and independence.

This spirit of nationalism and freedom certainly began to have its effect upon many of the national leaders of the churches in mission lands. Even though they scarcely knew how they could get along without the missionary and the financial resources made available from the missionary's homeland, they began to think in terms of how good it would be if they could enjoy the main positions of leadership in the church instead of the missionary. Many of these leaders were capable men and women, but for the most part Western missionaries considered them immature and not yet ready to assume responsible leadership in the church. Tensions therefore developed in many of the Movement's missions between our missionaries and the emerging leaders of the church. The most adverse situations revolved around the question of who was going to have the final say in the distribution of funds from America for the support of workers and churches.

All of this together gave many sensitive missionaries the feeling that the days of colonialism were fast coming to an end and that the spirit of colonialism in missions must also come to an end because it was not right in the first place. Numerous missionaries around the world, especially the younger generation of missionaries, began a serious study of a biblical understanding and a methodology that would bring forth a truly indigenous church in lands where missions had been operating for a number of years. Books were written about the methods the Apostle Paul used as he did his missionary work in Asia Minor and Europe, and about the tremendous success a missionary by the name of Nevius had in Korea in bringing forth an indigenous church—self-governing, self-propagating, self-supporting.

The big question in those days was this: How do you help a church become self-reliant when it has only known relationships with the mission that were almost identical to those that colonies had with Western colonial governments? There was a real awakening among missionaries that the time had come to discover ways and means to lead the church that had been mission oriented and mission dominated into a vibrant indigenous church. I was among that number as missionaries were struggling with this very situation in mission-church relationships in Lebanon.

One more event took place that must be mentioned. The International Missionary Council, which had come into being in Edinburgh, England, in 1910, had conducted two council meetings in 1921 and 1928, both of which were for missionaries only. My father, stationed in Beirut, attended the one in 1928 convened in Jerusalem. But in 1938 at Tambaram, just outside Madras, India, a revolutionary development happened. A few national church leaders from several countries were invited, although they were given no major responsibility. The chief topic of that IMC meeting was the development of the indigenous church. A considerable amount of material had been prepared in advance, and I was one of the many missionaries who read it all, even though I did not have the privilege of attending. All of us were searching for solutions to the situation in which we found ourselves, realizing quite well that the day of colonialism in missions had come to an end. We began to talk about fraternalism taking the place of paternalism. Little did we realize it would take years to bring about the transformation.

World War II emerged on the world scene, suddenly stopping any further development of the self-reliant church for almost a decade. In some places, however, the church began to realize that it could function without the presence of a missionary when the missionary was forced by the uncertain situations of war to leave the country where he or she was laboring. But now before we consider the effects of the war, we must return to the twenties and thirties to note important happenings in our movement's missionary outreach.

The Islands of the West Indies

The fast-growing work in **Jamaica** required more missionaries. A. E. Rather and family arrived in 1919; George and Maude Coplin, in 1923; and the Steimla family, in

1924. George and Nellie Olson were still looking after the work on the Cayman Islands and had visited again in 1920 the new work in Panama City, Colon, and the San Blas Islands. Some properties were purchased and registered in Panama for the developing congregations. For the first time the secretary of the Missionary Board, J. W. Phelps, paid a visit to Jamaica to see for himself what was going on and to encourage the church. Shortly thereafter a missionary residence was built for the Olsons next to the High Holborn Street Church, and for years this "mother church" and home were the headquarters of the Church of God in Jamaica.

In 1926, Nellie Olson, feeling the need for a better-trained ministry, opened the Jamaica Bible Institute. She observed immediately that most of the students had not yet completed secondary school, and so the very next year she opened a high school department at the institute. During that same year a young missionary, Edith Young, arrived to give full time to teaching at Jamaica Bible Institute, a position she held until her retirement many years later. Before the Great Depression became too severe George Olson, having a real vision for the future of the work, was able to purchase a large tract of land facing Ardenne Road and Hope Road on the outskirts of Kingston. It was not long before a new school building was erected facing Ardenne Road and was named Ardenne High School. Later on, several other facilities were erected for AHS. It has become one of the outstanding secondary schools in Jamaica. During World War II Jamaica Bible Institute was moved to a building facing Hope Road. Also during the war years the Olsons' daughter, Mary, became headmistress of Ardenne High School, a position she held until retirement. When Mary began her work there were only twenty-six students. Today there are over one thousand enrolled.

The One-Hundredth Anniversary of Freedom from Slavery was celebrated in Jamaica in 1938. Naturally there was great rejoicing throughout the island. Christian people became more enthusiastic in spreading the good news of freedom from sin. The Church of God continued to grow rapidly. By 1929 there were fifty congregations; by 1932, sixty-six; and by 1942, eighty-six. Unfortunately, there were only eighteen ordained ministers, plus local leaders. Jamaica has suffered through the years and even to the present time with an insufficient number of full-time trained pastors. In 1930 the ownership of all church properties belonging to the Church of God in Jamaica was transferred to the churches under the General Assembly. Since Jamaica is as close as it is to America, quite a few leaders from the church in America visited the work to encourage the saints. These included E. E. and Lucina Byrum, C. E. Brown, and E. A. and Pearl Reardon as well as Esther Boyer and Hester Greer. Of interest to me was that Edith Young was the first Church of God missionary to return to America for furlough by airplane. That required *twelve hours* from Kingston, Jamaica, to Miami, a distance of six hundred miles! By 1944 the church in Jamaica welcomed another missionary couple, Leslie and Nina Ratzlaff.

Over on the **Cayman Islands,** about two hundred miles west of Jamaica, several groups of believers were established through frequent visits by missionaries from Jamaica: the Olsons, the Steimlas, and Edith Young. A strong congregation in George Town, Grand Cayman, came into being, as well as a small congregation on the very small island of Cayman Brac. The small church building on Cayman Brac was destroyed by a hurricane and tidal wave in 1932, then was rebuilt and destroyed again by hurricane in 1945. All the islands in the Caribbean are subject to the fury of storms that bring property damage and destruction. It is a way of life in the tropics, but when disaster strikes, the people need assistance immediately for rehabilitation. Harold Andrews was the first resident missionary under whose ministry two more congregations were started in Grand Cayman. Leslie and Nina Ratzlaff were sent to Grand Cayman in 1941 to Triple C School, and American teachers Caroline Glassman and Wilma Ryder were enlisted. Both of these teachers later married men from Grand Cayman and remained for many years on the island teaching in Triple C School and serving the church faithfully.

Far to the southeast in the Caribbean and out into the Atlantic the movement was gaining ground on the island of **Barbados.** By the mid-thirties eighteen congregations had been established through the efforts of the missionaries serving during these two decades. It must always be remembered, however, that the real work of soul winning and establishing the work is done through highly motivated and consecrated national ministers and workers. So it was in Barbados. But like Jamaica, there was always a derth of full-time pastors. In 1928 Byron Chew married Zella, the Brookovers' daughter, and together with the Brookovers they served in both Barbados and Trinidad. During the early years of the church on both of these islands apparently no major effort was made by the missionaries to develop in the people a sense of responsibility for the work there. Offerings even in the larger congregations consisted of only a few British pennies. The churches did not support the pastors, and so they had to work in secular jobs to live; they did not have to keep the church buildings in repair, for the mission did that. As a result of the total situation a true understanding of evangelism and outreach was lost.

W. L. Brookover resigned and returned to America in 1937 and the Chews left in 1941. That left no missionaries in Barbados or Trinidad. That is when Ruthe and I were sent to the southern Caribbean as relief missionaries because we could not return to Lebanon due to the war. During the next three years as we served Barbados and Trinidad, the emphasis was initiated to bring the church to a position of self-understanding, leading ultimately to a position of self-reliance.

Growth in **Trinidad** was not as rapid as in Barbados, at least numerically. The situation was different. In Barbados the population was predominantly West Indian, originally African. But in Trinidad there was a mixed population of West Indians, Chinese, and East Indians who were originally from India. Only a relatively small work was ever developed by the Movement among the East Indians. But a strong congregation came into being in the second largest city, San Fernando. Also, three congregations started on the island of Tobago, which is a part of Trinidad. In 1920 the Board made available a car for Thaddeus and Katrina Neff to use in their ministry. Annual Church of God camp meetings were initiated. All-day meetings each quarter were conducted to bring the saints together for inspiration and teaching. Baptismal services were always held during the quarterly meetings. Good, adequate church buildings were erected, and most of the ten congregations were pastored by full-time ministers. These were capable leaders, including one woman, and they should have been encouraged and instructed early on how to bring into being an indigenous church. The potential had been there for years. But remember, this is in retrospect. In those early years in the southern Caribbean our missionaries seemed unaware of the necessity for missions to become churches so that the church could be the church without indefinite support from missions.

British Guiana (now known as Guyana) is a small country on the northeast coast of South America. It is the only English-speaking country in that continent, and its people are mainly West Indian and East Indian. For these reasons "B. G." has always been closely associated with the West Indian islands. Therefore, in our missionary outreach the developments in Trinidad, Barbados, and "B. G." were considered as a whole. Missionaries from the two islands made regular evangelistic journeys to "B. G." Soon several other congregations emerged, and when Adam W. Miller and Charles E. Brown visited there in 1935 there were three other ministers besides George Jeffrey. The John Street congregation in Georgetown became the "mother church." Jeffrey remained the dominant personality, with financial assistance received from America. He was known in the community for his welfare program on Bellaire Street, which was a "shelter for a motley collection of men, women and children who had fallen upon evil days."

The West Indian people many times moved about from island to island. Many of them made their way to New York City for temporary employment, and some went to Panama to help build the canal. This movement of people assisted in spreading the Reformation Movement. Significantly, Hannibal and Rose Boddie, who were originally from the island of St. Kitts, were converted in Elder Green's church in New York City. In 1932 they returned to **St. Kitts,** and conducted open-air meetings in Basseterre and throughout the island. Two years later Elizabeth Brewster, born in Barbados, arrived from New York City to join in the work. She purchased property and willed it to the church in Basseterre, and that is where the "mother church" in St. Kitts is located. Following her death, Wilhelmina Fraser came, held revival services, and became pastor of the Basseterre congregation. On the nearby island of **Antigua,** Wilfred and Christena Henry began services in the town of St. John's. They also had been converted under Elder Green's ministry in New York City. Francis and Mabel Lindo went from St. Kitts to the island of **Curacao** of the Netherlands West Indies just off the coast of western Venezuela so that Francis could work with the Shell Oil Company. Mabel had come up under the tutelage of Elizabeth Brewster in St. Kitts, who encouraged her to start a work of God in Curacao. She eventually did just that.

Central and South America

The Reformation Movement came to **Panama** primarily because West Indians arrived from several of the islands to seek employment as the Panama Canal was being constructed. Some of these were Church of God people. They discovered each other and started meetings in their homes. There were the visits by George Olson from Jamaica and George Coplin from Barbados. But it was not until the mid-thirties when A. E. and Rebecca Rather became resident missionaries in Panama that the work took shape. Remember these were English-speaking West Indians developing a work in Spanish-speaking communities. And so the congregations remained English-speaking for the first and second generations of the group in Panama. It has required many years of effort to assist these good people in becoming a part of the country in which they are now permanently residing by using the Spanish language in their services. It reminds me of some of our German and Greek congregations in America taking considerable time to become English-speaking in their meetings. The transition in Panama only now has about been accomplished.

The McHughs from the Church of God in Jamaica moved to **Costa Rica** and took the gospel with them. Others joined them to work in the United Fruit Company. A. E. Rather, visiting them from Panama in the mid-thirties, found the saints worshiping in the McHughs' home at Cimarrones. A church building was soon erected, and the work continued among the English-speaking West Indians who lived on the plain near Puerto Limon on the east coast.

Cuba will be mentioned here because it is Latin oriented and not related to the English-speaking West Indies. Earlier in this chapter I mentioned that E. Faith Stewart went to Cuba as an independent missionary because the Board had voted against her return as a missionary to India. She went to the home of an English-speaking Jamaican woman who was from the Church of God in Jamaica. Meetings were conducted in the English language in this woman's home. However, very wisely and deliberately the meetings were soon conducted in Spanish. Stewart began to learn Spanish, and when visitors came from America their messages were translated from English into Spanish. The next year Ray Jackson came from America for a five-week evangelistic campaign. Many people were converted. A larger place for meetings was needed and was subsequently rented. Hester Greer arrived the next year, 1932, and remained as a missionary for many years. Greer worked in the city of Havana itself, and Stewart labored in the suburbs. A few years later the Movement reached the adjacent island of the Isle of Pines. Unfortunately, Stewart could not get along with Greer. Also, Stewart refused to have the work in which she was involved placed under the supervision of the Missionary Board. Greer took the opposite position relative to the work she was developing. Stewart's work gradually separated itself and remained independent, while other missionaries arrived to work with Greer under the Missionary Board. The Rodriguezes and the Stephensons were among those. During the war years the church was registered with the government under the Missionary Board and several permanent congregations were established.

To escape the results of the 1917 communist take-over in Russia, Adolf Weidman and twenty-two families went first to Germany and then on to **Brazil** in 1923. This colony of German Church of God refugees settled in Santa Catarina. They formed a congregation and kept in touch with the German work in America centered in York, Nebraska. More German Christians, led by Edward Wagner, fled Poland and settled in Rio Das Antas in Brazil. Others, such as the Bosserts, took up residence in the state of São Paulo, while the Koenig family found a home in the city of Curitiba.

The first Church of God camp meeting in Brazil was held by the German believers at Nova Esperanza in 1929. By 1931 the Church of God in Brazil became officially registered. David Meier, a German American, and his family felt called to missionary service among the German immigrants in Brazil and arrived there in 1935. For some time he was forced to teach school to provide food for his family. Meier was the first evangelist to go to Argentina, holding meetings in Alem in Misiones Province. His work was also among German immigrants. Solomon Weissburger, his son Heinrich, and their families fled Germany as Hitler began to persecute the Jews. They settled in Rio Das Antas in Brazil. During World War II all these colonies of German Church of God Christians had to remain quiet. For a time the German language was forbidden in Brazil, and on occasion some people endured imprisonment just because they were Germans.

In **Argentina** Adolf Weidmann became the strong leader at Alem. Under capable leadership the work among these German-speaking people grew slowly but surely. And they were very German, reflecting their culture in almost every aspect of their lives. There were only rare attempts to do any evangelizing among the Portuguese-speaking people in Brazil or the Spanish-speaking people in Argentina.

More Happenings in Europe

Following World War I the Church of God regained its strength and carried on quite an evangelistic outreach. In 1922 the *Evangeliums Posaune* (German *Gospel Trumpet*) was published in **Germany** instead of in America. A well-established work among the German-speaking people in **Russia** was one result of their labors. The Malzons and the Doeberts went into the Ukraine and the Caucasus again and again, revisiting and holding evangelistic meetings. When communization was enforced under Stalin, attacks on the church were increased. Also, contacts diminished between the brothers and sisters in Germany and those in Russia. Finally, when Hitler's armies invaded Russia in 1941, the German-speaking people in Russia were sent to Siberia. Earlier, a real spiritual awakening broke out among the German-speaking people in **Poland.** But inflation in Germany, which reached its climax in 1923, hindered the awakening a great deal. It has been said that it required a wheelbarrow full of German marks to buy a loaf of bread. A new missionary home was built in Kassel, and a Bible school was started for training ministers. But the economic crisis prevented growth that the church would have otherwise enjoyed. It should be observed here that this expansion of the Reformation Movement into Poland, Russia, Brazil, and Argentina was really a missionary-inspired outreach of the Church of God in Germany, even though it was primarily a work among people of German descent. Eventually the church in Germany formed its own missionary board, known as Missionswerk. In the early twenties some penetration took place into **Hungary.** The first congregation was located at Tiszaszederkeny, and others were established at Kondoros, Gabrovo, Tschernitschevo, and Budapest. In 1938, on their way from Lebanon to America for furlough, my father and mother visited the churches in Hungary and Germany, encouraging the congregations as war clouds were gathering. They were amazed at the hold Hitler had on the minds and activities of the Christians of the Movement.

The *British Gospel Trumpet* started under the editorship of Adam Allan in 1921 in **Ireland,** and a Bible training school enjoyed a brief existence in the mid-twenties under the guidance of F. C. Blores. In 1926 a young minister named John Larmour became pastor of the Belfast congregation where he remained for a decade before moving to England. In **Denmark** J.P.N. Ikast and his family arrived from America in 1923. During the thirteen years Ikast labored there, major difficulties that killed the spirit of revival and brought division appeared among the churches. Pentecostalism had a devastating effect upon the Church of God, in spite of all the noble efforts of the Ikasts and Danish church leaders to reverse the trend. In 1927 Lars and Ellen Olsen were sent to Denmark to assist the Ikasts. Olsen edited the *Evangeli Basun,* the equivalent of the *Gospel Trumpet* in Danish. Somewhat discouraged with the church's situation in Denmark, the Ikasts left in 1936 and the Olsens in 1940, being evacuated through Italy during World War II.

J. Jeeninga began meetings in Waubach, **Holland,** in a remodeled barn in 1930. During the following ten years small groups of believers were established in Treebeck and Ymuidan. Overall, the work of the Church of God in Europe appeared in a holding position, except for that in Germany. The direct effects of the oncoming war would be devastating, even though individual Christians remained true to their Lord and faithful to the teaching of the Movement in spite of great suffering.

Growth in the Eastern Mediterranean

In **Egypt** right after World War I a woman by the name of Zaroohi Tabakian followed Ouzounian in the leadership of the large group of saints among the Armenians in Alexandria. During a five-year period following the war three Egyptians—Hanna Arsanious, Habib Yousef, and Abdul Talut Michail—cared for a growing work among the Egyptians as it spread from Cairo to other cities. I mention these names because they labored faithfully and to the best of their abilities without the presence of any missionary from America. They profited from the visit of F. G. Smith and E. A. Reardon in 1920 and from the several weeks spent in Egypt by H.M. and Minnie Riggle in 1921 on their way to Syria. The first issues of the *Buk-el-Ingeel,* the Arabic *Gospel Trumpet,* came out in 1921. Strong requests for missionaries continued, but it was not until 1923 that Thaddeus and Katrina Neff landed in Port Said and went on to Alexandria where they established headquarters for the mission in Egypt. Their arrival was a part of the new outreach following the war to assist in the eastern Mediterranean. The Neffs and their two children; John and Pearl Crose and their sons; Nellie Laughlin, returning to Syria following a furlough; Adele Jureidini, a Lebanese minister who had been with Nellie Laughlin in America; and Emil Hollander, a young missionary to Syria, were all on the same boat from New York to Port Said. During the next ten years the Church of God in Egypt grew rapidly. Places of worship were erected in cities and towns where congregations were established. Pastors to lead those congregations were found from other groups. Armenian congregations were started in Cairo as well as Alexandria. John Tabakian emerged as the Armenian leader in Alexandria and K. T. Sarian directed the work in Cairo. Work among the Greeks in Cairo began, and Nicholas and Rose Zazanis arrived in 1928. They developed a very large Greek congregation in Cairo and one of lesser size in Alexandria. My father was invited by Neff every year to spend a month in evangelistic meetings up and down the Nile. An Arabic printing press was purchased and one of the Egyptian brethren, Salib Farag, took charge of publishing the *Buk-el-Ingeel* in 1924 as well as printing other pieces of Christian literature, including a Church of God Arabic hymnal, word edition only. All this Arabic literature was used not only in Egypt but in Syria and Lebanon also. Nellie Laughlin was transferred from Lebanon to Egypt in 1929 where she assisted until her retirement in 1931. The William A. Fleenor family was transferred from Lebanon to Egypt in 1932. The following year the George Dallas and the William Conkis families arrived from America to assist in the work among the Greeks. Due to serious illness the Fleenor family returned to America in 1934. Thaddeus Neff also began to have health problems. Nellie Laughlin was asked to return to Egypt in 1937 and devoted the remaining five years of her life to a teaching ministry in Assiut.

In **Syria** immediately following World War I Nellie Laughlin made a very wise decision. She felt impressed that for the future welfare of the ministry of the Church of God in that country the work should be moved from the small village of Schweifat to the city of Beirut. F. G. Smith and E. A. Reardon visited the saints the next year and added their blessings to the move to the city. Then in 1921 H. M. and Minnie Riggle arrived from America in an effort to strengthen the work already begun. Riggle traveled far and wide, calling people to repentance and winning quite a few people to Christ. They remained in Syria while Nellie Laughlin took a well-deserved furlough, having spent those difficult years of World War I in Schweifat. H. M. Riggle completed his assignment by mid-1923, returning to America and writing his experiences in a book entitled *Pioneer Evangelism*. The Crose family and the Riggle family met in Anderson as the Croses were preparing to leave for Syria.

As an eleven-year-old boy I will never forger the journey by train across America. We stopped in several cities to visit churches on behalf of missions and spent some time in Anderson in the home of Russell Byrum. From there we moved on to New York where the group was coming together at the Missionary Home. I also remember the boat trip from New York to Port Said. We traveled in the stern of the S. S. *City of Lahore* where all the second-class passengers were missionaries going out after the war, many of them having had experienced missionary service before. These missionaries held nightly meetings on the boat, sharing their experiences in other lands. At Port Said the Neffs left the boat with Sister Neff critically ill. On the boat trip up the Palestinian coast to Beirut we made a stop offshore at Joppa where I believed I could see the house of Simon the tanner by the sea, and finally we were welcomed by the saints as we arrived early the next morning in the harbor of Beirut.

With an enlarged missionary staff, the influence of the Church of God in Syria increased and growth took place. Emil Hollander lasted as a missionary only one year. He stayed in our home and I shared a room with him where we had a lot of fun together. I always thought it was not quite fair to have taken a young man just out of Anderson Bible Training School, knowing nothing except the sidewalks of New York City where he grew up, and placing him in situations where he would have to rough it, such as traveling by horse or donkey for hours while engaging in village evangelism. Beirut itself was nothing more than a broken-down Turkish port following the war, so life was still difficult even in the city. In those days there was no form of orientation for new missionaries, and I had the idea that Emil really didn't know what he was getting into. He had been oversold on missionary service without proper preparation. In the end be became frustrated both emotionally and spiritually and left the field. But Emil remained my friend and I always saw him as I would come and go through New York City. The Missionary Board learned its lessons on recruitment the hard way.

In Beirut funds were received from America to erect an excellent church building in the Ashrafiyeh District, using Armenian refugee labor. This also provided facilties for a Church of God elementary school. A congregation was maintained in the city of Tripoli, and farther north in Syria village work was maintained by Ibrahim Maloof. William A. Fleenor and his family were sent to Syria in 1930 to relieve my parents, who returned to America for furlough after seven years on the field—the regular term at that time. I was appointed as a missionary to Syria in 1933, returning briefly to America during the summer of 1934 to marry Ruthe Hamon, who had been accepted by the Missionary Board. During the twenties and thirties the work of the church grew to a point and then seemed to level off for a couple of decades. In retrospect it appears the believers never really caught on to what their responsibility was as the church and in doing what the church under God should be doing. The work in Syria became too dependent upon the missionaries and the church in America, which supported the work of the mission. Several attempts were made to indigenize the work, but failure resulted time after time.

Constantine Nichols was a young Greek converted in 1915 in Cairo, Egypt, through the efforts of G. K. Ouzounian. He traveled to Chicago and began a work among the Greeks. While Nicholas Zazanis was attending Anderson Bible Training School he began editing the Greek *Gospel Trumpet*. At the same time Greek brethren from Chicago visited the Peloponnesus in Greece, making contacts and some converts. In 1932 Zazanis, who was a missionary in Egypt by then, made a trip to **Greece** to contact the brethren there. And in 1936 the publishing of the Greek *Gospel Trumpet* was transferred to Athens under the direction of Athanasius Chionos. However, no organized work of the Church of God in Greece was to begin until after World War II.

And Now to East Africa

H. C. and Gertrude Kramer had been in **Kenya** for several years as American Quaker missionaries working with the South Africa Compound and Interior Mission and were due a furlough. By then A. W. Baker in South Africa felt he could no longer sponsor and support his mission in Kenya, and so he asked the Kramers to seek out a church in America that would be willing to assume responsibility for the mission in Kenya. Baker said that mission should (1) not stress "the speaking in tongues"; (2) teach the Bible as the Word of God; and (3) teach the unity of God's people.

The Kramers had been receiving Gospel Trumpet literature irregularly for several years, and they had come to appreciate its teachings. So during their furlough in the spring of 1921, while visiting their sponsoring family in Pomona, California, they became acquainted with Abram and William Bixler, two brothers in the Church of God congregation there. Through the Bixlers' influence and that of the congregation, the Kramers embraced the truth. Upon hearing of the offer being made by A. W. Baker, William Bixler felt strongly that the Kramers should present the opportunity in Kenya to the Missionary Board. Correspondence with the Board took place, and the congregation in Pomona paid the train fare for the Kramers to be in Anderson for the camp meeting and the meeting of the Missionary Board. Baker's offer was presented to the

Board, including what it would cost. The price was fifteen hundred dollars plus the cost of Mabel Baker's residence and a residence for another missionary family. Board members were obviously interested in this opportunity to enter East Africa. But before a final decision could be made, some investigation was necessary. Since Sam Joiner and his wife had expressed an earlier interest in Africa, the Board sent them to Kenya. Together with W. J. Bailey they looked into the condition of the mission at Kima and sent back a favorable report to the Board. Transfer of the mission was negotiated and completed. In the end Baker turned over everything without cost to the Missionary Board. He was well pleased with the attitude of the Board and the beliefs of the Church of God. During the 1922 meeting of the Board, Henry and Gertrude Kramer were appointed as missionaries of the Church of God, as were the Joiners. Also, Mable Baker was accepted as a Church of God missionary. Ruth Fisher was appointed as a missionary to Kenya to teach the missionaries' children, and she went to Kenya with the Kramers.

Rapid growth took place. To the north in the Butsotso tribal area a mission was started at Ingotse by the Joiners before they were forced to return to the United States due to her health failure. In Bunyore they had led a boy to the Lord and he became one of the leaders of the church. His name is Jairo Asila, and he is alive yet today. In 1921 James Murray arrived in Kenya as a Salvation Army missionary, but he soon joined the Church of God mission. The William J. Bailey family was accepted by the Board in 1924 and stationed at Ingotse where they labored as agricultural missionaries for five years. Kramer laid the foundation for the large "cathedral" at Kima. It was known as BKKB because the churches in Bunyore, Kisa, Kakamega, and Butsotso donated money for it. The building was completed later under the guidance of J. S. Ludwig. Many people were being converted and baptized. Elders were being appointed. Children needed education, and so Mabel Baker initiated "bush schools" or village schools, along with Sunday schools in each location. A school for children was started at Kima. In 1925 James Murray married Ruth Fisher and they labored at Kima before being transferred to Ingotse when the boys' school that had been started at Kima in 1923 was transferred to there. They taught in the school and assisted in village evangelism. African evangelists were successfully active and many village churches were started.

John and Twyla Ludwig were sent as missionaries to Kenya in 1927. They threw themselves into the work with tremendous energy. Soon Twyla started a girls' school at Kima, for she carried a burden for the women and girls of Kenya. She taught them how to fight prevalent diseases and to take care of their bodies. In 1929 the Ludwigs developed an Elders Council, which was composed of twelve elders. That same year the Kramers left for America, not to return to Kenya. They left two of their children buried in the cemetery at Kima. Henry Kramer had helped to build many village church buildings and Gertrude had spent much time training "bush school" teachers and translating the New Testament along with Mabel Baker. A year later A. W. Baker from South Africa visited Kenya and was delighted with what he found developing at the mission he had helped to start and had turned over to the Church of God.

A young African, Musa Eshipiri, was converted in the Kisa tribal area and became an effective evangelist. He donated part of his land at Mwihila in 1934 for the beginning of a mission station. Homer and Vivian Bailey worked there first, followed by Jewell Hall, who started a clinic in 1939. This was a project taken on by the National Woman's Home and Foreign Missionary Society. In 1935 a maternity hospital was started at Kima. Missionary Freda Strenger was the nurse in charge, and a year later Lima Lehmer arrived to help in the nursing program. Soon afterward Rita Paulo became the first qualified African nurse.

Life was not easy for missionaries during that period of

time because disease was prevalent—especially malignant malaria (blackwater fever) and typhoid. In 1936 Ruth Murray died from a severe attack of typhoid fever. James Murray continued his services at Ingotse for four more years until he died from blackwater fever. Their graves at Kima, along with those of their three children who died in infancy, bear witness to their sacrificial service to the Africans. Soon a beautiful church building was erected at Ingotse and called the Murray Memorial Church. Following the Murrays, Homer and Vivian Bailey assumed responsibility for the work among the Butsotso people at Ingotse.

The tempo of the work picked up during the last few years of the thirties. On December 20, 1936, a never-to-be-forgotten day by the church in Kenya, the missionaries and African church leaders gathered at Kima and opened the first case of New Testaments printed in Olunyore by the American Bible Society. That was the fruit of persistent and dedicated labor over a number of years by Mabel Baker, Gertrude Kramer, and several faithful African Christians. Printing of other literature became necessary and as early as the mid-twenties a press was installed at Kima where it remained until 1959. Highly dedicated pastors and school teachers were on fire for God. African Christians were indeed turning their immediate world around them upside down. Villages were established with a Christian atmosphere. Converts were learning to live what they were being taught.

Looking East into India

Immediately following World War I the Floyd Heinly family was sent to **India,** becoming the first American missionaires of the Church of God to take up long-term residence in Calcutta where the headquarters of the mission was established. Mae Isenhart sailed with them but returned to America after three years due to health problems. Soon Mamie Wallace was sent to be the private secretary for Heinly. The Taskers arrived from furlough and worked in Calcutta. Josephine McCrie returned from furlough and brought with her Eva Goodwin, the first missionary to be sent out by the Church of God in England. Perhaps that was the first demonstration of partnership in mission. Both of these missionaries assisted the Taskers in Calcutta. When Faith Stewart returned from furlough in 1922 she brought with her two new missionaries, Mona Moors and Burd Barwick. When a home for boys was started the next year in Cuttack, Mona was put in charge. Mosir Moses and Floyd Heinly made a trip into Sikkim, a small country north of India, to see whether there were any possibilities of opening a work. That was not to be. In Calcutta A. D. Khan organized a mission to students a short time before his death, which occurred October 8, 1922. He died from a severe fever, probably influenza, when only forty-four years old.

That was a tremendous loss in leadership for the church in India. By all counts Khan was considered by missionaries and Indian Christians alike as chief among them. What D. S. Warner was to the Reformation Movement in America, A. D. Khan was to the Church of God in India. Both were dynamic leaders, evangelists, writers, publishers, and true pioneers. Both died at an early age but lived long enough to see the work well on its way. Shortly before his death Khan became greatly concerned about establishing a work in the general area of East Bengal, from which he had originally come. In consultation with the English Baptist Mission it was arranged that the Church of God would evangelize the Kurigram Subdivision of Rangpur District, an area where there was no mission at work among the predominantly Muslim population. These, of course, were Bengali-speaking people, the same as in West Bengal state in which Calcutta is located. The work was first started in Kurigram but soon centered in Lalmanirhat, an important railroad junction. It was decided that Floyd Heinly should be in charge, although his family did not move there until 1923. In the meantime a financial campaign was launched in America on Christmas Day, 1921, to raise funds to build "A Station in a Day," and over ten thousand dollars was made available immediately. A church building was erected and soon after a missionary residence, both of which remain in use today. New ways were initiated for communicating the gospel to Muslims and some Hindus in that area. Homes and secular institutions were visited. Books were loaned and tracts distributed. Meetings were conducted and inquirers instructed. Workers preached in the bazaars and used a stereoptican lantern to show pictures wherever a crowd at night would give permission. Soon a primary school was started at the mission in Lalmanirhat. Out in the villages Bible instruction was given along with moral lessons. There was preaching in the bazaars and visiting in the the homes. There were meetings with the women and children and showings of lantern slides at night. In these ways the gospel was brought to bear upon the Muslims in a nonoffensive way.

Farther south in Cuttack, Orissa, seven acres of land was purchased at the edge of the city, and a new, adequate facility was built for the Shelter. This was the first of several buildings erected on the compound. At that time there were 110 girls in the Shelter, each being educated through the seventh grade. Soon after Khan died some adjustments took place among the missionaries. There remained considerable dissatisfaction because the Indian leadership in the church thought they should make the decisions in the work and that missionaries were in India to assist the Indian church, whereas the missionaries felt they had been appointed by the Missionary Board to give leadership to the church and its Indian workers. There was also some difference of opinion between the Missionary Board and missionaries about methods to be used in the work. As a result, Faith Stewart and Burd Barwick left the field. Mona Moors took charge of the Shelter along with the Mundul sisters, Sonat and Nolini. E. L. and Martha Bleiler spent a term in Cuttack trying to make a success of the boys home, but that project died out. Josephine McCrie, who had been in India since 1904, resigned, as did G. P. and Minnie Tasker. This discontinued the work of the mission in Calcutta. Mosir Moses, the Indian leader and a convert from Islam, took charge of the congregation in that city, doing his best to carry on the work alone. And Andrew Shiffler, after twenty-five years of service primarily in literature work in northeast India, left for America at seventy-four years of age.

During this period of time the Church of God in South India was gaining ground under the leadership of P. J. Philip and J. M. Spadigum. Following Khan's death Field Secretary Floyd Heinly was in charge, and thereafter the work in South India was looked upon as a mission that was dependent upon the Missionary Board for support and direction. The congregations there were not considered self-reliant churches. P. J. Philip was ultimately appointed as a field secretary for the work in South India—another major blunder the Board made in its administration. Such an action perpetuated a mission complex. Far to the north in the state of Assam, today known as Meghalaya, the Movement was growing rapidly among the Khasi tribal peoples under the leadership of Evalyn and J. J. M. Nichols-Roy. By 1926 it was reported there were over two thousand adults in the Movement. Even though Nichols-Roy could not agree with many of the policies of the Missionary Board as related to the Church of God in India, he carried on in a self-reliant manner. Financially it was not easy, but the people were taught how to give. Nichols-Roy developed a fruit business of his own, while at the same time becoming a leader in the state government. Nichols-Roy was also a theologian in his own right, and he interpreted the New Testament from his own cultural perspective. Moore Wellson Laloo, a young Khasi man, was converted in 1933 and was destined to assume leadership of the work twenty-six years later. Unfortunately, "some strange teachings" were introduced to the work by Evalyn Nichols-Roy after she had been on furlough and had come into contact with the Foursquare Gospel, a Pentecostal movement in southern California. This ultimately caused a split in the work in Assam in 1941 when Aquilla Seige led a breakaway of twenty-four congregations. They formed their own assembly and erected their own central church building at Mawkhar in Shillong. Both groups claim loyalty to the reformation movement of the Church of God, but the division has not been healed even to this day.

Ellen High was appointed as a missionary to Cuttack in 1937, one of the very few new missionaries to go out during this period. With World War II already under way, Mona Moors returned to India following furlough in 1940. That same year the Heinlys left India, and my father and mother, John and Pearl Crose, were asked to go to India, as they were forced to evacuate Lebanon because of the war. They traveled constantly, visiting the churches and missionaries and endeavoring to create better relationships all around. The Taskers had returned to Bangalore, India, as independent missionaries, and Minnie Tasker died there in 1941. Soon thereafter George Tasker married Josephine McCrie, a longtime friend.

On the Rim of East Asia

When F. G. Smith and E. A. Reardon made their round-the-world trip in 1919 their first stop was in **Japan.** They sent an urgent message to the Missionary Board that someone must be sent immediately to relieve the Alexander family, who had been in Japan more than ten years without a furlough. My parents, who were supposed to be in preparation for going to Syria, were approached, and they accepted the challenge. The events of that February sailing between San Francisco and Yokahama that stood out in my mind as a seven-year-old boy were the ice cream and fresh pineapple in Hawaii and the typhoon we encountered, during which I almost got swept overboard. The Alexanders soon left for America, having served the Japanese people faithfully. The center of the work moved from Musashi Sakai to the large two-floor Mission Home in the Hongo District of Tokyo. A. U. Yajima was pastoring the congregation that met in a large room on the second floor. He and his family of several children and grandmother lived in a wing of the first floor. Zuda Chambers, the single woman missionary, and Shojima San, the Bible woman assisting "Aunt Zuda," lived in a part of the first and second floors, while our family lived mostly on the second floor. The kitchen and Japanese bath were on the first floor. We all lived together, yet separate, with all things in common.

With all the potential present for developing a good work in Tokyo, the effects of overwork were soon noticed. My father spent many hours each day in language study, attending a language school in downtown Tokyo. In addition, he preached, conducted classes for university students, and visited among the people. In late 1920 a cable was received by the Missionary Board that declared, "Chambers and Crose overworked and underfed." After a year and half my father suffered a complete nervous breakdown and was put on a boat where he was expected to die before reaching San Francisco. Axchie Bolitho was sent to Japan in 1921 to help Zuda Chambers, and Adam and Grace Miller went in 1922. Zuda Chambers returned to America later that year, having completed five years of service. During the early and mid-twenties the church grew and expanded. The Mission Home was only one mile from the Imperial University and many students were reached through English classes, some being converted to the Christian faith. Evangelism produced results, and there was effort put forth to develop church leadership. This wave of advance was quite unique in a predominantly Buddhist country, but many young people were searching for something other than the traditional religions in Japan. This provided opportunity to present the good news of salvation through Jesus Christ. Both of the Millers and Axchie Bolitho began to feel the strain of heavy responsibilities by late 1925, and so in mid-1926 Bolitho returned to America, followed by Adam and Grace Miller in early 1927. There may have been some financial reasons why they could not be replaced, but it appeared to both the missionaries and the Missionary Board that the Church of God in Japan could be termed indigenous, no longer needing resident missionaries, as mentioned earlier in this chapter.

There were four congregations in the greater Tokyo area—Hongo, Mishigahara, Miyanaka, and Nerima—each having a Japanese pastor. Consequently, no more missionaries from America were sent to Japan until after World War II. At first there was some talk by the Japanese leadership about closing down the work, but through the faithfulness of A. U. Yajima, Choko Shimizu (who is still living), and Taniguchi Sensei, the situation started on the upward swing by 1930. Some financial assistance continued to be sent on a monthly basis by the Missionary Board. The Japan Bible Institute was opened, receiving official recognition from the Deprtment of Education, and the first General Convention of the Church of God was held in 1931. When the people of China suffered from a great flood the Church of God in Japan raised 6,111 Yen, which was a lot of money in those days, to send to the Hunnexes in Shanghai to help relieve those who were suffering. By 1932 there were ten meeting places, and the churches were beginning to use kindergartens as a means of reaching people with the gospel. That same year A. U. Yajima, a highly respected leader in all Christian circles in Japan, died. In the mid-thirties contacts were made with the brethren in Korea. But late in that decade the church in Japan began to face other difficulties as war against China developed in Manchuria. There was strong pressure from the Japanese government that only *one* Christian church be officially recognized. *Danippon Kirisuto Kyodon,* the United Church in Japan, generally known as

Kyodon, came into being. There was considerable uncertainty in the Church of God as to whether they should join Kyodon. All through the thirties correspondence was maintained with the Missionary Board. But that communication abruptly ended with Pearl Harbor, which put America at war with Japan. Nothing was heard from Japan until after that country's unconditional surrender in 1945.

Christian witness in **China** has traditionally been difficult even though modern Protestant missions have poured millions of dollars and hundreds of missionaries into that country. Shortly after World War I, it was estimated that after 110 years of Christian witness there were only a total of ten converts for each missionary engaged over that period of time. It was also estimated that it cost missions 558 gold dollars to convert one Chinese. But the Church of God was in China to stay, whatever happened to missionaries. Early in the twenties William and Gloria Hunnex left China permanently. Mission headquarters were moved from Chinkiang to Nanking, but Pastor Dong and his family remained in Chinkiang to shepherd the group of believers. Isaac Doone, prosperous businessman in Hong Kong today, is a son of that family and remains loyal to the Church of God. A missionary home was started in Shanghai, with Pastor Lee giving Chinese leadership. Karl and Hazel Kreutz sailed as missionaries to China in 1923 and worked in Yangchow fifteen miles from Chinkiang where Daisy Maiden and Bell Watson were stationed. Strong emphasis was being placed upon self-support. This was fortunate because there were only a few times when missionaries were able to serve in China during the years ahead.

Civil war caused by a communist-nationalist take-over in 1927 made it necessary for all our missionaries to flee to the foreign concession in Shanghai: the Kreutzes from Yangchow, Maiden and Watson from Chinkiang, and Charles and Annabel Hunnex from Nanking. Belle Watson sailed for America, but the Hunnexes remained for a while in Shanghai. Daisy Maiden sailed home by way of India,

Egypt, and Syria. She remained in Syria (now Lebanon) about a year, assisting in the Lord's work where she was greatly needed. That is where I as a youth in high school first knew Daisy. The Kreutzes went to the Philippines where they lived for many years. A second evacuation occurred in 1937 when China was invaded by the Japanese military. Daisy Maiden was forced to leave again. The Hunnexes, who were on their way to China at that time, stopped off in the Philippines for nine months until they could get back into Nanking. Unfortunately for them, they remained in China too long and were held by the Japanese in an internment camp in Shanghai for two and a half years. The Kreutzes were caught by the Japanese in the Philippines during World War II and were held as prisoners in the Santo Tomas Internment Camp in Manila. But in spite of all this uncertainty of missionary presence, the ravages of civil war, and the presence of Japanese military forces, the Church of God continued to exist as a Christian entity, but with little chance for growth.

As mentioned earlier the Reformation Movement spread to **Korea.** Some Korean ministers representing eleven congregations visited one of our churches in Tokyo. They became seriously interested in the Church of God and severed their relations with the Church of the Nazarene. At the request of K. Y. Kim, Adam W. Miller and A. F. Gray visited this group of people in Pyengyang during their tour of East Asia in 1937. That city is in what is now known as North Korea and was at that time the main seat of Christianity in Korea as a whole. These congregations were mostly self-supporting, and they carried on under their own leadership, encouraged through correspondence with the Missionary Board. It was not until the mid-fifties that Church of God American missionaries were sent to South Korea.

In the early thirties in the **Philippines** a man by the name of Celestino Matias contacted the Church of God in Montesano, Washington. He embraced the Truth and returned to his home at Laoag on northern Luzon Island and began a congregation. It was on the beaches of Laoag that the Japanese first landed in their attack on the Philippines during World War II. Matias died, but his son Fernando took over and tried for a while to enlarge the work. A small chapel was partially built in 1938. Encouragement was given by the Hunnexes and the Kreutzes, along with Adam Miller and A. F. Gray during their brief visit. But that little work all but died out during a period of twenty years, after which it sprang to life again.

"Man Is Destined to Die Once" (Heb. 9:27, NIV)

By the close of this twenty-five-year period of time several more of the Reformation Movement's first-generation missionaries had died. They included the following:

Mae Isenhart	192?	India
Zuda Chambers	1933	Japan
Opal Brookover	1934	Trinidad
Nels Renbeck	1934	Denmark
The Hopwoods	1936	England
Ruth Murray	1936	Kenya
James Murray	1940	Kenya
Minnie Tasker	1941	India
Nellie S. Laughlin	1942	Egypt

We should also note the deaths of several national church leaders: A. D. Khan and Mosir Moses in India and A. U. Yajima in Japan. These, along with those mentioned earlier and even perhaps some I have overlooked, should be credited for having laid, for the most part, a good foundation in other lands for the Church of God reformation movement. I have stood several times before the tombstones of the Maidens, Opal Brookover, the Murrays, Laughlin, and Yajima and have prayed that I might be faithful to follow their examples. During the next period of thirty-five years more fruit was destined to spring from the seeds that were sown by these early saints of God.

The Years of World War II

Contact with the church leaders in Japan was immediately lost when Pearl Harbor was attacked in 1941. Charles and Annabel Hunnex were interned for the duration in Shanghai by the Japanese. Mona Moors and Ellen High remained in Cuttack, India, but Floyd and Maude Heinly returned to America for a much-needed furlough. John and Pearl Crose had just returned to Lebanon when war broke out in 1939, and so they remained until forced evacuation in 1941 took them overland and by sea to India, a most hazardous journey, to cover for the Heinlys until they could return to India in 1942. Ruthe, our daughter Alta, and I, having completed one full term of service in Lebanon, sailed from Beirut in December 1939 on board one of the last American passenger boats to enter the eastern Mediterranean. This was at the advice of the American consul, who was anxious to get Americans with children out of the war zone. Caught in America by the war, we were sent by the Missionary Board to Barbados and Trinidad as relief missionaries for three years to relieve Byron and Zella Chew. The Ludwigs from Kenya were caught on furlough in America at the outbreak of war, but they were able to bring together a great deal of needed material and equipment, find a boat that would accept nonmilitary freight and a woman passenger, and reach Kenya where they remained for the rest of the war. Thaddeus and Katrina Neff were forced to flee Egypt twice during heavy military attacks on Egypt, but each time they were able to return. During one air raid over Egypt the wife of one of the Church of God pastors was killed. The Zazanises fled Egypt, returning to America. In Germany most of the work was destroyed; church buildings were reduced to rubble and church members were scattered. In other parts of Europe church work as such came to a standstill, although individual Christians remained faithful, finding comfort and courage through their trust in God. Throughout the West Indies the difficulties experienced took the form of scarcity of food and building supplies to maintain church buildings and living quarters. This was due to the presence in the South Atlantic and Caribbean waters of German U-boats, or submarines, whose commanders worked havoc with Allied shipping during the course of the war.

As fighting came to an end, most of the countries of Europe and Japan stood in dire need of all kinds of assistance as the people of the world struggled to bring themselves back to some form of peaceful existence. Tremendous adjustments were necessary, requiring several years of time to change from war to peace. A few countries, such as Lebanon, had profited, and its people came out of the war with far more economic blessings than was their status when war was declared six years earlier. This was in unbelievable contrast to the way in which the Lebanese people had survived World War I.

We will now look at what took place in the missionary enterprise of the Church of God immediately following VE and VJ Day. The Missionary Board had passed a resolution in the early forties "to hold all positions, even during the war" and that "missionaries would leave only if forced to do so." Now the Board was ready to go beyond a holding position.

Chapter 4

Regaining Momentum

(1945-1955)

PEACE WITH some degree of normality does not come easily following five years of violent conflict such as the nations experienced during World War II. Japan and Germany lay devastated. Many other countries, such as England and Greece, showed to a greater or lesser degree horrible scars of war. Relief and rehabilitation assistance of all kinds were needed and activated. Many Americans felt a special burden for the family of God in Germany, and so food, clothing, and materials for rebuilding were made available. Christians of our Movement demonstrated love and compassion especially for those of the Reformation Movement who were suffering as a result of the conflict.

The war had its effect on missionary activities and on the life of the church, particularly in countries directly affected. And there were indirect effects in countries where there was no actual combat. Unemployment and other economic problems abounded. Shortages of the necessities of life, especially staple foods, were experienced. Rationing had to be maintained in many places. Uncertainty about the immediate future caused many to lose hope.

However, all of these factors put together provided a rare opportunity in many lands to present the "balm in Gilead" to suffering humanity. In America the war effort had produced a degree of financial prosperity that made more funds for missionary outreach available to the church.

Adam W. Miller, first as executive secretary-treasurer of the Board (1933 to mid-1947) and then vice-president and finally president, had given wise guidance to the movement's missionary enterprise in bringing it out of the Great Depression, through the uncertain years of World War II, and on into a new and challenging era of missionary endeavor. The war's end presented an almost unparalleled opportunity to discover first the nature of the new world in which people now had to live and secondly the most effective ways to present Jesus Christ in such a world. C. Lowery Quinn served as executive secretary-treasurer (mid-1947 to April 1954) during this difficult ten-year period. More than five years of war brought changes in how people thought about themselves and the society in which they lived. How nations thought about one another had a direct effect on how missionaries would be received or not received in a growing number of countries. What did it mean to be an American missionary in this new world environment? That is what missionaries going out immediately after the war had to discover for themselves to make the necessary adaptations.

On the world scene several colonial countries took up their struggle for political independence immediately after the war. The hatchets of xenophobic nationalism had been buried during the war in favor of joining the armed forces of the Western Allies in the struggle against their common enemies. But now with pent-up fury the spirit of nationalism was revived and the struggle was renewed against colonialism and imperialism. India was a classic example. That nation's armed forces were loyal to Great Britain during the war and its strategic geographical position provided many advantages for the Allies. In most colonies the struggle for independence was accompanied with violence.

But in India, Mahatma Gandhi led nonviolent protests that at times brought imprisonment to the leaders. Within two years Britain gave India its independence. The only violence took place when Britain, to please strong religious elements among the people, partitioned India, creating a new nation known as Pakistan. The plan was to move all the Hindus living in West and East Pakistan into India and all the Muslims in India, especially northern India, into the two Pakistans, which were divided from one another geographically by over one thousand miles. The result was a bloodbath. Literally thousands of Indians were slaughtered on the roads and along the railways. Masses of people tried to move in one direction or the other, depending on their religion. They were not only *in* buses and trains but on top of them and hanging on the sides. The killing began when the vehicles in which the people traveled stopped at stations along the way. Blood literally ran alongside railroad tracks. Our new missionaries, Robert and Frances Clark, had just arrived in India, and they witnessed some of this. It should be noted that this division of India divided the work of the Church of God in that country geographically, for it was the state of East Bengal that became East Pakistan, and our mission work centered in Lalmanirhat found itself in a new country.

Other areas of the world experienced frequent outbreaks of violence. France was having difficulty in Indonesia, which led to France's withdrawal and ultimately to America's involvement in Vietnam. Egypt and other countries of the Arab world maintained their revolts against Britain and France until freedom was finally granted. Nationalist movements among the British West Indies colonies gathered strength. Colonial possessions in Africa began to give trouble to the imperial powers. Also, the British were handling the situation in Palestine somewhat clumsily. They were in a losing battle against the Jewish immigrants escaping from Europe; so in 1948 they partitioned Palestine, creating the state of Israel. This action brought immediate adverse reaction from all Arab countries, especially against America. Our missionaries in Cairo, Alexandria, and Beirut made themselves scarce on the streets for a number of days. However, all of these attempts to gain political independence from colonialism had only nominal influence on the work of missionaries. As a matter of fact, most missionaries sympathized with those who were attempting to gain their independence, for the era of colonialism had obviously come to an end. Indeed, most of the colonies were ready for their independence. This change of events also spoke to the feelings of Christians in the churches found in those countries and began to influence relationships between missionaries and national church leaders. As a whole, these developments challenged the missionary movement. Most missionaries, however, were optimistic.

The Missionary Board in America was also helpful. As it entered this decade of recovery and regained momentum, its members saw the opportunity for rapid advance in almost every area of the world where the Movement maintained missionary activity. After picking up the pieces and sorting things out, the Board went on record "to start a new era of expansion after the trials of the past few years." Members felt "the need for a forward-looking program, well designed within the framework of present-day mission strategy." Early in the decade the president of the Board wrote in his annual report that if the gospel is to challenge the whole world, "there are four imperatives:

1. Make clear the distinctive character of the Christian faith,

2. Explain the faith in terms people can understand,

3. Discover new ways to make the Gospel effective in the lives of men and women, and

4. Assist in the demand for unity."

Board members and missionaries alike began to see opportunities to serve the people of the world through four general types of missionary endeavor: evangelism, education, medicine, and agriculture.

The Church of God reformation movement in America was now ready to send out a wave of new missionaries, a fourth generation. My parents and their peers represented the second generation of missionaries, and, as mentioned earlier, there were only a handful of third-generation missionaries, due primarily to the Great Depression. As will be revealed later on in this chapter, numerous missionaries were sent out during this ten-year period from 1945 to 1955. There were volunteers and there were funds with which to send them. Ruthe, our two children, and I were, I believe, the first to leave America following the war, sailing from New York in August on the second sailing of the M.S. *Gripsholm,* which was taking American personnel into the Mediterranean. E. A. and Pearl Reardon were on the same sailing, going to Kenya to help solve a major problem that had been developing in that mission. The ravages of war were still very evident as we stopped in Naples and Piraeus, the port for Athens.

Due to the influx of this new generation, a period of adjustment was required on some fields between the older and the younger missionaries, especially between some of those in the second generation and the new fourth generation. This was due to new concepts emerging in postcolonial missions and to considerable change in attitudes and methods in the American church. It was not easy for many of the older generation of missionaries to understand that where missions had been at work for several decades there should now be a church emerging with its own identity to be the church and to do its work. Paternalistically minded missionaries expressed fears that the national church was not yet mature enough to be on its own without some kind of missionary oversight, and that its leaders were not yet ready for total responsibility.

Fortunately, many of those new fourth-generation missionaries who went out soon after the war had been provided the opportunity by the Missionary Board to prepare themselves for service. One of those places of preparation was the Kennedy School of Missions, and before it closed a number of years later many of the Movement's missionaries received training there. They went to the field, knowing something of what they faced in contemporary missions. They arrived on the field eager to aid the church through leadership training and to enter a transition period through which the mission would decrease and the church would increase in responsibility. In some countries the transition was smoother than in others, as we shall see.

All the Movement's missionaries were helped at this and many other points through a new Missionary Manual put out in 1947. This was the only new manual since the first one was printed in 1923. It brought numerous missionary concepts, strategies, and relationships up to date. Two quotations from the manual are worthy of note here.

> The supreme aim of foreign missions, therefore, is to make Jesus Christ known to all men as their divine Savior, and to persuade them to become His disciples; to gather those disciples into churches which shall be self-propagating, self-supporting and self-governing: to co-operate, as long as necessary, with these churches in the evangelizing of their countrymen and in bringing to bear on all human life the principles of Christ.

> The mission is not a permanent institution though it is a necessary one in the first stages of evangelization. It aims to build up as soon as possible an indigenous church which shall be self-supporting, self-propagating and self-governing, and it prepares and encourages the entire native church to complete the work of evangelization in the way best suited to its own national genius.

The significance of those statements was slow in being understood by some missionaries who maintained a colonial concept of missions, even some of the new fourth generation. The new Missionary Manual also made a change in name of the missionary on the field who was the liaison between the Missionary Board and the mission on the field. The old term was *field secretary,* and for a long time it had smacked of colonialism—the man wearing the white sun helmet. The new term was *mission secretary-trea-*

surer. Dropping the title field secretary was not appreciated by some who used it to indicate the authority they carried in the work and especially the privileged position with the church on the mission field. But the change was necessary in the new climate in which missions operated.

It was during this period that the Missionary Board lost the accumulative wisdom of several persons. In 1946 E. A. Reardon died soon after arriving in America following the year spent in Kenya. His wife, Pearl, had to bring his report to the Board. She had been with him in Kenya and had kept copious notes. Reardon was a charter member of the Board and had given valued service for thirty-seven years. J. W. Phelps also died in 1946. He had served earlier for sixteen years (mid-1912 to mid-1929) as secretary-treasurer of the Board. In 1947 F. G. Smith died suddenly. He had been a Board member for thirty-two years. The following year H. M. Riggle did not have his expiring term on the Board renewed. He was a charter member and had served thirty-nine years, three of which were as secretary-treasurer (1929-1932). In 1950 C. E. Brown resigned as president of the Missionary Board. He had held that office since 1931. Brown was elected as a Board member in 1921 and remained as such until 1958. It is always good to have new blood on the Board, but those first few years following the war showed an unusual turnover and the loss of considerable continuity. The Board, however, was existing in a new day in missions and needed new members to introduce fresh concepts commensurate with the changes in mission policies and strategies in the postwar world.

A number of the second-generation missionaries were reaching the age of retirement. Contemporary feeling in the church required that something be done to provide for its missionaries in old age. Three things developed. In 1949 the Board worked out a Retirement Allowance Schedule to care for those missionaries already retired. At the same time all active missionaries were placed in the newly established Pension Plan of the Church of God. Some were near retirement when they entered the plan; so they still required some supplement from the Retirement Allowance Schedule. Then came Social Security as it was made available to missionaries who were eligible. It was entered on a voluntary basis and would ultimately take the place of the supplemental retirement allowance. That was a great boost for the morale of the third- and fourth-generation missionaries. It meant they would more likely make missionary work a career. This also demonstrated the church's expression of loving concern for the welfare of its missionaries. It was in keeping with trends in American society.

The offices of the Missionary Board found a new home in 1949. The National Woman's Missionary Society, World Service, the Board of Christian Education, and the Missionary Board of the Church of God cooperated in building the Missions Building just east of the Gospel Trumpet Company. Today the building is called Church of God Executive Offices and is just east of Warner Press. This structure provided much more adequate facilities for the Missionary Board as it moved from very small quarters in the old tower of the Gospel Trumpet Company building.

In 1950 the National Council of Churches of Christ was formed and the Foreign Missions Conference of North America became the Division of Foreign Missions within the framework of NCCC. The Missionary Board reconsidered its relationship carefully, for the general feeling in the Movement was opposed to relationships with the NCCC. However, involvement in DFM provided the opportunity to give and receive valid services and to experience many helpful relationships with other missionary boards. Our Board decided to retain its membership with the Division of Foreign Missions. Later on, when the NCCC was reorganized, requiring church bodies to be members in the NCCC before they could be full members in any of its divisions, the Missionary Board became an associate member of the DFM. Furthermore, in more recent years since the National Association of Evangelicals has within it a missions department, the Missionary Board has also gone in that direction to serve and to be served on behalf of the cause of missions.

Another united move took place in 1951. Instead of publishing three separate magazines the Board of Church Extension and Home Missions, the National Woman's Missionary Society, and the Missionary Board of the Church of God combined their efforts and came out with a jointly controlled and supported *Church of God Missions* magazine. That publication has been a great informative and educational tool within the Movement ever since. Another good thing happened in 1953 when the General Ministerial Assembly voted that it must ratify the names of all chief executive officers of the general boards and agencies, following their election by their respective bodies. The Missionary Board voted in favor of this move, which indicated quite well the excellent relationship always maintained between the Assembly and that Board.

As the church in America entered the decade of the fifties, its men, sparked by the enthusiasm of Everett Hartung, an outstanding layman residing in Anderson, Indiana, organized themselves in a campaign called Mid-Century Building Fund. The goal was to raise two million dollars, primarily for special capital fund needs demonstrated by the Missionary Board of the Church of God, the Board of Church Extension and Home Missions, Anderson College, Pacific Bible College (now known as Warner Pacific College), and the international campgrounds in Anderson. There were included some noncapital fund needs for the Board of Christian Education and the Board of Pensions. Men of the Movement rallied around the slogan "We Build for the New Age." Banquets for men were held in strategic places across the nation where they were challenged by dynamic speakers such as W. Dale Oldham and Everett Hartung. Many volunteers were involved in getting men to sign pledge cards. Enthusiasm ran high. Never before in the history of the Reformation Movement had such a large sum of money been raised. What the women of the church had done during the Great Depression its men were now doing to help the movement with capital funds at this important time when the Church of God was beginning to regain its momentum following World War II.

The Missionary Board needed capital funds desperately to meet financial obligations it could not include in its regular operating budget. Over five hundred thousand dollars was ultimately made available for overseas missions. Numerous church buildings and missionary homes were erected and some ten automobiles were supplied that otherwise could not have been made available. Generous amounts were given for building needs at Bible schools in Trinidad, Jamaica, and Germany. A mission center in Alexandria, Egypt, was made possible. The first main unit of the Hunter Memorial Hospital at Mwihila, Kenya, was erected and a large generator was installed to provide electricity for that station. Considerable assistance was given to the completion of the new church building in Athens, Greece. All in all this was a major demonstration of what the church could do once it was informed, for the financial potential was there. The campaign did not impinge adversely upon the giving to World Service. It was a real victory for the men of the church!

Ruthe and I came to America on furlough from Egypt in the late spring of 1952. We had been out for seven years and it was good to be home again among relatives, friends, and leaders of the church. I had the exhilarating experience of being caught up in this unprecedented Mid-Century Building Fund campaign at two points: (1) In the fall of 1952 I was loaned by the Missionary Board to the project to assist in setting up the campaigns in numerous places and, at times, to take part in some of them as a missionary to tell about the needs, and (2) in the spring of 1953 I was asked to become director of the campaign from an Anderson office. These two assignments provided me with considerable exposure to the Movement across the country, and I was delighted to make what little contribution I could to such a successful happening in the church.

An interesting phenomenon emerged during the late forties and early fifties. Several younger men of the church decided on their own to travel out into the world and visit Church of God mission stations. They wanted to see for themselves what was being done and to be "missionaries to the missionaries." Some of them took it upon themselves to present reports to the Missionary Board. Among the several were Maurice Berquist, Ralph Starr, Frederic Pinyoun, and Wade Jakeway. I speak from my own viewpoint and experience by saying that these visitors were able for the most part to be a blessing to the family of God wherever they went, and they were in an excellent position to bring back to the church in America a different perspective about what was going on out there. This was the beginning of a time when Church of God pastors and laypersons would make their own trips or join tours to visit mission stations. This has done much to stimulate a greater interest in missions.

An administrative transition in the Missionary Board took place in 1954. C. Lowery Quinn resigned as executive secretary-treasurer after having served for seven years. Those were difficult years administratively, as the missionary cause of the Church of God was quickening its pace. Quinn had never been a missionary and it was therefore difficult for him to comprehend all the factors in difficult situations in other cultures. But he was faithful and dedicated to his work. The Missionary Board elected the writer to succeed Quinn, and I came into the office April 1, 1954, not being quite sure about the significance of the date. I was ratified by the General Ministerial Assembly that June. In Egypt, Wilbur Skaggs was appointed as mission secretary to succeed me in that responsibility. I mention all this to let you know how difficult it is to determine God's will in such matters. I had spent twenty-one years as a missionary and was just beginning to feel at home with the Arabic language. Ruthe and I were in a position to make our greatest contribution on the mission field. But others thought differently, and they seemed to feel they had the mind of the Lord in requesting that we remain in America in a new administrative position so vital to carrying on the church's obligation to take the Good News to the whole world.

Now we must turn from the general to the more specific developments on the mission fields during this decade from 1945 to 1955. Through it all you will notice the hand of God leading his people on to greater involvement in missions.

The English-speaking West Indies

The Church of God in **Jamaica** was still growing. By 1947, when it celebrated the fortieth anniversary of the Olsons' arrival on the island, Jamaica had ninety-one congregations with approximately twenty-five hundred members. Sixty-seven pastors were assisted by seventy-six evangelists and helpers. Visitors from America continued to give encouragement, among them C. Lowrey Quinn, Nora Hunter, W. Dale Oldham, Ross Minkler, Maurice Berquist, and Frank Towers. The Olsons moved out of Kingston to a residence called Mount Joy located on the hillside just outside the city. George Olson tried to develop better interisland relationships by attending the Annual Convention of the Church of God in Barbados and Trinidad. In 1951 Hurricane Charlie hit Jamaica, destroying ten chapels of the Movement and badly damaging six more.

This was also a period of transition in missionary leadership on the island. Quinn, present for the 1952 Annual Assembly, publicly announced the resignation of George and Nellie Olson as missionaries, although they were granted a brief extended period of service. Nina and Leslie Ratzlaff arrived back from furlough, and Leslie was to be the new mission secretary. Those changes did not come easily. The Olsons elected to remain in Jamaica, for it was thought George Olson could assist Leslie Ratzlaff when asked.

This period of transfer had its effect on the Church of God in Jamaica. With considerable uncertainty pastors and lay leaders alike experienced this "changing of the guard," which was the first of its kind in the Movement's history in Jamaica. The following year Edgar and Mildred Williams arrived to strengthen the missionary force. They had been evacuated out of China and visas could not be secured for them to enter India; so they graciously accepted the call to Jamaica. In December of that year George and Nellie Olson went into full retirement after having given forty-six years of leadership in Jamaica.

Good things were happening in the two institutions in Jamaica. In 1946 Charles and Florence Struthers arrived as missionaries to teach in the Jamaica Bible Institute along with Edith Young, already there. The Strutherses remained for twelve years in that very important task of training leaders for the church. Ardenne High School had become a government grant-aided secondary school by 1948, and in 1950 a new science laboratory was built. The school enjoyed 100 percent passes in Cambridge examinations in 1951 and again in 1952. And 1952 marked the twenty-fifth anniversary of Ardenne High School with 345 students enrolled. Mary Olson was headmistress, being assisted by very capable Jamaican teachers.

Two hundred miles to the northwest on the **Cayman Islands** more missionary teachers were being sent to assist in the work of the church and Triple C School (Creative Christian Character). Emilia Blaskowsky arrived in 1947, remained for two and a half years, and was transferred to Barbados. Max and Neva Hill and Ethel Jeffcoat gave full time to teaching. Raymond and Elna Mae Hastings helped the church from 1951 to 1954. Numerous persons gave leadership for special occasions as they came from America and Jamaica. Finally in 1954 the first long-term missionaries were sent, Arthur and Mary Kluge, with the assignment to help the church become self-reliant as quickly as possible.

In **Trinidad,** not too long after the arrival of Clair and Retha Shultz in 1945 and Ralph and Ruth Coolidge in 1947, plans were set in motion to begin a Church of God training school. For many years this had been a need throughout the southern Caribbean. The churches were in dire need of trained leadership. In the beginning it was necessary to accept dedicated students where they were educationally, for most had not completed the equivalent of high school. A vocational department was a necessity from the beginning to provide training in woodwork for the students as well as income so that they could pay their way. In 1952 Oakley and Veryl Miller were sent as missionaries so that he could head up the vocational department and she could teach Christian education courses. In that same year, land with a good residence was purchased at La Pastora in a valley over the mountain from Port of Spain. Also, a building program was soon under way for housing the vocational department and a combined dormitory-classroom unit. The West Indies Bible Institute became a going institution and is known today as West Indies Theological College. This was the beginning of a most effective training program for the church's leadership in the central and southern Caribbean. Regular visits were made by the missionaries to the island of **Grenada** where a work of the Church of God had started.

Further out in the Atlantic the Church of God on the island of **Barbados** was enjoying increased missionary leadership. Lars and Ellen Olsen, missionaries to Denmark who had been caught in America during World War II, were sent as relief missionaries to Barbados to relieve Ruthe and me in 1944 so that we could be ready to leave America for Lebanon immediately at the war's end. The Olsens left Barbados in 1946 and were soon back in Denmark. They were followed by William and Hope Livingston and then Walter and Margaret Tiesel in 1947. The Livingstons moved on, but Emilia Blaskowsky arrived in 1949 from Grand Cayman. Aaron and Kathryn Kerr were also in Barbados for a brief time. It was Walter and Margaret Tiesel who remained for a number of years and strengthened the church, leading them toward complete self-reliance. While I was working in Barbados during the war I discovered that even though all the properties of the Church of God on the island were registered in the name of the Missionary Board of the Church of God, the Missionary Board was not registered on the island as an alien not-for-profit corporation. That placed the eighteen or nineteen properties in jeopardy. I began the legal process immediately to rectify the situation, but it was not until 1949 and through the persistent efforts of Walter Tiesel that, by an act of the legislature signed by the governor of Barbados, the Missionary Board legally owned those properties. All of this was in preparation for the transfer of the properties to the General Assembly of the Church of God in Barbados more than a decade later.

The West Indian and East Indian work in **British Guiana** took on new life. George Jeffrey, the strong national leader who had come with the Church of God a number of years earlier, died in 1959. Aaron and Kathryn Kerr were transferred from Barbados in 1950 to give leadership to the work but were transferred to East Pakistan after a year. When Herman and Lavera Smith returned home from Kenya they were sent as long-term missionaries to British Guiana. When they arrived in Georgetown there were only three congregations of the Movement in that British colony.

Soon things began to happen. Out in the Corentyne District an East Indian Hindu, Ramalingum Armogum, was converted. He soon became a Christian leader and has now pastored in that area among the East Indians for many years. The Smiths remodeled the old home for the needy at Bellaire Street in Georgetown, making it into a church with numerous rooms for a large Sunday school. Lavera Smith developed the first departmentalized Sunday school in the entire colony. The Yussig Abdool family, East Indians living in Georgetown, were converted to Christianity from Islam, and they have remained faithful down through the years. Training institutes for Sunday school teachers were started as were vacation Bible schools. The concept was to reach children, have them grow up in the church, become converted as young people, and later establish families in the church. British Guiana was one of the first colonies in the Caribbean to have the "Christian Brotherhood Hour" broadcast over government radio. The broadcast was heard throughout the colony. In 1955 a very successful youth revival was conducted in the John Street Church in Georgetown. It was led by a young student from St. Kitts named Theodosia Francis who was studying in the West Indies Bible Institute in Trinidad. She later became the wife of Carlton Cumberbatch, who was destined to become the first West Indian president of the West Indies Bible Institute. By 1955 there were six congregations of the Movement in British Guiana.

The small works on the islands of **Antigua, St. Kitts** and **Curacao** began to develop under the assistance of the Missionary Board of the National Association of the Church of God headquartered at West Middlesex, Pennsylvania. These efforts were sponsored by many of the black churches in America. Bernice and Monroe Spencer emerged as the strong national leaders in Antigua. Both were ministers, although Monroe devoted considerable time to his very profitable business through which he was able to assist in meeting the financial needs of the growing church. By 1953 there were five congregations. That same year the Brewster house in Basseterre, St. Kitts, was demolished and the present church building erected. Willa Davis from Dayton, Ohio, was appointed by the National Association as a missionary to St. Kitts in 1948, but unfortunately she died two years later. In Curacao, David Wade began a second congregation of the Church of God. This was the beginning of a situation destined to give trouble over many years. The Wades developed loyalty with the National Association in America while the Lindos, who had started the first congregation of the Church of God in Curacao, chose to remain closely associated with the Missionary Board of the Church of God.

Central and South America

From the very beginning the work of the Church of God in **Mexico** had its leadership from very short-term evangelistic ventures out of America, especially from the Spanish-speaking congregations that had grown up in Texas and southern California. Because of this the Board of Church Extension and Home Missions looked after and gave direction to what was taking place in Baja California and northern Mexico. By 1953 that Board sent the first long-term missionaries, Maurice and Dondeena Caldwell, to Saltillo. Within a year they had seen the need for and had started La Buena Tierra, the first Bible training school of the Movement among the Spanish-speaking people of Latin America. And by the following year there were brought together in united fellowship and organized effort nine congregations of the Movement in Mexico. In addition to receiving training in the Bible, the students learned about small animal husbandry, which would help them as they went out from the school to live in village situations where the churches were at the time.

To the south of Mexico in **Guatemala City** there was a young Costa Rican student studying in a Presbyterian seminary. As a dynamic evangelist he visited America, seeking Christian fellowship. He happened to attend a camp meeting in the Northwest where Max Gaulke was the evangelist. Isai Calderon's heart was moved. Entirely on his own he then attended the International Convention at Anderson, observing, praying, and feeling very warm toward the fellowship convened there. Calderon then decided he would become identified with the Church of God reformation movement. Therefore, he returned to Guatemala City where he had already married a Guatemalan named Cheney, and they began an independent work in that city. Under their leadership the work grew and spread to Puerto Barrios, Delores and San José de las Minas. Contacts were made with Max Gaulke in Houston, Texas, and with the Missionary Board. Fortunately, by the

108

mid-fifties the opportunity was seized upon to allow this new work to grow as an indigenous church from the beginning. Even though there has never been a resident missionary of the Church of God in Guatemala, the church in America through the Missionary Board has been able to assist Latin leadership so that the church could function as a church and not as a mission. In future chapters the results of this bold attempt will be seen as having been very successful.

In 1948 in **Costa Rica** "Mother" McHugh, who really began the work of the Church of God on the coastal plain, died. Although seven persons were baptized that year, the small group of English-speaking West Indians was left without any kind of leadership except as the missionary in Panama might make a visit once or twice a year. In 1945 Ralph and Mary Collins were sent to **Panama,** and in 1947 Ernest and Grace LaFont were commissioned as missionaries to Panama. After three years the Collinses retired from the field because of ill health. The responsibilities in Panama and the Canal Zone were so great that very little contact was maintained with Costa Rica.

The Latin work in **Cuba** and the Isle of Pines continued to take shape, although the congregations that were predominantly West Indian continued to use the English language in their services. Several of the local leaders were bilingual, and this helped communications. While doing some missionary service in Cuba in 1946 Ellsworth Palmer met a young lady named Hilaria, who soon became his wife. By 1950 they were appointed as missionaries to Cuba and were starting a new group in Matanzas. It was entirely Spanish speaking. Another missionary couple, Earl and Freda Carver, was soon sent, adding to the emphasis on reaching the Spanish-speaking people of Cuba. Within a period of four or five years all the congregations of the movement in Cuba were using the Spanish language. The work had now reached the center of Cuba at Coscorro, and there were three congregations on the Isle of Pines. Several church buildings were erected. Good progress continued until the end of the decade when something happened about which you will read in the next chapter.

During World War II the German immigrants in **Brazil** maintained a low profile. When peace came, however, they renewed their efforts to evangelize, primarily among their own ethnic group. During this time there were periodic attempts to reach the Portuguese-speaking people of Brazil. David Meier returned from America and decided to start a new work in São Paulo, and within two years a building was going up in a newly developing area of the city. Heinrich Weissburger began a Bible training school in Rio das Antas, and soon a printing press was purchased and a magazine named *Missionsbote* was being published. By 1955 there were twelve congregations in Brazil, eleven outreach missions, and ten meeting houses. These were served by eleven ministers and ten helpers.

Rebuilding in Europe After World War II

The people of Europe were in a state of shock when the carnage and devastation of war finally ended. It would require considerable time for them to emerge from war's rubble to normal life again. It took most of a decade for those related to the Church of God reformation movement to regroup their people, begin earning a livelihood, rebuild their churches and homes, and start functioning as a church. This was especially so in **Germany.** But the leaders of the church led the people through a realistic rehabilitation program as quickly as possible. In 1948 Ernst Kersten began the new Bible school at Fritzlar. Gerhard Klabunde in Essen served as pastor of the first church to reconstruct its building in 1948. The Missionary Board sent Wick and Grace Donohew to Europe for two years to give whatever assistance possible. That was a great encouragement. In the basement of the new building in Essen, Klabunde founded the printing shop called Wickenburg Press. By 1955 the first World Conference of the

Church of God was held in Fritzlar. It astonished the delegates to see what the church in Germany had been able to accomplish in ten years by extreme sacrifice and plain hard labor.

In other parts of Europe it was also a struggle to regain momentum in the life and work of the church. Lars and Ellen Olsen, after their stint in Barbados, were sent to Karlstad, Sweden, where they spent three years before transferring to Aalborg, **Denmark.** The situation in Sweden seemed hopeless, and the work of the Church of God there has never recovered. However, the Olsens were able to start a small Bible school in Denmark, endeavoring successfully to train several young men for the ministry. This was the first step toward the Movement's becoming completely self-reliant in that country during the years to come.

The year after the war ended Adam Allan died in **Ireland,** leaving his daughter Naomi to carry on the publication of the *British Gospel Trumpet.* A wooden Quonset-type structure was used as a church building in Belfast. In 1953 Pastor McCloy withdrew from the work after having served for seventeen years as pastor in Belfast. Sam Porter, a stable layman in the congregation, assumed responsibility. John Larmour, originally from Belfast, was in **England** endeavoring to revitalize the congregation in Berkinhead. Meanwhile, across the Channel, one new group in Leeuwarden was added to the small work in **Holland.**

When Stalin died in 1953, the German-speaking people held prisoner in **Russia** were released from the Siberian concentration camps. Many of those in the Church of God fellowship returned to their former homes in the Ukraine and the Caucuses. To the credit of our brothers and sisters living in Europe at that time, having survived the horrors of war, they accomplished an almost unbelievable comeback during that first decade immediately following the conflict. This was done with what I would call a minimum amount of assistance from outside.

Recovery in the Eastern Mediterranean

After a wartime holding pattern throughout the congregations of the Church of God in **Egypt,** everyone was ready to move forward. Egypt was still smarting under some remnants of British colonialism, but within the new decade complete independence from Britain would be achieved and through a bloodless coup the monarchy overthrown in favor of an elected president. This change did, however, bring less freedom for Christian witness because Islam became the official religion of the government, whereas under British rule considerable religious freedom had been enjoyed by the Christian community. This was to affect the activities of the church and mission for years to come.

Thaddeus and Katrina Neff were back in Egypt several months before the end of the fighting and William Fleenor went out alone from America in the spring of 1945 to assist them. Wilbur and Evelyn Skaggs were appointed to Egypt, arriving in November of that same year. Nick and Rose Zazanis also returned to Egypt. Missionary leadership appeared adequate. But William Fleenor soon returned to America to be with his wife, who was very ill. The Kenneth Crose family was in Egypt for about a year. In 1948 a training center was started in Cairo, but it had an on-and-off history until 1954. That summer the Neffs went to Italy for a time of complete rest due to Thaddeus's poor health. In the spring of 1949 I was called to Egypt from Beirut to help in some difficulties that arose in the mission. That summer Ruthe and I and the family went to Egypt to live in the Neff residence in Alexandria while the Neffs spent the summer in America on health leave. We endeavored to care for the responsibilities carried by them. Thaddeus Neff had been able to purchase good properties in the Camp Cesar District of Alexandria and the Shoubra District of Cairo for the further development of the work in those two cities. The Zazanises were forced to leave Egypt in 1946. They became *persona non grata* because the Greek Orthodox archbishop in Egypt brought pressure on the government to expel the Zazanises. It was felt that too many Greeks were being converted. There was a very large congregation of Greeks in Cairo and a smaller one in Alexandria, and so the archbishop used the only method he knew to stop this work of evangelicals. Panayote Dendrinos, a capable layman in the congregation in Cairo, assumed pastoral oversight of the congregation. He maintained this leadership until most of the Greek people left Egypt, including Dendrinos, due to pressure from the government a few years later.

In 1950 Ruthe and I were transferred from Lebanon to Cairo. We had closed out the mission in Lebanon, for the church had become self-reliant. But instead of returning to America at the end of that five-year term in Lebanon the Missionary Board asked us to spend another two years in Egypt before taking our furlough. We agreed to do this to help in the transition taking place in the mission in Egypt. The Neffs retired from the field in 1951 just prior to the return of the Skaggses from furlough. Accompanying the Skaggses was William Fleenor, who was being sent to Egypt for a three-year term. His wife had died earlier. Youth centers developed in both Cairo and Alexandria and turned out to be a new approach to reach university students and young professionals. Downtown offices in Cairo were rented, providing facilities for leadership training. Two missionary residences were purchased in Maadi, a suburb of Cairo. The former residence of the Neffs in Alexandria was remodeled and named Neff Christian Center. Another missionary couple was considered necessary to have a well-rounded staff, with the new personnel to devote full time to leadership training. Consequently, the Missionary Board transferred Ernest and Grace LaFont from Panama to Egypt. In 1954 Jean and Ruth Kilmer arrived in Egypt as numerical missionary replacements for Ruthe and me. I had been asked while on furlough to become the chief executive officer of the Missionary Board. The future of the Church of God in Egypt was looking up, and there was enthusiasm expressed throughout.

Back up now to **Lebanon** right after World War II. This little country had gained its political independence from France during the war. When Ruthe and I arrived back on the field in mid-1954 we found the church doing well with a large number of younger people, some with leadership potential. Fouad Melki was among that group. My parents were badly in need of a furlough, and so they were in America from mid-1946 to mid-1947. It could be said that during the five-year period following the war the Church of God in Lebanon was being led toward and prepared for becoming a self-reliant body. It was a period of struggle and uncertainty for both missionaries and the church. Careful and continuous review of what an indigenous church was and the potential the church possessed toward being one indicated the possibility was present. But the will was lacking on the part of some. Then in May 1948 the world gave birth to the state of Israel. That provided the setting within which it would be possible to initiate a planned withdrawal of missionaries from Lebanon. Americans became an embarrassment instead of an asset in Lebanon. Consequently, negotiations began between the Missionary Board, the mission in Lebanon, and the Church of God in Lebanon, believing that then was the time for the church to become self-reliant without the presence of resident missionaries. It was decided that John and Pearl Crose would leave Lebanon in mid-1949 and that Lester and Ruthe Crose would remain one more year to close out the mission before transferring to Egypt.

One should understand the combination of reasons leading to this decision, for when we arrived home on furlough in 1952 I found the church in America to be quite unaware of what was taking place in the world of missions following the war. Many people still thought that nothing could be done in the work overseas without the presence of an American missionary. Here are six reasons why it was thought imperative that the church in Lebanon be allowed to be on its own. (1) It would give the native church opportunity to assume the initiative in leadership. (2) Continued political unrest, resulting in tensions, made it difficult for the missionary to work. This was especially true for smaller missions that were engaged primarily in evangelism. (3) Lebanon and Syria continued to be unproductive fields compared to worldwide missions. Permanent visible results were not commensurate with efforts expended. (4) There was a trend on the field by larger missions to turn over church work to native administration. (5) Operational costs for the mission in Lebanon were high compared with other fields. (6) There was an apparent lack of funds with which to expand, such as for a student center and equipment for the two mission schools.

Although this appeared to be a bold step and quite unprecedented in the work of Church of God missions, the plan was carried out and the experiment was successful. The last resident missionaries were out and the church in Lebanon became from that moment entirely self-governing, self-propagating, and self-supporting. God has blessed the church there with success. The Movement in Lebanon has maintained contact with the worldwide church in an interdependent relationship.

It had long been the desire of Nick and Rose Zazanis to start a work of the Church of God in **Greece.** So when they were forced to leave Egypt it was only natural for them to be transferred to Athens. The Greek people suffered much during the war, and so for several years relief was necessary. In 1946 Church of God congregations in America sent to Greece more than eight tons of clothing, which the Zazanises distributed among the needy. A centrally located hall was rented in Athens. Four groups of Christians were soon found in the Athens area. A place was rented in Patas, and Nick Zazanis was preaching in numerous places. Since the Greek Orthodox church is the state church in Greece, persecution against evangelicals materialized. The Zazanises were thrown in jail in Corinth at one time. Three of the four places of worship were closed in Athens. But Nick Zazanis persisted. He finally got the Evangelical Church of God registered with the government. Then he began the arduous task of buying a lot and erecting a church building in Athens, a project that everyone said could not be done in that Greek Orthodox-dominated country. But it was, and in mid-1955 a beautiful three-story church building was dedicated in downtown Athens. There were many converts. Zazanis edited the *Greek Gospel Trumpet*. Literature of all kinds was distributed, and there were signs that the work was on the verge of expansion.

Building on Foundations in Kenya

Postwar conditions in the East African British colony of **Kenya** provided opportunity for a new face-off in our missionary activities; therefore, numerous new missionaries were sent. A period of transition was required. The postwar missionaries saw situations differently from earlier missionaires. There were differences in approach, methods used, organization of the growing church, and appreciation for the postcolonial attitudes rapidly appearing among the Africans. In mid-1945 immediately after the war E. A. and Pearl Reardon were sent by the Missionary Board to Kenya to rectify a situation that had developed around John and Twyla Ludwig. It was not until 1947, however, that the Ludwigs returned to America on furlough, during which time the Missionary Board voted that they should not be sent back to Kenya because John Ludwig had reached retirement age. In 1945 the first teacher training class was started at Kima to provide qualified teachers for a growing number of Church of God elementary schools. By the next year Frank and Margaret LaFont and Herman and Lavera Smith were serving at the Kenya mission, the Smiths having been transferred from Trinidad. More nurses were needed, and so Ruth Sanderson and Lima Lehmer were appointed. The Boys' School was moved to Ingotse where Ruben C. and Nora

Schweiger were to work. The Teacher Training School was moved to Mwihila with Jewell Hall in charge and soon to be joined by James and Glenna Yutzy. Irene Engst was sent to the Mwihila station and lived with Jewell Hall. Both of these moves were a disappointment to the Bunyore African Christians around Kima due to tribal jealousies. Evangelism was producing many strong village churches. The newly formed Woman's Missionary Society in Bunyore raised funds to send their own missionary, Obed Kutera, to another tribal area, Kisii, in southern Kenya. A station was started at Ibeno. Lydia Hansen was sent to Kima, and she and Lima Lehmer formed a strong team at that station.

When the Ludwigs left for furlough in 1947 Herman Smith was appointed as mission secretary. He was the first to provide a democratic organization for the church by developing a General Assembly with appropriate bylaws. This encouraged a much greater involvement and more cooperation by the many pastors and elders. It became a delegated assembly. When the Smiths went on furlough to America and were then transferred to British Guiana, Wick and Grace Donohew were transferred from Europe to Kenya and Wick became the mission secretary. These were good moves by the Board. Both Smith and Donohew, over a longer period, gave stability to the mission and to the church. By virtue of his office and according to the bylaws of the General Assembly, Donohew was chairman of the Assembly. It required twelve years before the church was ready to accept an African chairman. But change had to come.

One of the first achievements by Donohew was to start a Bible school, which was the first attempt at providing regular training for pastors. When I made my first visit to Kenya at the end of 1955 to participate in the Fiftieth-Year Jubilee of the Church of God mission in Kenya I was introduced to the first twelve students who were to graduate from the Bible school. These fine men had to be accepted and taught from where they were educationally. No one had more than a second-grade education and one was illiterate. That was no discredit to them. But teaching had to be at that level. Within a few years the picture changed completely due to the rapid advance in general education in Kenya.

Education was indeed given priority throughout Kenya. Christian missions were much involved by request of the British colonial government. Many of the Church of God village churches began elementary schools. Calvin and Martha Brallier were sent out and stationed in Mwihila, and from there Calvin gave supervision to these elementary schools. Velma Schneider was sent to Kima to teach in the Girls' School, which was an intermediate school. Margaret LaFont had become headmistress after the Ludwigs left.

In 1951 the Missionary Board voted to establish a hospital in Kenya, and within a short time David and Elsie Gaulke were on their way there to oversee the project. Nora Memorial Hospital was sponsored by the Woman's Missionary Society and the Mid-Century Building Fund. Hazel McDilda and Vera Martin were sent as nurses to be ready when the first two units of the hospital, a duplex for American nurses and a doctor's residence at Mwihila, were ready for occupancy in early 1956. In these two areas of education and medicine the mission worked very closely with the government. Much of it was subsidized by government grants, for the colonial power at that time had a policy of working through the various missions in caring for the needs of the people, especially those in the interior provinces. That relationship was to be modified in subsequent years.

The Asian Sub-continent: India and East Pakistan

After one hundred fifty years under British rule **India** gained its independence from Great Britain in 1947 but remained a member of the British Commonwealth. At the same time, as mentioned earlier, two states of India became a new country named Pakistan. The work of the Church of God mission in India centered at Lalmanirhat found itself in East Pakistan with an Islamic government. Floyd and Maude Heinly discovered that they and the mission were responsible to new authorities. This left only Mona Moors and Ellen High as missionaries in India, giving most of their time to the care and education of the girls in the Shelter at Cuttack. Mosier Moses, the only capable Indian leader in Calcutta, had died during the war. Also, there were very few contacts with the Nichols-Roys in the northern state of Assam.

In the southern state of Kerala, P. J. Philip was in control, having almost no contact with the two groups of the Church of God centered in Cuttack and Shillong. The entire mission in India came out of the war in a weakened condition. In 1949 P. J. Philip made a journey to America to be present during the International Convention in Anderson and to meet with the Missionary Board to secure more financial aid for South India. Actually, there were only two strong leaders of the Church of God in India at that time: J.J.M. Nichols-Roy in the northeast and P.J. Philip in the south. Nichols-Roy was a leader in government, in business, and in the church. I recall the time he showed me a large picture of the special congress convened by the government to draft the constitution for the newly independent country of India. There were only a half-dozen Christians in that large assembly of Hindus and Muslims. Yet their influence as Christians was strong in demanding religious liberty in India, a secular state. And so it is found yet today in India's constitution. P. J. Philip in the early fifties was selected as chairman of the Malayalam (the language of Kerala state in South India) Bible Revision Committee of the Indian Bible Society. He was also chosen as the vice-president of the Kerala Christian Council. But both Nichols-Roy and Philip, though able men, were getting on in years and there was need for younger leadership. In 1950 the doors of Miller Bible Insti-

119

tute were opened in Chengannur, South India, but it had an up-and-down history and finally closed, due primarily to lack of qualified and continuous leadership.

After having served in East Pakistan for a year, Aaron and Kathryn Kerr moved to South India to work with P. J. Philip. The Kerrs were the first American missionaries of the Church of God to reside in South India. At that particular juncture relationships did not work out too well for the Kerrs. Three men were ordained to the Christian ministry: P. C. Zachariah, P. D. Varughese, and K. K. Mathai. All three gave many years of leadership to the Movement in South India. The Bodhini Press began operation in Chengannur, printing many kinds of Christian literature, including the church paper called *Atma Bodhini.* Philip was editor. After three years in South India the Kerrs left the country and their replacements were Gordon and Wilhemina Schieck from the Church of God in Canada. P. J. Philip soon turned over administrative responsibility to Schieck and shortly thereafter died. One should keep in mind that he was one of the young men who had been converted and had enjoyed contact with A. D. Khan in 1907. He had been been with the Church of God for forty-nine years, and his death was a loss to the entire Christian community in South India. P. C. Zachariah then became the new editor of *Atma Bodhini.* Up to the northeast in Cuttack a chapel was built for the Shelter. Mona Moors, after giving thirty-one years of service to India, retired from the field to marry G. P. Tasker, whose estranged relations with the Church of God had been resolved ten years earlier. Also, permits were finally received from the Indian government to allow Sidney and Jean Johnson to take up missionary service at Cuttack. It appears to have taken almost a decade following the war to regain some momentum in India.

But a new day had dawned for Christian missions in India. Soon after gaining political independence the government of India began to bring pressure on all Protestant Christian missions by restricting the entry of American missionaries. In fact, India was being flooded with many independent missionaries, and unethical means were frequently employed to gain converts. As a result of the government's adverse reactions, long-standing missions in India suffered along with the offenders. The Movement was fortunate to have qualified Canadians whom the Missionary Board could send to India. Canadians did not need an entry visa because they were members of the Commonwealth and therefore could not be denied entry into India. Gordon and Wilhemina Schieck were the first of several Canadian missionaries of the Church of God to be sent to India during the next decade. The government also brought great pressure on long-standing missions in India to transfer their property holdings to the Indian church of their respective denominations. In 1955 the Missionary Board went on record with a resolution to make such a transfer of properties it held in India to the Church of God in India as soon as a representative body of the church became a legal entity capable of holding property. And that, as we shall see, required a number of years.

East Pakistan was even slower in picking up after the war. The mission station at Lalmanirhat had been requisitioned by the United States Air Force during the last two years of the war as a base for flying "the hump" into China. Robert and Frances Clark, however, arrived in India (soon to be East Pakistan) early enough to have about a two-year overlap with the Heinlys before the Heinlys' retirement from the field, which for them was necessary due to poor health and age. As mentioned earlier, Aaron and Kathrym Kerr were with the Clarks at Lalmanirhat for about a year before going to South India. The Clarks labored diligently, and by the time of their first furlough they felt they were beginning to experience some breakthrough in reaching Hindus. There had been ten baptisms, and four Sunday schools were being conducted. A little later they had their first preaching mission among Muslims. But the going was difficult and visible results were small. Considerable relief work was also necessary on a perennial basis due to floods and other natural causes. At one time considerable feeling was generated in the Missionary Board to close out this nonproductive field. Fortunately, good Christian common sense prevailed. Regardless of the small number of converts to Christianity, the Hindus and Muslims need the witness of Christian faith in their midst. That is explicit in the Great Commission.

Out of Dust and Ashes in East Asia

The Japanese people were badly shaken by the time the peace treaty was signed with America. The atomic bomb used by America ushered in a new era for the world. Thousands of Japanese had been killed and many more wounded. Their homes and factories lay in ruins. Here was presented to the Western church the opportunity to demonstrate mercy and love. And, strangely enough, American missionaries were to be readily accepted. But the question was how to regain contact with the few scattered Japanese Christians. One of the Church of God servicemen stationed in Japan, Ralph Morton, wrote to Adam Miller, secretary of the Missionary Board, asking for information on how to find any Church of God people. He was given an address. By December 1945 Morton was able to discover Choko Shimizu.

It was learned that the large building at Hongo had been destroyed as well as every other church building except that at Nerima. Almost unbelievably no Japanese of the Church of God had been killed during the war, although some almost lost their lives. Many had lost their homes and businesses. Direct contact with the main Japanese church leaders was established. Taniguchi Sensei called for many missionaries to come to Christianize Japan. Shimizu Sensei wrote about being visited by five Christian Americans of the occupation forces. One of these was Nathan Smith, who within five years was out of the armed forces and back in Japan as a Church of God missionary. In spite of all the problems encountered in entering Japan at that time, it was unfortunate that the church in America was not prepared to do what, in retrospect, could have been accomplished in Japan when the time was ripe for salutary Christian evangelization. We can be thankful, however, for what progress was made during the ten-year period immediately after the conflict.

Policies must be flexible to meet the needs of changing times. Even though the church in America had sent no missionaries to Japan since 1927, the Church of God in Japan was now in desperate need of missionary assistance and encouragement. Early in 1949 Kyodan (the United Church of Japan) was building a model community in Shinjuku District of Tokyo and approached Shimizu Sensei to have the Church of God start a congregation there. A good location on top of a hill was offered, and this became the Toyama Heights Church of God. Obstacles were overcome and by November 1949, Arthur and Norma Eikamp reached Tokyo. At first they had to live in the YMCA, but when the new church building was erected at Toyama Heights they were able to live there in a couple of rooms.

Within a year and a half Nathan and Ann Smith were sent to join the missionary family. A new church building was erected at Nerima, another district of Tokyo. To show the resilience of the Japanese Christians and also their way of demonstrating their appreciation to the American Church, the Church of God in Japan sent seventy dollars as a contribution to Christ's World Service Day in 1951.

Nathan and Ann Smith started a work in Tachikawa near an American military base where some Church of God members of the American armed forces had made contacts with several interested Japanese. Within three years Philip and Phyllis Kinley reached Japan and assumed responsibility for the work at Tachikawa, leaving Nathan and Ann Smith free to move southward to the island of Kyushu where a beginning had been made at Imajuku by Church of God military personnel. Also nearby in the city of

Fukuoka another congregation was developing under the leadership of Morito Tajima and his wife, both professors at a university. They were ably assisted by Nakahara Sensei, one of the leaders from Tokyo dating back to the mid-twenties. The son of the late Japanese pioneer of the Church of God, Keiji Yajima, a businessman in a large department store, was transferred to Osaka, the second largest city of Japan located about halfway between Tokyo and Fukuoka. He initiated children's meetings out of which grew a congregation. At Toyama Heights Shimizu Sensei, a very capable pastor and leader, was willing to get along without missionary assistance, and so Arthur and Norma Eikamp moved to Tamagawa, another district of the great city of Tokyo. A mission home was built for them, and soon the congregation was large enough to warrant a building. And it was at Tamagawa that Arthur Eikamp, encouraged by the Japanese church leaders, began what is known today as *Tamagawa Sei Gakuin,* a school for girls, through which it was hoped homes in the area could be reached with the Christian message. A five-year plan was sponsored by the Missionary Board, during which time the school became well established and was soon to become one of the best and most well-known intermediate and secondary schools for girls in Tokyo.

There were other educational approaches to the Japanese people through which the gospel could be communicated. As local congregations began again after the war, they started kindergartens for small children in the community. This provided ready access into nearby homes and provided some partial support for the pastor, who was always head of the kindergarten. Christian teachers were employed, and the overall influence in the communities through the children was significant. The American church's missionaries in Japan and the Japanese churches were further assisted during this period of time by another influence. While American occupational forces were in Japan the United States government provided what were known as Dependents' Schools for the children of American families. These schools required American teachers, and some of them, such as Alfred Lange and his family, were from the Church of God. The Langes requested to be placed in the Dependents' School in Fukuoka so that they could assist in the work of the church. Their ministry was a real blessing. One of these teachers, Freda LaFoe, became a full-time missionary after completing her assignment with our government when the schools for dependents were closed out. She taught in Tamagawa Sei Gakuin for a number of years. A new training school was felt necessary for educating potential leadership for the church. This was a night school and only religious subjects were offered. As we shall see later on, this was not adequate training for the otherwise highly educated Japanese young men, and another form of training emerged. Another missionary couple, Donald and Arlene Goens, arrived in Japan to become involved in direct evangelism, helping to develop new congregations. Contacts were maintained with America through infrequent visitors, such as Adam and Grace Miller and Dale and Polly Oldham.

With all of these efforts, and especially through the hard work of the Japanese Christians, the work of the Church of God in Japan came out of complete chaos in 1945 into a growing church through the subsequent decade. That growth is best seen through these statistics:

	1949	1951	1952	1953	1955
Congregations	4	4	7	9	11
Sunday Schools	4	5	8	14	16
Church Attendance	90	145	230	310	350
Sunday School Attendance	170	575	900	1500	2000

On the mainland in **China** the missionary endeavors of the Church of God got off to a good start immediately after World War II but came to an abrupt end when the communists invaded and took over China in 1949-50. In Shanghai, Charles and Annabel Hunnex were released from the internment camp where they had been held captive by the Japanese for two and a half years. Their health was somewhat impaired, but they remained in China to assist and give guidance to the new missionaries arriving. Daisy Maiden returned to work in Soo Chow. David and Elsie Gaulke along with Milton and Eleanor Buettner were taking special courses at the University of California at Berkeley in preparation for their assignment in China and in 1946 found themselves in Yunnan Province of West China as Christian witnesses at the Peace Memorial Hospital in Tengchung. Lovena Billings arrived shortly thereafter.

David Gaulke was the first medical missionary doctor to be commissioned by the Missionary Board of the Church of God. Elsie Gaulke and Eleanor Buettner were nurses, and Lovena Billings also assisted in the hospital. Milton Buettner did evangelistic work and also taught English in the government middle school. The following year Edgar and Mildred Williams were appointed to China where they were involved in leadership training and administrative work in East China. Just when some encouraging results were beginning to appear through the efforts put forth in both East and West China, the communist invasion of those areas began, ending in subsequent take-over. This meant immediate evacuation by all American missionaries. Charles and Annabel Hunnex and Daisy Maiden left immediately for America and all three retired from active missionary service. About the same time Edgar and Mildred Williams left for America.

While studying in a Peking language school Lovena Billings had met a young medical doctor from Bristol, England, P. K. Jenkins. He was preparing for missionary service in China. They were married in July and in December evacuated to Hong Kong. There they began working in a medical clinic through the Emanuel Medical Mission. David and Elsie Gaulke and Milton and Eleanor Buettner evacuated West China southward to Burma. The Gaulkes then went to Kenya to check on the possibilities of enlarging the medical services of the Kenya mission, and the Buettners served for several months in Cuttack, India, before returning to America. From that point on in China our only contact with our Christian fellowship has been through the underground. Most of the Christians remained faithful, but opportunities for public witness were no more. In fact, the entire Christian church in China went underground.

The year following the end of the Second World War M.C. Sergeant, a major in America's armed forces, made contact with the group in **Korea** who had earlier identified themselves with the Church of God. Several Church of God chaplains also encouraged the group, who were already beginning to suffer from communist pressures. By 1950 severe persecution of the Christians in what we now know as North Korea had set in. Many were killed. Seventy-five to eighty percent of the Christian ministers were either captured or killed by communists, and many churches were burned. Christians fled by the hundreds to the southern part of the country. Then came the Korean War with the subsequent division of Korea into North and South. After the conflict was over two Church of God chaplains, Gerald Weaver and Ralph Adamson, made contact in and around Seoul with the Christians of our fellowship. Arthur Eikamp went over to Japan to give encouragement. The Korean church was requesting missionary assistance as they were starting life all over again. They especially wanted someone who could teach in the Bible school they were beginning. The Missionary Board brought John and Pearl Crose out of retirement and sent them to Korea to offer the mature guidance needed at that time. They remained in South Korea only one year.

Another gradual change was taking place in the Movement's missionary outreach. Practically all of the second-generation missionaries of the Church of God had by 1955 made their contribution in overseas service. They had served faithfully and well during very difficult years of the world's history from the end of World War I to around a decade following World War II. The few third-generation missionaries, among whom were Ruthe and me, were still much involved, acting as a bridge between the colonial and postcolonial eras of missionary history. But it was primarily the new wave of fourth-generation missionaries who were now to carry the burden of taking the Good News to people around the world. Naturally the process of change from one generation to another is always gradual and has a great deal of overlap.

Chapter 5

Churches Emerge from Missions
(1955-1965)

BOTH EXCITEMENT and concerns were generated during this particular decade as congregations of the Church of God reformation movement extant in countries other than America began to recognize and cherish their identity as something quite unique and different from the foreign missions that brought about their existence. As suggested earlier, these dynamic feelings within the overseas churches ran parallel with the rapid appearance of new nations as they gained their political independence from colonial powers. In Africa alone during this ten-year period, thirty-seven new states or countries representing two hundred million people emerged from colonialism to gain control over their own destinies. An atmosphere conducive to the indigenization of churches was created. If these countries could do it politically, why couldn't the churches do it in their relationships with the "mother" church? I had gone through this experience in Lebanon shortly before assuming responsibility in the Missionary Board, and I was aware of what could take place in Barbados, Trinidad, and Egypt. Indeed, the possibilities that appeared to be present in most countries where the Church of God had missions were very exciting.

The entire missionary outreach of the Reformation Movement in America was entering a period of its history when a new understanding of its mission surfaced, especially as it related to churches in mission fields that had been in existence from ten to fifty years. As the church was growing and maturing in each country, the mission had been acting as a kind of scaffold around the structure from which missionaries helped shape the church. Now it was time for the scaffolding to come down, allowing the church to stand alone as a biblical entity, an indigenous church.

The Indigenous Church

What is indigeneity? A clear understanding of this term is necessary to visualize what was happening in missions during the 1950s and 1960s. Most people in the American churches had only a very nebulous concept of the meaning of the indigenous church as applied to mission churches. Many missionaries considered the major goal to be self-support. Mission churches usually perceived it as being a plan perpetrated by colonial missions to withdraw financial support and missionaries. If there was any degree of understanding it was always in terms of the three selfs, as they were called: self-supporting, self-governing, and self-propagating. Self-support always came first in the eyes of American Christians. I consistently maintained that self-government and self-propagation were primary. Once any new group of Christians were able to govern itself according to the Word of God and was experiencing new births into the kingdom of God, the third "self" would come naturally and with greater ease than by having the monetary factor stressed first, as so many missions were doing.

Look at it more closely. A plant is indigenous when it grows naturally in the soil of the country where it is planted, takes root, and flourishes. The same is true in church planting. When the seed of the gospel is planted by missionaries in the hearts of the people of another country it dies but later springs forth in the lives of new Christians of another culture. Another reflection of the incarnation of God among people takes place. Jesus becomes one of or identifies with the believers found in that particular culture. And the gospel becomes relevant only when this incarnation takes place. A church becomes indigenous only when this becomes a reality. But this is not all. When incarnation occurs in another culture certain adaptations or adjustments are necessary—cultural adjustments, to be precise. The seed of the gospel planted in the new soil of another culture will spring up as the gospel, but it will not be identical in every respect to the seed originally planted. The Christian faith will make the necessary accommodations to the new culture but without losing its absolute identity with the gospel.

There must be limits, however, to these adjustments or accommodations. A core of basics representing the pure faith or pure truth as revealed through the Holy Spirit will always endure as the Word of God is studied diligently. When any accommodation would do damage to that core of truth, it should not be considered. If an accommodation does not damage the core, it could be accepted as a cultural adaptation. If this is properly understood and practiced it is possible to avoid syncretism or the union of Christianity with paganism. On the other hand, to understand this principle is to assist in achieving indigenous Christianity wherever missions go. True, the gospel is above culture, but it must be presented in meaningful cultural patterns to be effective. Who decides what adaptations to make and not to make? It is not the responsibility of the missionaries, although they could very well be resource persons if they are wise and have the confidence of the people among whom they are working. Primarily the decisions should be reached by the Christians living in a specific culture, guided by the Holy Spirit as the Word is studied.

All of this removes the colonial approach as a missionary introduces the gospel into new cultural patterns. Some new religious forms or ways of doing things in the church will gradually emerge. For instance, church architecture will reflect local cultural styles. Hymns will not merely be translations of Western hymns using Western music, as is sometimes necessary in the beginning, but will in due time be born from the soul of Christian poets and musicians within the culture. Musical instruments reflecting the culture will be used during the meeting together of believers. There are indeed different ways each culture has to express the feelings of the Christian life and experience. These accommodations relate the gospel to people and not to a "foreign" religion.

Missionaries who find themselves in fields where totally Western cultural patterns have been used in planting the church can use these concepts in providing opportunities to discover and implement whatever accommodations should take place to allow the church to become truly indigenous. But that takes time. The missionaries themselves will probably retain most of their cultural likes and dislikes, at the same time making the necessary adaptations to the culture in which they live in order to exist comfortably and effectively among the people. But they must not impose their own cultural forms on the Christians of the other culture. Furthermore, we must also recognize that cultures do change with every age, at every level, and with each generation. This occurs as new conditions emerge that naturally create change in the culture of any society.

I have spent considerable time explaining the indigenous church, because without a correct understanding it is impossible to comprehend what was taking place on the mission fields during this decade of time. During the twenty-one years of my administrative ministry in missions I made many trips to the countries where the Movement existed and to the American church. I tried to explain to the church in the United States and its leadership, to our missionaries on the field, and to national church leaders in other countries the biblical concept of the indigenous church and the manner in which the church should become indigenous. I tried to impress upon the American church that the day of colonialism in missions had passed and that our missions in other countries had to maintain the initiative during a transition period to the end that an indigenous church would emerge from a mission church. I tried to indicate that the American church must learn not to violate the integrity of the indigenous church coming into being, but rather it should relate to the church in a spirit of fraternalism, not paternalism.

In more recent years a new term has come into good usage: *self-reliant*. A church that is self-reliant depends upon itself and not upon a mission from another country. I wish we could have had this term in popular usage in the late 1950s as the attempt was being made to help the church of the Reformation Movement in other countries to be the church and not to depend on a mission from America to do the staffing, supporting, and administering. The American church had to understand that as indigenous churches came into being it did not mean the end of missions. Cross-cultural missions will remain imperative to the end of time, for there will always be in some parts of the world those who have never heard the name of Jesus. A proper concept of the self-reliant church is necessary to understand some of the situations that developed in mission-to-church and church-to-mission relationships. These will be observed as we continue in this chapter.

The goals set and reset in all these undertakings were not achieved overnight. They required the diligent effort of all persons concerned throughout the time span of 1955-75, roughly twenty years, or a generation of time. That is just about what it required—a new generation in the church—to bring the Church of God reformation movement into being in countries around the world. But at this point I must bring to your attention some concepts and plans that were linked closely with the indigenization of the mission church.

General Assemblies Come Alive

In most countries where our missions had functioned for a number of years and where there were several congregations, the emerging church followed the general congregational polity of the Church of God reformation movement. During the decade of the 1950s, General Assemblies became evident—some for the first time and others showing themselves for what they indeed were. But in most situations where resident missionaries were present those General Assemblies assumed a secondary position. Unfortunately, the mission held the primary position. The 1947 Missionary Manual called for the organization of the mission staff to carry out the objectives of the mission. When this happened, as it did in most countries, it turned out that the mission staff on each mission field fairly well controlled the affairs of the church. This was not a common practice at the local congregational level, but rather at the point of the overall work of the Church of God in that country. Instead of the mission's working with the church that had come into being, as was the intent of the statement in the Missionary Manual, the church worked with the mission.

I sat in many mission staff meetings in Kenya, Jamaica, Japan, India, Barbados, Trinidad, and British Guiana during the late 1950s and early 1960s when the missionaries would strategize and plan the implementation of all the efforts to be put forth by the church. The mission would report the thinking and decision of the missionaries to the General Assembly. The church had no national representative present in mission staff meetings. But many times missionaries held most of the key positions in the General Assembly, serving as chairmen, secretary, treasurer, and chairmen of committees.

In retrospect, perhaps all of this happened as part of the evolution of the indigenous church. But it should not surprise anyone that this method of operation would be challenged. Colonialism in missions had to cease. I was asked by national ministers at that time what was going on behind closed doors of a mission meeting that should eliminate the presence of a national church representative.

This was indeed the beginning of the end of mission control of the church in countries where there was a church large enough to be organized. But the process of demissionizing was not easy and in most cases required several years of transition. To make the change suddenly and completely by mandate of the Missionary Board would have been disastrous. Most missionaries were not ready for it. They thought the church leaders were not mature enough. Some were afraid of the "young rebels" or the "radical element" in the church wanting to gain control. And strange as it may seem, most people at the local church level were not wanting it. Missionaries thought they were doing what they had been sent to accomplish. Church people, particularly the older ones, were afraid of being on their own and still wanted the last word on any issue to come from missionaries, especially from the mission secretary. It was generally agreed that the treasurer must be a missionary, since there was a lack of confidence in a national Christian by both the people of the church and by the missionaries. But the times demanded change, which was soon to come.

The first move was to strengthen the General Assembly, allowing it to function according to its own bylaws, representing the voice of the church. This was not always easy. I observed in 1957 in South India that the church was known as the "Church of God Missions." I told the leaders that it should be called the "Church of God in South India." But it required years for the congregations there to reach that objective, with a viable General Assembly. In several other countries missionaries took the initiative by declaring that they would refrain from serving as officers of the General Assembly or as chairmen of committees. That became a process extending over several years until national leadership was finally in control of the General Assembly. However, it did not entirely eliminate missionary presence. Missionaries agreed to serve on committees and boards if elected by the church to serve, the same as any other person, and not because they were missionaries.

This was the beginning of the period when the official position of the organized mission would decrease in influence and the rightful position of the church would increase. The mission began to carry less and less responsibility for the work of the church with missionaries performing major functions. The church began to assume more and more responsibility for its own life and activities, since national ministers and church workers were being trained to carry on. All the functions of the church were now to be looked after not by the mission but by the General Assembly. It was interesting to note that most of these General Assemblies became members of the national councils in their respective countries, such as the Kenya Christian Council, the Assam Christian Council and the Kerala Christian Council in India, and the Jamaica Christian Council. This was to give General Assemblies of the Church of God considerable strength as a part of the total Christian population in their respective countries.

It must also be noted that from the very beginning and by choice of the church in each country, the General Assembly of the Church of God was a delegated body. Furthermore, it represented through its membership the laity of the church as well as its pastoral leadership. Our Christian brothers and sisters in other countries experienced no theological problem at this point, but it did tend to make these General Assemblies more official with greater influence over local congregations. Part of our recognizing the validity of the overseas General Assembly was to understand and develop proper relations with it. If the General Assembly had integrity, it should have the privilege of making its own decisions, which the mission, its missionaries, and the Missionary Board should recognize and respect. Within a few years the Missionary Board began to seek the feelings of each General Assembly relative to the kind of assistance the church wanted from the church in America and the type of missionary it might want. This was not always easy for the Missionary Board or for the missionaries to accept. It was a shock to a few missionaries to hear from the General Assembly that their services were no longer needed. And it was difficult for members of the Missionary Board, for example, to understand the General Assembly thought differently from them about how an institution should be operated or staffed. But let it be said here that in every situation the spirit of Christ was demonstrated within the framework of mutual love and respect.

Employing the Concept of Grant-In-Aid

One of the major problems as the church on mission fields moved toward being indigenous was that of finance. The problem was how to become self-supporting when the church had been so dependent financially on the mission for so many years. In most situations the mission had supplied the total or partial support of ministers and other church workers as well as amounts required for the activities of the church through institutions or other services. Could the problem be solved by the Missionary Board's giving notice that as of an early date all financial assistance would be cut off abruptly and entirely? Hardly. There were a few who advocated that approach saying, ''Let the churches sink or swim. They have received financial assistance long enough.'' But when reviewed carefully, that plan appeared inadequate to reach the desired goal. In fact, it could have well destroyed what had already been achieved on the mission field after many years of diligent and sacrificial labor. Even colonial governments continued assisting through financial grants the new independent nations that had formerly been their colonies. Survival was important and necessary.

Therefore, during the late 1950s and early 1960s the General Assemblies of the Church of God in countries where our missionaries had labored for many years were approached one by one to enter into an agreement with the Missionary Board on a plan called "Grant-In-Aid on a Decreasing Subsidy Basis." It was a simple concept that would allow the Missionary Board to continue financial support where actually needed, but the amount would be decreased each year over a period of ten or fifteen years until the time would come when the church would indeed be self-supporting. Each agreement had to be worked out with each General Assembly. There was no rigid pattern to follow. The situation in each country was different from that in another.

It was not long before the Movement's churches in Japan, Kenya, Egypt, Denmark, Jamaica, Barbados, Trinidad, and Panama were well on their way in the plan. When the shock of the first or second year's decrease of income from the Missionary Board was survived, it became obvious that a strong emphasis on all-of-life stewardship must be implemented. In countries where most of the pastors' support came from the Missionary Board, pastor-congregation relations were being strained. The pastors much preferred receiving their support from a trustworthy foreign mission rather than being dependent on their congregations. The congregation was slow in accepting responsibility for its pastor, feeling it was the mission's responsiblity. Most pastors thought it was begging to ask their congregations to support them. The solution required a strong educational program aimed at both the pastors and the congregations. And that could best be done, although with problems, through the General Assemblies.

To help the churches feel responsible to their General Assembly and to assist the General Assembly in feeling responsible to aid the churches, both of which were necessary if the Grant-In-Aid plan was to be successful, the Missionary Board suggested that the entire amount of the monthly Grant-In-Aid be sent to the treasurer of the General Assembly and not to the mission secretary-treasurer for disbursement. The General Assembly would then use the funds according to an agreed-upon budget schedule. As a matter of fact, the General Assembly could probably determine more accurately the needs of pastors, churches, and programs. This placed a great deal of responsibility upon the General Assembly, but that was good. It was no longer the mission or the missionaries who were managing the finances of the church. This plan liberated the mission secretary-treasurer from one of the most difficult tasks in relation to the people. I was made aware of this after having served in that position in four different countries. Now members of the General Assembly through its various committees had to determine how the Grant-In-Aid would be distributed to persons and programs.

But adverse situations were not over. It was soon learned that the Grant-In-Aid plan had to be flexible in order to be practical. On occasion I had to sit with a General Assembly or its Executive Council to review the possibility of adjusting the amount being sent or to extend the number of years over which the decrease of amounts was to be made. Those were always difficult sessions. It was not always easy to determine the accuracy of presentations. A certain degree of pressure had to be maintained to indicate to individuals who were not living up to agreements that the Missionary Board meant business. And yet undue suffering could not be tolerated. The question of how to be hard-nosed and compassionate at the same time is not an easy one. And there were valid reasons for adjustments or for declaring, on occasion, a moratorium on the decrease for one or two years. Sometimes economic problems in the country were of such a nature that the common people were actually suffering. Disasters such as severe drought, famine, flood, or even war made it imperative to grant certain considerations. One or two specific situations presented special concerns. Sometimes the cost of living in a country would increase tremendously. To impose the agreed-upon cut in salary or program would amount to a double blow. Or if additional pastors or workers were taken on as the work was growing, they would not always fit into the Grant-In-Aid scheme without adjustments. Much grace and wisdom were required by all involved, and I always found the members of the General Assembly to be understanding and willing to make adjustments and concessions if the Missionary Board would do the same. In some countries it required more grace than in others.

What happened to the funds that were withheld by the Missionary Board each year when the decrease was made in remittances sent to General Assemblies involved in the Grant-In-Aid scheme? Naturally that question would be raised by members of those Assemblies. At first they felt the amount of the decrease in any given year should remain in the country for some special need or project. On the other hand, the Missionary Board was being hard-pressed to start new missions in new countries, and the increase in income in America was not permitting much, if any, expansion. Therefore, funds released through the decreasing subsidy plan helped the Missionary Board, but not sufficiently. It was during this period that demands were made for expansion and more missionaries were sent out. But overextension brought about deficit spending. That soon came to an abrupt end as reserves were depleted. For two or three years what was known as an austerity budget was implemented, although neither missionaries nor the Missionary Board appreciated it. Hence, any savings through the decreasing subsidy plan to General Assemblies was desperately needed at that particular time to maintain fiscal integrity.

Toward the Transfer of Properties

The Missionary Board began to encourage each of the various General Assemblies to become a legal entity recognized by its respective government. This was stressed to allow the church in each country to hold its own properties rather than the Missionary Board's holding them. Up to this time when the Missionary Board was responsible for the work of the church, the Board had registered as an alien corporation in that country and therefore held church properties in its name. But related to the indigenization of these churches was the desire expressed by both the Missionary Board and the General Assemblies that in a country where the church existed that church should own the properties. Consequently, each General Assembly revised its constitution and bylaws to allow for the holding of properties and became a legal entity in its own country. That process required time—in some countries much longer than in others. Then the transfer of all the church's properties could take place. But eventually it happened. Occasionally there was discussion about the possibility of including movable properties such as automobiles, house furnishings, and equipment. As a rule, movable properties were not transferred. The Missionary Board, however, did turn over all office equipment to the offices of the General Assembly when the transfer of responsibility was made from the mission to the church. It also made available at a token price mission-owned automobiles. There was always a deliberate attempt on the part of the Board to be as generous as possible at such times. Of course, the transfer of church properties itself provided the church with assets running into thousands of dollars. Furthermore, it was understood that once the transfer had been made, the church would be responsible for the maintenance and upkeep of those properties. Since in most situations there were no vast institutional buildings to maintain, no major problems evolved at that point.

Indigenous Churches from the Beginning

As the Church of God reformation movement began to spread into new countries, opportunities prevailed to start these new works as indigenous churches from the very beginning. In order to grow they would not require a mission to be established by the Missionary Board. At the same time, however, the Board could relate and assist as mutually agreed upon by sending an occasional missionary to perform some specific and needed function. Financial assistance could also be provided without violating the integrity of the church. This could be done without giving the young church the idea that it was being controlled by the church in America through the Missionary Board. There were times and places where the people of the country were actually very poor and required some form of assistance from the affluent American churches. But the giving had to be done in such a manner that it did not make the recipient subservient to the donor.

A new set of relationships materialized with these fresh and enthusiastic beginnings in other countries even though they were not initiated by the Missionary Board. For instance, we began to have good relations with the start that Carl and Lova Swart were making in Australia, a country that had not been considered a foreign mission field. The start in Guatemala and the Philippines was made by nationals of those countries who became burdened for their people and who desired to begin a work of the Reformation Movement. In Denmark, a Grant-In-Aid scheme continued even after a resident missionay was no longer necessary. In Germany, the church had moved to the place where our relation with it was one of church-to-church. There was the unique situation in Okinawa where Church of God American military personnel started a children's work that quickly developed into an adult program. They wanted the Missionary Board to come in and take over. Instead, since Okinawa had belonged to Japan, the Board encouraged the Church of God in Japan to send one of its ministers to assist in Okinawa. The Japanese gave the young minister ten years to build an indigenous church. Later on in this chapter more details will be given about each one of these situations. The point to make here is that in all of these new starts the attempt was made not to burden the young church with a mission, but rather to assist it to be the church from the very beginning. This allowed for the formation of General Assemblies, the registration of those legal entities with their respective governments, and the handling of any church properties from the beginning. This bypassed the earlier route of establishing a mission, developing a church, and then demissionizing that church so that it might become indigenous. When the young indigenous church was given guidance by the Missionary Board, the possibility of fragmentation or anarchy was avoided.

By now the Church of God reformation movement was beginning to be seen, heard, and felt around the world. Not only was the missionary outreach gaining momentum, but individuals and groups were interested in starting a work wherever they might happen to be.

As I visualized the world and the work of the Movement around the world, I developed the concept that there were certain spheres wherein the Church of God had influence. I called them *orbits of the Church of God*. Beyond the American and Canadian sphere there were seven orbits of Church of God influence: the English-speaking Caribbean, Latin America, Europe, the Middle East, East Africa, South Asia, and East Asia. We will now look at what was going on in each one of these orbits during the late 1950s and the early 1960s.

The English-speaking Caribbean Orbit of Influence

The Church of God in **Jamaica** after fifty years of growth on the island was entering a period in its history when the influence of American missionaries and the Missionary Board was decreasing and the leadership and authority of the General Assembly and the leadership of the Jamaican church was increasing. And that was good. Years before, missionary George Olson had led the church in assuming ownership of all church properties. The Missionary Board

143

still held title to the land and buildings of Ardenne High School, Jamaica Bible Institute, and missionary residences. Except for a very small grant from the Missionary Board to assist in the support of pastors, the congregations were assuming major responsibility for the support of their leadership, although the pastors were poorly paid. Also, most of the pastors shepherded from four to six congregations in a circuit system, assisted by sometimes very capable lay leaders.

But difficulties were encountered as control and administrative responsibilities of the General Assembly, Ardenne High School, and Jamaica Bible Institute shifted from the Church of God mission to the Church of God in Jamaica. These situations required face-to-face consultations. I visited Jamaica twice in 1955 and then again in 1956, 1957, 1958, 1959, 1960, 1962, and 1964. Many days were spent each time in discussions with the church's leadership and the missionaries. Most of the older believers, especially those in the country churches, did not want change. They preferred authority within the church to remain with the missionaries. There were highly qualified and loyal laypeople in the church, especially in the Kingston area, who were having an increasing influence in the churches and in the General Assembly. The Assembly was lay delegated. Because there were so few qualified full-time ordained pastors, compared to the large number of congregations, the laity began to have greater influence. But, in retrospect, I can say that this was a challenging and interesting period of time during which the church was readying itself for complete indigeneity within the next ten to fifteen years.

Nellie Olson, who had come to Jamaica with her husband in 1907 to begin the work of the Church of God, did not live to enjoy the Jamaican Church of God's fiftieth anniversary celebration. She died April 23, 1956, one of the few missionaries who spent their entire careers in one place, contributing so much toward the growth of the church. In July of that same year a large assembly hall was dedicated at Ardenne High School and named Olson Hall. That same month a new church building was dedicated at Constant Spring Road within the Kingston corporate area, its first pastor being missionary Edgar Williams. During the annual Assembly in 1957 the fiftieth anniversary celebration took place. Adam W. Miller represented the Missionary Board, and Ocie Perry, Hallie Patterson, and Nellie Snowden represented the National Woman's Missionary Society. In July a special service was conducted at Port Antonio on the north coast of the island to celebrate the landing of the Olson family fifty years earlier. I was present and felt something of the pioneer spirit as I stood on the now broken-down wharf where the boat carrying the Olsons docked.

There was now talk of reorganizing Jamaica Bible Institute to initiate an accelerated program. But that, along with some other situations, required some changes in missionary personnel. It was agreed that Charles and Florence Struthers and Edgar and Mildred Williams would leave, to be replaced by Raymond and Elna Mae Hastings and Clair and Retha Shultz. The General Assembly wanted a change in mission secretaries, but some members were somewhat fearful about Clair Shultz's being transferred from Trinidad. They thought he might try to use the "big stick." But upon arrival the Shultzes calmed that fear and were able to help the church on toward complete indigeneity. William and Emelia Fleenor, evacuated from Egypt during the 1956 Suez crisis, were sent to Jamaica to assist a number of congregations in evangelistic efforts. As a means of strengthening Jamaica Bible Institute, a vocational department was established so that the students could earn their way through their educational programs. Ralph and Helen Little were sent so that Ralph could direct the work at the shop. Further strength was given to JBI as Kenneth and Elizabeth Jones were sent to Jamaica so that Kenneth could teach in the school's ministerial training program.

145

A large science building at Ardenne High School was dedicated in 1961. That was also the year when the government of Jamaica voted against the West Indies Federation, which was an attempt to develop a new nation by uniting several of the British West Indies islands, chiefly Jamaica, Trinidad, and Barbados. Jamaica's decision to go it alone spelled failure for the federation. I mention this to indicate the influence political events have on the people even within the body of the church. The fires of independence were being fanned.

The big event the following year in Jamaica was the celebration of independence from Great Britain. That did something to the entire population and helped to stimulate the desire within the church to go it alone. After all, if it could be done politically, why not within the church? That same year Clair and Retha Shultz were transferred to Kenya where he would replace retiring Wick Donohew as mission secretary. The vacancy in Jamaica was filled by the arrival of Tom and Dorothy Pickens.

On April 25, 1963, George Olson died, having given fifty-six years of service to the people of Jamaica. Kenneth and Elizabeth Jones had left Jamaica and were replaced by James and Gwendolyn Massey. But time was running out for our missionaries in Jamaica. Edith Young retired after thirty-seven years of teaching at Jamaica Bible Institute. The Masseys were to remain for only three years. The Littles were on their last term. Also, someone had to be found to replace the Pickenses, who were being transferred to London, England, to pastor a West Indian congregation of the Church of God. Meanwhile, there was a move on to replace Mary Olson with a Jamaican headmistress at Ardenne High School. By now there were 730 students enrolled in the school. In terms of the Jamaican work as a whole, there were eighty-eight congregations of the Church of God, but only fourteen full-time ministers to care for that number of churches.

On the **Cayman Islands** Arthur and Mary Kluge were endeavoring to fulfill their assignment by encouraging the congregations and the one institution, Triple C School, toward indigeneity. Missionary Vivian Phelps, principal of the school, was urging a better school organization. It was a mission school, but Phelps thought responsibility should rest with the church. There was some question whether the school should be a private school or one responsible to the church. It required several years to get all of this settled, including the school's relationship to government and to the one other secondary school on the island. On Grand Cayman the church had no legal entity to hold the properties of the four congregations on the island. They were held under a trusteeship, and some of the trustees had moved away or had died. It was necessary, therefore, for the General Assembly to be regularized and duly constituted to hold its own properties for the church. Vivian Phelps was transferred to Kenya in 1959. A five-year plan was initiated to make Triple C School entirely indigenous but responsible to the Church of God General Assembly in the Cayman Islands. One of the most severe problems for the Caymanian church was related to pastoral leadership. For some reasons very difficult to understand the church appeared unable to produce its own ministers, let alone teachers for the school. When Dewey and Thelma Johnson replaced Arthur and Mary Kluge in 1963, it was understood that the Johnsons would be the last resident missionaries for Cayman. And the Johnsons did remain until 1970. During the 1960s every attempt was made to assist the Church of God in the Cayman Islands to develop and employ Caymanian pastors. Even to the present time any attempt on the part of the church to do that has been unsuccessful and North American pastors have been asked to serve. There has been a rapid turnover of these expatriate pastors because the congregations do not pay adequate salaries even though they have the potential for doing so.

Farther south, in the Caribbean on the island of **Trinidad,** missionaries and national church leadership began thinking in terms of the indigenous church and how to achieve it. Donald and Betty Jo Johnson were transferred from British Guiana in 1956 and assumed roles of leadership in the West Indies Bible Institute. By 1958 William and Emelia Fleenor had come down from Jamaica to provide evangelistic emphasis among the fourteen congregations on the islands of Trinidad and Tobago. Meanwhile, Clair and Retha Shultz were transferred to Jamaica. It was becoming obvious that the official position of the mission was beginning to diminish. In fact, in Trinidad both missionaries and leaders of the General Assembly talked in terms of the integration of the mission and the church. Questions were raised, such as to what extent the missionary was subject or responsible to the national church. It was a time of testing several approaches to the situation and learning from the process.

When Clair Shultz left Trinidad it provided opportunity to consider a West Indian as president of WIBI. Fortunately, Carlton Cumberbatch agreed to accept that position. He was the son of the first ordained minister of the Church of God in Trinidad, and he still retains this post. By the early 1960s graduates coming out of WIBI were assuming roles of leadership in the Church of God throughout the southern Caribbean. The General Assembly in Trinidad and Tobago accepted a scheme for Grant-In-Aid on a decreasing subsidy basis over a ten-year period of time. Throughout that decade the church was faithful in carrying out the plan. In 1959 a new chapel was dedicated at WIBI and named the Houston Memorial Chapel in honor of the First Church of God in Houston, who had donated the funds. Walter and Margaret Lehmann served as missionaries from 1961 to 1964. In 1963 Donald and Betty Jo Johnson left missionary service at the end of a term, and Walter and Margaret Tiesel were transferred from Barbados to Trinidad. The General Assembly in Trinidad began the process of incorporation so that it could be recognized as a legal entity to hold the properties of the church. It was obvious to all that the time was soon coming when the Church of God in Trinidad and Tobago would be indigenous and the West Indies Bible Institute would no longer be a school administered by the mission but a school responsible to the Church of God in the southern Caribbean and administered by a board of trustees representing the area.

Further out in the Atlantic the Church of God in **Barbados** continued to mature. In the late 1950s the General Assembly and the Missionary Board worked out a ten-year plan for decreasing financial subsidy through the Grant-In-Aid concept. At the same time, work began to incorporate the General Assembly so that it could become the legal entity to hold the properties of the church. In order to change the image of the mission, The Grange building was sold. This large building, formerly the residence of the postmaster general, was purchased earlier as a residence for our missionaries. But it always appeared that the missionary was living in a luxurious place compared with the homes of the church people. Also, it was costing the Missionary Board too much money to maintain the building. From the sale of The Grange two modest residences were purchased, one for the one remaining missionary family in Barbados and one nextdoor to the Chapman Street Church in Bridgetown to be used as a manse as well as for headquarter offices for the General Assembly.

The fiftieth anniversary of the Church of God in Barbados was celebrated in 1962 during the annual Assembly. An island crusade was conducted with Dale Oldham as guest speaker and Doug Oldham as song leader. At the appropriate time a special service provided opportunity for me to hand over all the deeds of church properties to Augustus Banister, chairman of the General Assembly, thus transferring those properties to the church. They represented seventeen pieces of land, nineteen church buildings, and four manses, with a value totaling approximately one hundred thousand dollars. Here as well as in other countries where transfer of property took place I explained that it was never the intent of the Missionary Board to take its investment in properties back to America when the mission ceased to exist in any given country. Rather, the investment by the American church in properties was part of the total contribution made in order to help establish the church.

About this time the General Assembly was experiencing difficulty in keeping up with the decreasing subsidy of the Grant-In-Aid plan. A revision was necessary, which the Missionary Board accepted. When Walter and Margaret Tiesel were transferred to Trinidad, LaVern and Darlene Root were sent as replacements. One very positive outreach by the church in Barbados materialized. The people became vitally interested in their own missionary project on the island of St. Vincent. I was amazed when I saw the manner in which the offering plates would be filled with contributions for supporting their own missionary outreach. That brought new enthusiasm and vigor to the church. Such a method will do it every time wherever it is tried!

During this period of time in **British Guiana** missionary leadership was undergoing change while at the same time several attempts at expansion were initiated. In a small village called Whim and farther up the Demerara River at a settlement called Wismar, there were small groups of believers associated with the Church of God. For health reasons Herman and Lavera Smith left the field in 1959 and were replaced by Aaron and Kathryn Kerr. Within two years the Kerrs left and Raymond and Elna Mae Hastings were sent, followed by Edward and Meriam Oldham when the Hastingses were transferred to Saltillo, Mexico. With such a rapid turnover in missionary personnel it was not easy to maintain stability in the work. The church leaders were never quite certain whom to follow.

It was during this time, however, that British Guiana was in the last stages of gaining its independence from Great Britain, and that provided the right atmosphere in which to encourage the church toward becoming indigeneity. Racial and political tensions produced strikes and riots between the East Indians and the West Indians. In the church, for the most part, racial tensions did not surface, although most of the East Indian congregations were found in the Corentyne, a district to the east of Georgetown. The church was still in a season of growth. Ralph and Ruth Coolidge were sent to the colony to give additional missionary support. Several young women and young men were returning from the West Indies Bible Institute, prepared to work in the church. The big question discussed in the General Assembly was how to carry on planned expansion and with whose financial support.

There were now thirteen congregations of the Church of God in British Guiana and twenty-five Sunday schools. Only six congregations had church buildings. The greatest growth was among the East Indians in the Corentyne. Up the Demerara River real potential existed for a strong work at MacKenzie and Wismar, centers of the lucrative bauxite industry. Farther into the interior two attempts were made by the church to start a work among the Amerindians, the primitive people of the jungles. Mr. Dover, who was a corporal in the police force, along with his wife—members of the Bellaire Street Church of God—was sent to the Northwest Territory to keep law and order among primitive peoples and those who were coming in to open up the area. Mrs. Dover started a Sunday school in their home. Unfortunately, a severe border dispute between British Guiana and Venezuela forced the Dovers to leave the interior—a move that closed the opportunity there.

The Church of God in British Guiana was making strides toward self-reliance. The General Assembly adopted a revision of its constitution and bylaws, giving it strength and authority. For the first time a national minister became chairman of the Assembly in place of a missionary. A Grant-In-Aid scheme was adopted, even though there were fears that it would not succeed due to the terrible state of the country's economy. Also, the fiftieth anniversary of the Church of God in the colony was celebrated. As in the other countries celebrating the year of Jubilee in the church, I was privileged to be present to assist in the joyous occasion. At the end of their first term of three years Edward and Meriam Oldham returned to America, but Ralph and Ruth Coolidge remained to give encouragement to the church.

The Latin American Orbit of Influence

Sustained efforts were maintained to keep the small yet growing work in **Guatemala** indigenous from the beginning. As the small group of believers began to enlarge and reach out under the dynamic leadership of Isai Calderon, the question was raised as to what extent should the American church assist. The Missionary Board did not want to inject a mission with a resident missionary. But there were needs that the American church could provide through the Board. Frequent visits by American church leaders assisted in revivals and conventions. Missionaries provided encouragement through visits by Earl and Freda Carver from Cuba, William and Emelia Fleenor from Trinidad, and Keith and Gloria Plank from Costa Rica.

By 1962 there were ten congregations of the Church of God, and those had come into being in less than ten years. There was a lack, however, of trained leadership for these groups of believers. Isai Calderon recognized the need for doctrinal teaching and strong moral support. Occasional grants were made available. By 1963 land was purchased on the Pan American Highway where it passes through Guatemala City, and a year later construction began on a beautiful and adequate church edifice, primarily sponsored by the First Church of God in Houston and the Missionary Board. It became necessary for the Missionary Board to hold the properties of the church in Guatemala until such a time as its organization would become strong enough to be a legal entity. But the Reformation Movement in Guatemala was well on its way as a viable indigenous group of believers.

The time came when resident missionaries were needed in **Costa Rica** if the English-speaking West Indian believers were to be encouraged to expand into the Spanish-speaking community. Consequently, in 1958 Keith and Gloria Plank were sent as missionaries. They lived in the capital city, San José, where they studied Spanish at a language school. They started meetings in their home as well as making occasional visits to the two small congregations on the plain. Another missionary, Paul Ashton, was sent to assist in reviving the congregation in Puerto Limon. Also, a new work in Siquirres came into being. The Planks and Paul Ashton left in 1964, and Sidney Bennett, a Costa Rican returning from his studies at West Indies Bible Institute, along with his Trinidadian wife, assumed responsibility for the two congregations of Cimerrones and Siquirres. Leroy Nicholls, a Trinidadian who had just graduated from WIBI, and his wife from Barbados came as missionaries to care for the work in Puerto Limon. Leroy and Monica Nicholls went through all the culture shock and the necessity of learning Spanish the same as any missionary from America.

In **Panama** the Reformation Movement was still primarily among the West Indian people with all the meetings being conducted in English. A move was on, however, to shift from English to Spanish, for now second and third generations were coming along who had been educated in Spanish. English was the language still spoken in the homes and church services. There was also the desire to reach out to the Spanish-speaking people. A new face-off in the work took place when Dean and Nina Flora were sent to Panama as missionaries, replacing William and Hope Livingston. Strong emphasis was placed on the need for the church to move toward indigeneity. The church began to organize itself in a more responsible fashion, and it was not too long before the General Assembly accepted a Grant-In-Aid scheme over a ten-year period. A new spark of enthusiasm was generated in the church when contacts were made with a number of converts among the primitive people the Cuna Indians on several of the small San Blas Islands. This was to mature into a strong segment of the total work of the Church of God in Panama.

Progress continued in **Cuba** during the late 1950s, but difficult days were soon to be experienced. A Woman's Missionary Society was organized and a Spanish language broadcast entitled "Light from Heaven" was started. Four young men of the church were in training at an interdenominational Bible school at Placetas. A National Assembly of the Church of God in Cuba became a reality, and a new church building in the Finlay section of Havana was erected. The first youth convention in Cuba was held with great success. But political conditions began to bring adverse pressure on all Christian work on the island. Unsettled conditions prevailed as Fidel Castro began his takeover. There were mixed feelings about Castro, as the population was glad to be rid of the Batista government. The church, however, began to suffer. The government closed the Placetas Bible School. Earl and Freda Carver were forced to leave, followed by Ellsworth and Hilaria Palmer. The Palmers settled in Miami, Florida, and began to work among the Cuban refugees who were streaming into America to escape the Castro regime. This was the beginning of a Spanish Church of God in Miami.

Back in Cuba the Church of God continued with almost no interference from the government. Meetings continued and properties were maintained. There were, however, certain regulations to abide by, and secret service men attended meetings regularly. All evangelical pastors had to register with the government and had to pay 11 percent of their earnings. Fortunately, there was a good core of capable leadership for the church: Remberto Ortiz at Matanzas, Arturo Fumero at Cascorro, Gerino Blanco at Finlay (Havana), Jaime Beil at Diezmero, and Andres Hines on the Isle of Pines. As time went on, fewer and infrequent contacts with the church leaders in Cuba were enjoyed, even by way of correspondence.

At the beginning of the 1960s German immigration into **Brazil** remained high, including people from the Church of God. The Missionary Board knew almost nothing of what was taking place among the German believers in the Church of God in Brazil and Argentina. The Church of God in Germany took on the work in both countries as a missionary project, sending evangelists and pastors as needed. Publication work was under way in Rio Das Antas and Bible classes began in Joinville. As David and Lillian Meiers returned to Brazil they soon found themselves in the new settlements in and around Rondon in western Brazil. The general headquarters of the work seemed to be in Curitiba. As early as 1960 the Missionary Board was giving some consideration as to what might be done to assist in the work in Brazil and Argentina. Approaches from certain German people were received, but during that decade prime responsibility remained with the Church of God in Germany. There were only feeble attempts to reach the Portuguese-speaking population.

Something new was started in **Peru** by Paul and Mary Butz and their family as they felt called of God to leave America and take the gospel to the people in the interior of Peru. Paul hired on with Le Tourneau, who had developed a center at Tournavista and was developing agricultural projects south of Pucallpa for the government. Paul and Mary were self-supporting missionaries. They had visited with the Missionary Board on their way south and wanted to keep in touch. During the first four years the Butzes worked with the settlement of American Christians at Tournavista. They wanted, however, to reach out to the people of the country. When Paul lost his job with Le Tourneau and became employed by Zachry Construction Company, he launched out on his own in doing gospel work. He built his home at Campo Verde and began a congregation. Soon a church building was erected, and a Peruvian worker by the name of Salomon Cabanillas was assisting. A little later on, 125 acres of land was purchased between Campo Verde and Pucallpa where eventually a

Bible school would be established. Here is a classic example of what individuals can do in missionary service with the knowledge and blessing of the Missionary Board when the Board is unable to extend its financial commitments.

The European Orbit of Influence

Something out of the ordinary was taking place in **England.** Due to severe economic pressures in many of the British West Indian Islands of the Carribean, many West Indians were emigrating to England to seek employment. They could enter Great Britain easily, for they were citizens of the British Commonwealth. Included among them were many Church of God people from Jamaica, but there were also several from Trinidad and Barbados. As they discovered one another in the great city of London, they came together to form a new congregation of the Church of God reformation movement, the only one in London. The other two older congregations were further north in Birkenhead and Liverpool. The group started in 1960 in a rented Anglican church hall and was led by one of its number, Shirley Miller.

Lars and Ellen Olsen left **Denmark** in 1957, having assisted greatly in training several young Danes for Christian service. Their replacements were James and Esther Fair. Esther was the daughter of J.P.N. Ikast, who had served earlier in Denmark. She knew the Danish language, having grown up in Denmark. The Fairs had a five-year goal to develop an indigenous church. Six major activities occupied all their time, First, the Bible school was expanded. Consequently, effective church leadership emerged. Carl Carlsen and David Anderson, the two main leaders of the church in Denmark today, were the first two graduates. Second, since the only religious materials available were those printed by the Lutheran church, the state church of Denmark, translation of some basic materials for the Church of God was undertaken. This was a laborious job, but it was well worth the time and effort expended. Third, a new hymnal in Danish for the Church of God was printed in 1962. Fourth, to break down the isolation of the Church of God in Denmark, interchurch cooperation was encouraged with evangelical groups. In 1960 the Church of God became a member of the Danish Free Church Council and the Danish Sunday School Association. Fifth, James Fair invited Church of God pastors in Denmark, England, and Germany to meet in Denmark to discuss ways and means whereby there could be more cooperation in the Church of God in Europe. By 1960 the first European Ministers' Conference convened in Bochum, Germany, with ministers present from Denmark, England, Greece, Holland, Germany, and Switzerland. This conference now meets every two years and is a unifying factor for the Reformation Movement in all of Europe. And finally, Fair encouraged the Church of God in Denmark to become a free-standing body. A lay-delegated General Assembly was organized, *Guds Meinghed's*, with an Executive Council, *Representantaskak*. The Fairs returned to America at the end of their first five-year term, having accomplished the goal. The Church of God in Denmark was self-reliant, with a revised scheme of Grant-In-Aid that would be decreased over a fifteen-year period.

Progress continued throughout the Church of God in **Germany.** In fact, the movement in Germany became the focal point for all the work in Europe, mainly through the biennial European Ministers' Fellowship, which I have mentioned before, but also as a result of the second and third World Conferences of the Church of God convened in Essen in 1959 and in Bochum in 1963. More about these World Conferences will be mentioned later in this chapter. In West Berlin, which was like an island stranded in the midst of communist East Germany, the Church of God maintained a congregation under the leadership of F. Besteck. As I stood at the church one day in 1963 I could almost feel the strong pressures militating against the Christian forces in West Berlin. In Essen the publishing work of the Church of God under Gerhard Klabunde was given the opportunity to build a new facility for the printing of gospel literature. It was on the same property in Essen that a beautiful new church building had been erected two years earlier.

Continuing to exist under numerous handicaps, the Movement in **Hungary** maintained its viability under the leadership of Janos Vigh in Budapest and Attila Vigh in Tiszaszederkeny. One new work came into being at Imaeden, **Holland.** And in **Switzerland** the congregation in Zurich came under the pastoral care of younger people, Willi and Edith Krenz, who soon brought more youth into a congregation composed of mainly elderly persons. Enthusiasm was also generated in that congregation to work toward the time when it could have its own property, for up until that time it had always convened in rented quarters.

The Middle East Orbit of Influence

It does not happen very often to missionaries, but just as the Apostle Paul experienced shipwreck, so did Ernest and Grace LaFont and their son Leland as they were returning to America for furlough from **Egypt** in mid-1956. The passenger ship *Andrea Doria,* on which the LaFonts were sailing, suffered a collision with a Swedish liner, the *Stockholm,* and sank. The accident occurred not too far out of New York. Most of the *Andrea Doria's* passengers were rescued, among whom were the LaFonts, and many were brought into the harbor on board the crippled Swedish boat. Upon hearing the radio news of the disaster at sea, I boarded an airplane to New York and caught up with the LaFonts just as they arrived at their hotel in New York. They had escaped, of course, with only what they were wearing at the time of the accident. Fortunately, Ernest had the family passport in his pocket. So before closing time that afternoon we went out on a shopping spree to buy toothbrushes and toothpaste, combs, brushes, shaving equipment, and clothing for further travel to Anderson. Everyone in New York was kind and considerate toward the survivors of this major sea disaster.

In November of that same year the crisis over the Suez Canal exploded and all nonessential American citizens were advised by the American Embassy to leave Egypt at once. Jean and Ruth Kilmer, William and Emilia Fleenor, and Evelyn Skaggs with her two children were evacuated by the United States Navy to Italy along with most of the other missionaries in Egypt. It was agreed by the mission staff that only Wilbur Skaggs would remain in Egypt to look after the work of the church and the affairs of the mission. Since there was need in Kenya, the Kilmers were sent there from Rome. The Fleenors and Evelyn Skaggs with her two children were brought home to America. You will remember that the Fleenors were then sent on to Jamaica to assist in evangelistic work.

The Suez Canal crisis proved to be a turning point in the political life of Egypt—a turning point felt by both the church and mission. There was a strong upsurge against imperialism, colonialism, and the state of Israel. With a revival of the state religion of Islam many legal requirements were laid upon Christians and churches, including the holding of meetings only by royal decree. Missionaries suffered in the backlash. Because it appeared the days of missionaries in Egypt were numbered, strong emphasis was placed upon the nationalization of the church in that country. The Missionary Board felt the work should go on in Egypt, but with a change in emphasis by the missionaries. They now had to expend every effort to prepare the church for complete self-reliance. Therefore, within a year Jean and Ruth Kilmer were returned to Egypt from Kenya. Also, Evelyn Skaggs and the two children returned from America. Unfortunately, Evelyn suffered a severe illness that terminated the missionary career of the Skaggs family. Ernest and Grace LaFont returned to Egypt. Antiforeign and anti-Christian forces gained momentum throughout the valley of the Nile. It was a time of testing through subtle persecution experienced by all Christians.

In an attempt to maintain a helpful missionary staff in Egypt, James and Sybil Simpson were sent to Cairo, but they remained only three years. Difficult situations were developing within the General Assembly of the Church of God in Egypt. The decreasing subsidy schedule of the Grant-In-Aid scheme had failed and adjustments in the plan were required. In Egypt this always brought tension between the missionaries and the leaders of the church. At the end of their term on the field Jean and Ruth Kilmer returned to America to stay. James and Elizabeth Royster, however, were transferred from India to Egypt. The Indian government had refused to renew the Roysters' resident visas.

After two years a need developed farther to the south in Kenya, requiring the services of James Royster; so when the family was transferred from Egypt to Kenya in 1964 it left only one missionary couple in Egypt, Ernest and Grace LaFont. Because of the uncertainties of the future, all Church of God properties in Egypt remained under the ownership of the Missionary Board. These were uneasy months and years for the Arabic-speaking congregations. The Greek and Armenian congregations were dying due to emigration to other countries. Foreigners saw no future for themselves in Egypt. But all was not dark. The youth centers in both Cairo and Alexandria were booming. University students and young professionals from various ethnic backgrounds came together in these places in Christian fellowship to strengthen one another and to minister to others. Out of the group in Alexandria, Franco and Beatrice Santonocito felt called to the ministry, went to Lebanon for training in a Bible school, and returned to Alexandria to assume leadership of the youth center there. In 1965 the Church of God mission in Egypt joined in partnership with three other evangelical missions in Egypt to operate the Nile Christian Bookstores, taking over a British-sponsored Nile Mission Press, which had been asked by the government to leave the country. This proved to be an unprecedented opportunity to witness in a Muslim land through literature.

To the north in **Lebanon** the work was really beginning to grow as a self-reliant entity. Fouad Melki and Adel Mussry were ordained to the Christian ministry. A campsite was purchased in the Lebanon mountains by some of the church members in Beirut and a small colony of believers began development of a community that is now called Theopolis. Evangelistic efforts fired the body of believers to involvement in Kingdom work and the Church of God in Lebanon began to receive the attention of the entire Protestant community. To the northwest in **Greece** a revival broke out among a group of Gypsies in Tragano, which is located in the southern Peloponnesus. The Zazanises needed help; so Dan and Aleta Dallas were sent to Greece. The Dallases encouraged a large youth group in the Athens congregation and assisted greatly in Tragano. Unfortunately, that work among the Gypsies collapsed because an opportunity opened for them to emigrate to Germany where employment was available. Following the Dallases, Savas and Olive Joannides were sent to Athens to replace the Zazanises, who were retiring. It was a moving experience for me to be present with the congregation when Savas Joannides was installed as pastor and the farewells were being said to the Zazanises. It should be noted that in Greece, where the Greek Orthodox church is the state church, it was most difficult for any evangelical group to grow. In fact, the strength of the Greek Orthodox church politically was such as to prevent by force any major growth of any evangelical group.

The East Africa Orbit of Influence

The fiftieth anniversary of the Church of God in **Kenya** celebrated in 1955 was the beginning of a decade of very rapid growth. Evangelistic efforts of the church resulted in many village congregations springing up, worshiping in large grass huts for the most part. Many times elementary schools began in connection with and at the birth of the local church. To keep up with the opportunities and needs of this growth, the Church of God mission in Kenya was enlarging numerically and broadening its services. Missionaries were laboring with a passion to bring into being a church worthy of the name, although many times rather strong colonial methods were employed.

In Kenya, more than in any other country where the Church of God had missionary activity, the Missionary Board employed the institutional as well as the evangelistic approach. This was due no doubt to the educational and medical needs of the people. Most certainly they also had urgent spiritual needs because of the strong hold animism had on the people.

The British colonial government showed considerable interest in giving direction and financial grants to Christian missions involved in education and medical services, for the people would thereby be enabled to develop their country more rapidly. Missionaries entered into these services motivated by a spirit of Christian love and compassion, feeling that many people would thereby be reached with the good news of salvation. By the early to mid-1960s the American Church of God reached its largest investment of missionaries in Kenya, averaging around forty-five for any given year. Roughly one-third of these were involved in educational work, one-third in the medical program, and one-third in direct church-related work. It was not always easy to maintain a balance in these various kinds of services, for institutionalism has a way of demanding personnel, equipment, and an operating budget which, although necessary, tends to leave lesser amounts for direct church-related expenses. At one point we had so many institutional buildings and so many missionary residences in Kenya that a full-time maintenance missionary was required.

But the rapid advancement of the African people of Kenya could never have taken place without all of these combined efforts. With all the criticism leveled at colonialism, and most of it justifiable only in retrospect, it must be said that the British more than any other colonial power endeavored honestly to prepare developing peoples for political independence. Independence came to Kenya on December 12, 1963, when the Union Jack was replaced by the national flag of Kenya. The British had trained public servants for government offices as well as provincial and district officers for governing the interior of the country. It should also be noted that a parallel situation existed in the Church of God in Kenya during this period of time. Missionaries were involved in basic services of all kinds that would prepare Christians for the time when the church would become indigenous—a time not far away.

As I look at the record I am amazed at the rapid growth of the mission's medical department. Over a very few years numerous buildings were erected, especially at Mwihila. Nora Memorial Hospital, generally known as the Church of God Hospital, started with only the main unit of the facility, an outpatient clinic, one doctor's residence, and a duplex for American nurses. Within less than ten years the investment included a men's ward, a women's ward, and a maternity wing as units attached to the main unit of the hospital, in addition to rooms for surgery, x-ray, offices, and classroom space. Then two more residences for missionary doctors, an African nurses' residence, an African male dresser's house, a kitchen and dining hall, a laundry, chapel, morgue, and graduate nurses' home were built. Added to that was a larger outpatient clinic, including offices for two doctors.

All of this plus missionaries who were living at the same station involved in educational work created a small village in itself, for which adequate water supply had to be found and electricity generated by the mission's own generator brought in from America. The American church invested close to a half-million dollars in this one project.

In addition, there was development at the Kima Hospital, which offered mainly maternity service as well as excellent clinical attention. There were at least six clinics scattered out in other parts of the Western Province, staffed by American and African nurses and visited regularly by the doctors stationed at Mwihila. A strong nurses' training program was established at the hospital at Mwihila.

Missionaries who worked in the medical program during this decade, although not necessarily the entire period of time, were Deloris Beaty, Darlene Detwiler, Rosa Bollmeyer, David and Elsie Gaulke, Lydia Hansen, Candace Heinly, Merlene Huber, Harold and Donna LaFont, David and Joan Livingston, Vera Martin, Hazel McDilda, Jene Nachtigall, Ruth Sanderson, Richard and Donna Smith, Naomi Sweeney, Edna Thimes, and Arthenia Turner.

Elementary education spread rapidly by way of the church and mission and was subsidized by the government. Intermediate schools sprang up at Kima where the Girls' School was located, and schools for boys were established at Mwihila, Ingotse, and Emusire. For a number of years our mission provided the Teacher Training Center at Mwihila and staffed it with missionaries to provide qualified graduates to teach at the elementary level. A few of our missionaries were involved in intermediate education, for there were not enough Africans prepared to teach at that level.

Within almost no time, pressure was on for more secondary schools (equivalent to our high schools) due to the demand from students graduating first of all from elementary schools and then from intermediate schools. Competition to enter the very few secondary schools throughout Kenya was fierce. The government hastened to make the necessary provision. The Mwihila Teacher Training Center was changed to a secondary school for boys; the Bunyore Girls' School at Kima was changed to a secondary school for girls; the intermediate school at Ingotse was changed to a secondary school for boys, and the intermediate school at Emusire was changed to a secondary school for both boys and girls. These and similar changes throughout Kenya created staffing problems, for there were only a few Africans in Kenya who had a bachelor's degree in education.

As Africans went forth to Europe and America to train, having completed secondary education in Kenya, American short-term teachers by the scores were required immediately. Many Church of God teachers responded and made a marked contribution at a very critical time in the overall development of Kenya, but especially within the Church of God in Kenya. African Christians were so intent upon providing education for their children that *harambee* schools were started. This African word means that the people pulled together to start their own schools, struggling for a few years until they could qualify for government grants.

Missionaries who were in the educational program during this decade, although not necessarily the entire period of time, were Alta Abrams, Esther Beaty, Calvin and Martha Brallier, Olive Fiscus, Jewell Hall, Harry Nachtigall, Carl and Eva Kardatzke, Margaret LaFont, Velma Schneider, Ruben Don and Jenny Schweiger, James and Dorothy Sharp, Richard and Georgia Woodsome, and James and Glenna Yutzy.

While all this was going on, rapid developments also took place in other institutions related more directly to the church and mission. The Kima Bible School was upgraded rapidly so that as young men came out of intermediate and then secondary schools, feeling the call to the ministry of the church, they could be adequately trained on a commensurate level. More space and buildings were required. By 1962 the name was changed to Kima Theological College, and adequate facilities were being provided over a period of years. It joined the East African Theological Association. This institution was a definite asset to the development of the Church of God in Kenya.

A self-help program brought forth a tannery and leather-craft industry where Christians could find employment in a local business and thereby become self-reliant more quickly. Unfortunately, this experiment did not end with success, and this brief attempt at self-help went out of existence. As the extremely outdated printing press was abandoned at Kima, a modern offset press was installed in a building at Mwihila and, through the efforts of Douglas Welch, a strong literature program called Church of God Publications was started. An African church paper was initiated.

One more institution, which was strictly American, was born. Within the numerous Church of God missionary families stationed in Kenya there were many children who were too young to be sent off to boarding school at Kijabe where the Africa Inland Mission maintained an excellent school for American children. Consequently, the Church of God mission started the Baker Elementary School at Mwihila where missionary Vivian Phelps, transferred from Grand Cayman, taught in a modern one-room school for children in grades one through six. After that they would go to Kijabe. Baker Elementary School remained open for almost fifteen years and then closed its doors, for there were no longer any missionary children in that age bracket to educate.

A new mission station was opened at Ibeno in Kisii. It was to provide additional assistance beyond what had been given by the African missionary, Obed. Lima Lehmer and Lydia Hansen were especially helpful in getting this station started, serving there for a time. Soon medical and educational facilities were established, and the work of the church in the Kisii area expanded. Roy and Magaline Hoops, who were independent Church of God missionaries stationed in Shitoli to the northeast of Mwihila, were appointed by the Missionary Board, bringing the few congregations in the Idakho area into the mainstream of the Church of God in Kenya.

Other missionaries who served in church-related work

were Samuel and Jane Betts, Irene Engst, Lew and Wanda Goodrick, Frank LaFont, Vivian Phelps, Simon and Mae Robinson, Ruben and Nora Schweiger, Clair and Retha Shultz, James and Beth Royster, and Douglas and Ruth Welch.

Each one of the numerous missionaries who served in Kenya during this period of unusual development and expansion deserves the highest praise for work well done. Many times adverse circumstances prevailed. Language had to be learned. Malaria was still prevalent. Dirt roads made travel difficult during the rainy season. It was not always easy to make the necessary adaptations to fit into the African culture, but there was always the positive side. Satisfying joy was found in service, and gratification came from an unusual dedication to the task assigned. God supplied the missionaries with physical strength and spiritual graces beyond the ordinary. And above all, the African Christians were always grateful and showed their appreciation in so many gracious ways.

By 1965 real signs of a self-reliant Church of God began to appear. The General Assembly of the Church of God in East Africa was making the necessary adjustments and approaches to the government to become a registered legal entity in order to hold property that the Missionary Board was soon to transfer to the African church. For the first time an African, Daudi Otieno, became chairman of the General Assembly. replacing a missionary. He was the son of the chief who gave the land in the beginning for the Kima mission station. The Kaloleni Church of God had been established in that section of Nairobi on the plot of land given by the government for the establishment of the only Protestant church. Also, the Mariakani Christian Center was erected in another part of Nairobi on land given by the government. Altogether there were twelve congregations of the Church of God in Nairobi, the capital city.

The Church of God was being established in other urban areas such as Nakuru, Eldoret, and Mombasa. Africanization was well on its way in the institutions. Boards of governors were placed in administrative control of the four secondary schools, the hospitals at Mwihila and Kima, and Kima Theological College. The manner in which members were appointed to these boards provided the possibility for the Church of God to maintain control, thus making them truly institutions to serve the church in East Africa. Throughout all this administrative development the Church of God in East Africa was primarily evangelistic in character, resulting in church growth. Much of this direct evangelism was done by Africans, making it especially effective.

The year 1958 found Stanley and Marion Hoffman and Ralph and Gertrude Farmer in Kenya as independent Church of God missionaries from Canada. They were being sponsored by the World Missionary Fellowship with headquarters in Medicine Hat, Alberta. For a time the couples worked with J. S. and Twyla Ludwig in Nairobi. Early in 1959, however, the Hoffmans began a mission station in a primitive place in **Tanzania** called Kaiti. Later that same year the Farmers moved to Tanzania to start another station not too far from Kaiti near the small town of Mbulu.

Two years later Stanley Hoffman began another station farther south at Mirambo. These were strictly pioneer missionary ventures of faith requiring much hard work. Slowly but surely over the next five years the stations at Kaiti and Mbulu became centers of Christian nurture and outreach. Missionary residences were constructed, and several other buildings were erected on each station to facilitate the work. Following evangelistic efforts, small congregations came into being in surrounding villages. Limited clinical services were provided. Training classes developed into Bible schools at Kaiti and Mbulu. At Mbulu the school was called ABLE, which stands for African Bible And Leadership Education. A few other persons from Canada came to both stations on very short terms of service. Before long there were a number of pastors and evangelists. God was blessing the efforts of these missionaries in spite of some of the difficulties inherent in independent missionary outreach.

Missionaries and a few African church leaders from Tanzania visited the Church of God in Kenya, attending an annual convention there. It dawned upon all that the work of the Church of God in East Africa should be one. This seemed to suggest that the mission in Kenya and the mission in Tanzania ought to be one. In 1965 Clair and Retha Shultz and I were invited to visit this development in Tanzania. That was a beautiful experience of fellowship and sharing concepts related to the unity of God's people and the missionary work in which they are engaged. A tentative schedule was agreed upon, pointing toward the time when the work in Tanzania would come under the administrative guidance of the Missionary Board of the Church of God. This subject, however, takes us into the next chapter.

The South Asia Orbit of Influence

On the **Indian** scene, the government was struggling with its political independence. This decade of time that we are now considering encompassed three five-year plans through which the nation was attempting to improve communications, industry, and agriculture. The British were forgotten, but English was the only common language of India where more than four hundred languages and dialects are spoken. An attempt was being made to enforce the teaching of Hindi in all schools. The aim was to eventually make it the common language of the country, but it did not work.

Within the Church of God in India this was also a time of change and progress, including the ways in which Church of God missionary efforts in that country related to it. To the south, in the state of Kerala, Gordon Schieck was endeavoring to bring the church together in a unified approach. The first General Assembly of the Church of God in South India convened in Chengannur, with the three ordained ministers and Gordon Schieck forming the Executive Committee. A number of the church properties were held in the name of the late P.J. Philip, and so the first step was to have them transferred to the Missionary Board of the Church of God and then to wait until the All-India Assembly of the Church of God formed a legal entity to which all the properties held in the name of the Missionary Board of the Church of God could be transferred to the Indian church. Farther north, in the state of Orissa, Sidney Johnson was feeling his way and gaining confidences. The main emphasis in Cuttack was placed on the institutional work of the Shelter and the schools. The one congregation claimed to be indigenous, and so little assistance was given by the missionaries. It was not long before Sybil Holmes became the first Indian home superintendent at the Shelter instead of a missionary. The small group in Calcutta had dwindled. In Cuttack the Sonate Nalini Girls' High School was dedicated and in place of a missionary being responsible to give guidance, a management committee assumed control. Farther to the north, in the state of Assam, I had the privilege of spending several days renewing relationships with James and Evalyn Nichols-Roy. This opened the door for future contacts to be made with them by our missionaries in India. It was a period of reaffirming fellowship within the one body of Christ.

At the very southern tip of India there lived a seventy-two-year-old man named D. M. Devasahayam. He was the leader of a group of three thousand Christians called the Bible Faith Mission. They were looking for fellowship and affiliation with a larger group and had been recommended to the Church of God because their beliefs were almost identical to those held by the Reformation Movement. In 1957 it was my joy to be with Gordon Schieck when the first official contact was made with the twenty congregations. My notes reveal a few exciting moments wherever

Schieck and I appeared and were honored in processions with horns, flutes, drums, and garlands. At one place a public address system played Sousa's "Stars and Stripes Forever." It was like a wedding ceremony at times. In fact, Devasahayam expected the marriage of the two groups to take place immediately. But obviously more time was necessary for complete understanding. A year later an affiliation agreement was signed, integrating the Bible Faith Mission with the Church of God in South India. It reminded many people of the Day of Pentecost when three thousand persons were added to the body of believers.

There were other signs of advancement by the Church of God in India. In the state of Orissa the government granted permission for the Church of God to enter Keonjhar District, which was 99.64 percent Hindu. This challenge was taken up by the congregation in Cuttack. The small group in Calcutta again began meeting under the leadership of Hridoy Mundul. Later the congregation was assisted by Glenn and Alice Beach, Canadian missionaries appointed to India.

A feeling was growing among our missionaries and a few of the Indian church leaders that it would be good to bring all the work of the Church of God in India more closely together. It was said, "How can we believe in unity and live in isolation? Something similar to the early camp meetings held in Cuttack from 1905 to 1920 should be revived." So it happened in October 1961 that the first meeting of the All-India Assembly convened in Cuttack, Orissa, with Church of God delegates present from the states of Assam, Kerala, Orissa, and West Bengal. This brought about a feeling of oneness and strength throughout the Church of God in India. Only a provisional committee met in 1962 due to Chinese infiltration into northeast India, severe food rationing, and difficulties in transportation. But the scope of the Assembly was outlined, a planning and coordinating committee was formed, and an outline of some basic beliefs of the Church of God was reviewed.

By 1963 the first draft of a Trust Memorandum was considered as the initial step toward the formation of the All-India Trust for the holding of properties. Four very important papers were presented to the Assembly, designed to develop a oneness in understanding major issues in the church. Also, a monthly periodical, *High Calling*, was started for the English-speaking ministers of India and East Pakistan.

The result of all this was that the missionary force of the Church of God in India was strengthened in spite of mounting restrictions and difficulties in securing visas. Glenn and Alice Beach were in West Bengal assisting at Calcutta; Clifton and Mary Morgan were in Orissa soon to help at the new outreach at Keonjhar after land was purchased and a multipurpose building erected; and James and Elizabeth Royster were in Kerala with an assignment to study carefully the problem of theological training for upcoming Church of God leaders in India. As a result of that study, the All-India Assembly decided to use primarily Union Biblical Seminary, located at Yeotmal in the geographical center of India. The Missionary Board concurred and became a member of the Cooperating Home Board in America, which gives assistance to the seminary. When Ellen High left India for furlough in 1958 after eleven years of service, she did not return to India under the auspices of the Missionary Board. During this period of time there were losses in Indian leadership. J. J. M. Nichols-Roy died in Shillong, November 1, 1959, after fifty-five years of service in the ministry. In 1960 Banchu Sahu, pastor of the Mount House Church of God in Cuttack, retired after fifty years of labor. Four years later in Cuttack, Jonathan Mohanty died. He was a dedicated lay leader, an educator, and early pioneer in the Church of God. That same year, in September, Evalyn Nichols-Roy died in Shillong. You will remember she had come to India as a young missionary in 1904, married young J. J. M. Roy in 1906, and had given her entire life to the Khasi people over a period of sixty years.

In September of 1962 I met in Calcutta in the Red Shield Hostel of the Salvation Army with twelve of our missionaries in India and East Pakistan. This was the first and last conference of its kind, but it was necessary at that juncture. Understanding and consensus were necessary as relationships of missionaries to the Indian church were experienced. My notes taken at that time reveal several items discussed: the development of the indigenous church, the All-India Assembly, Grant-In-Aid on a decreasing subsidy basis, the possibility of an All-India Trust to hold properties, ministerial training and theological education, ecumenical relations, institutional work and the development of the local congregations. These topics were carefully studied over a period of five days. A ten-year plan emerged, outlining certain strategies, one of which was that by the year 1972 the Missionary Board would have no more *resident* missionaries in India. But observe that in the Calcutta conference there was not one Indian church leader present. It was agreed from that time forward that the All-India Assembly should be the body to strategize and plan. And so during the next few years the missionaries worked closely with that body regarding all the issues at hand. Each time I visited India, I did business directly with the Assembly and had wonderful Christian fellowship. The church indeed was emerging from a mission.

Some signs of progress appeared in the Church of God mission in **East Pakistan,** but pressures from an Islamic government were keenly felt. An indigenous church was extremely slow in forming. Paul and Nova Hutchins were new missionaries living at Lalmanirhat while Robert and Frances Clark moved into a rural area at Kakina, endeavoring to identify with the Pakistanis by adopting their life-style as much as possible. In 1960 the Hutchinses moved to Nilphimari to help build the work. Just across the border in India is a frontier town called Siliguri, and a new group was developing under the leadership of P. K. Misra. Since this was so close to Nilphimari it was thought

173

best to have the missionaries in East Pakistan give encouragement. Of course, as the work grew in Siliguri it became an integral part of the Church of God in India.

About this time there was a discovery in the Sylhet District of northeast East Pakistan. A number of years before, when East Pakistan was the East Bengal state of India, a large number of Church of God Khasi Christians from Assam settled in the Sylhet area. But no contact had ever been made with them after the partition of India took place and Pakistan became a new and separate nation. So it was with a great deal of enthusiasm that this large group in the Sylhet area was brought into the fellowship with the Church of God in East Pakistan. They spoke the Khasi language rather than Bengali, but this did not prevent regular contacts being maintained with them.

When Robert and Frances Clark returned to America at the end of their term in 1961 they terminated their services in East Pakistan. In order to keep at least two missionary families in that mission, Joseph and Ramona Spires were sent by the Missionary Board. They resided at Lalmanirhat. On that mission station the Lalmanirhat Mission Middle English School was providing elementary education through the eighth grade. There were 287 pupils, 12 percent being from Christian families, 74 percent Muslim, and 14 percent Hindu. The school had been operating for ten years without a government permit, but there was never any question from the authorities. One of the pressures that finally had to be obeyed, however, was the teaching of the religion of Islam to the Muslim students only. Christian mission schools in all countries where Islam was the state religion struggled with this pressure, but they agreed that it was still worthwhile to keep the schools with an overall Christian influence open rather than to have them closed and thus lose all contact through children. The Missionary Board, therefore, authorized the missionaries in East Pakistan to comply with the law.

There were basic weaknesses in the work of the Church of God in East Pakistan. Traditionally, the people were dependent upon the mission. Poverty prevailed, making it easy to fall into a system of "rupee diplomacy" whereby almost everyone received financial assistance in one way or another from the mission. Considerable thought was given to developing some kind of a self-help project in this rural area, and sometime later a large fish pond for raising fish to market and a small cooperative farm were tried. For reasons difficult for Westerners to understand, both projects never really reached the goals set for viable self-help projects.

The East Asia Orbit of Influence

By the beginning of this decade Donald and Arlene Goens and Philip and Phyllis Kinley were new missionaries in **Japan.** Through the efforts of the four missionary couples then present in Japan and the enthusiasm of Japanese church leadership, the Church of God continued to grow. New church buildings were erected in Imajuku, Fukuoka, and Osaka. Nathan and Ann Smith moved southward to Kyushu Island where there was potential for Christian growth, with starts that had been made at Imajuku and Fukuoka. Donald and Arlene Goens helped Japanese leadership at Fukaya and Menuma north of Tokyo. Another new work in Tokyo was started in Nishi-Kunitachi. At the request of Remmi, the Japanese church's General Assembly, Arthur and Norma Eikamp moved from Tamagawa in Tokyo to the Osaka area. The Church of God in Japan was beginning to have three points of emphasis: the greater Tokyo area, the Osaka-Kobe area, and Kyushu Island to the south.

Instead of starting a Church of God seminary for theological education in Japan, it was finally decided to use excellent Christian seminaries already in existence in Tokyo and start what was called a Seminary House. This would be a kind of hostel where the few Church of God seminary students would live and from which they would attend the seminary chosen. Philip Kinley was requested by the Japanese to head up this program. The Kinleys would live next to the Seminary House and offer guidance and fellowship to the students. Two important courses would be taught by Philip Kinley: Church of God Doctrine and Christian Education. Kinley always worked closely with the dean of the seminary where the students attended, particularly at the point of field work in Church of God congregations. This Seminary House program provided excellent theological training commensurate with the level of education enjoyed by Japanese young men who felt called to the Christian ministry. The number of those called, however, was not great, and so the number attending seminary through the Seminary House during any given year was anywhere from two to six students. But this was felt adequate for openings available in the Church of God in Japan.

Tamagawa Sei Gakuin, the school for girls, was enlarging its enrollment from 450 pupils in 1960 to 515 in 1962, and was reaching for 750 students. This required additional building and equipment facilities as well as additional faculty. Freda LaFoe left teaching in United States military schools in Japan and became a full-term missionary, teaching English in Tamagawa Sei Gakuin. This school provided great opportunity for Christian witness not only in Tamagawa District but also in Tokyo as it became known for its excellence in education. Quality leadership was found in Taniguchi Sensei, who was principal for a number of years.

As I sat in the meeting of Remmei in 1962 I heard individual reports, translated quietly into English by Arthur Eikamp, from fourteen congregations and preaching places. These represented a total of 422 adults attending morning services and an average of 1,090 attending Sunday school. That is a very good record of achievement considering the church started from zero immediately following World War II. In Japan less than one-half of 1 percent of the population is Christian, including Roman

Catholics and Protestants. It is not easy and requires considerable time to bring a person reared in the major non-Christian religion of Japan to an understanding of Jesus Christ. It should be observed, however, that for a number of years following World War II there was an interest expressed by many Japanese to discover a better way. But culture and society continued to have strong influence, preventing many from following Christ.

Near the end of World War II one of the bloodiest landings by American forces took place on the little island of **Okinawa** as General MacArthur's forces moved closer to the mainland of Japan. Once taken from Japan it remained under the control of the United States Civil Administration of the Ryuku Islands for many years. The island was considered the keystone of the Far East. About 1960 interest on the part of several Americans stationed on Okinawa seemed to converge. These were persons of the Church of God who were interested in winning people to Christ. First of all, there was Mr. McGarvey's wife, who was of Japanese background. McGarvey was employed by the occupational forces, and his wife had been converted to Christianity in the Church of God in El Paso, Texas. Somehow she made contact with William Caylor of the air force, Richard Rudman of the navy, and John Williams of the army, along with their respective families, all of whom were Church of God people. Altogether they were interested in starting not only a Sunday school but also a congregation. They had gone into Ameku, a suburb of the capital city, Naha, and started work among the children of the community. Almost all of the homes they visited were Buddhist. Among this group of Americans only Mrs. McGarvey knew the Japanese language.

I was invited to stop at Okinawa during one of my trips to East Asia, and there I observed a real opportunity to do something for God. Members of the American armed forces stationed in Okinawa were already supporting the activities with their finances. In fact, they had already purchased a small lot in Ameku and were hoping to gain assistance to build. Nathan Smith was asked to come down for a visit from Japan. Okinawa is about halfway between Japan and Taiwan, and so it was not far from where Smith lived on Kyushu Island. I suggested that perhaps the Church of God in Japan would like to take on this opportunity as a missionary outreach, especially since the people of Okinawa were Japanese speaking. Remmei, the Japanese General Assembly, accepted the challenge, and Masahiro Orita was sent to Okinawa as their first missionary. It is interesting to note that the church in Japan gave Orita Sensei ten years to bring about a totally self-reliant work in Okinawa or they would consider his efforts a failure. By 1964 all of these Church of God Americans had left Okinawa, but they continued to support the work as best they could while on the island. Orita Sensei carried on the work as it grew and spread to several other locations on the island.

Following the Korean War the leaders of the Church of God in **Korea** began requesting assistance from the American church. Perhaps as a result of a guilt complex, the Christians of America began pouring millions of dollars into that country. The Korean Church of God established the Seoul Bible Institute, known in Korean as *Han Yang Shin-Hak-Won*. The main leaders at that time were H. C. Ahn in Seoul and Jai Kun Kwak in Mok Po. The church had established two large orphanages in Mok Po and Suwon as well as a boy's high school in Mok Po. Many Church of God people in America gave liberally to the support of the widows and orphans in Korea.

The Missionary Board decided to provide thirty thousand dollars to get a resident missionary to Korea and to assist in capital fund needs at the Bible school. Kenneth and Sue Jo Good were sent in 1961. First, they spent two years in language school and then devoted the remainder of that five-year term to teaching at the Bible school and assisting in general church work as the church leaders desired. A Grant-In-Aid plan was set up to assist in the support of the Bible school, where there were twenty-five students and nine faculty members, although they were not all full time. Everything appeared to be going smoothly and the work was growing as students began to graduate from their training programs. It was unfortunate, therefore, when seeds of division were sown by an independent American by the name of Carl McIntyre. This was certain to affect not only the Church of God in Korea but every other Protestant group. In another chapter you will read what happened.

In **Hong Kong,** P. K. and Lovena Jenkins were serving the Chinese people in that British colony. He had become medical superintendent of the Junk Bay Medical Relief Council, which supervised the Haven of Hope Tuberculosis Sanatorium, Rennie's Mill Christian Medical Center, and the Sunnyside Children's Hostel. Staff was secured from evangelical Christians in Europe and America. Following several visits to Hong Kong I was being encouraged to have the Church of God contribute a staff person. But it required several years for this to materialize. Contacts were made with Isaac V. Doone, the son of one of the early pastors of the Church of God in China. Doone was and still is a successful businessman. Through him and other underground sources the Missionary Board was able to maintain some contact with the believers in China.

Rolando Bacani, a Filipino working on an American base in Guam, became a Christian under the influence of William Rife, went to Gulf-Coast Bible College in Houston, Texas, to complete his education, and returned home to Manila, capital of the **Philippines,** to begin a work of the Church of God. This proved to be another successful attempt at starting a church that would be indigenous from the beginning. That is to say there would be no long-term resident missionary sent to oversee the development. In 1959 Bacani started meetings in his home and within two months moved to a larger rented place. During those early years of the work I stopped by occasionally to provide encouragement. Nathan Smith made a visit or two from

Japan. Bacani made contact with the earlier congregation of believers in Laoag to the north. By 1962 there were three Church of God congregations in the Philippines and the following year the Pacific Bible Institute was initiated.

Vacation Bible schools flourished in both Manila and Laoag, and the Church of God in the Philippines incorporated so that the congregations could hold their own properties. By 1964 a chapel and parsonage were built for the First Church of God in the Valenzuela District of Manila. Rolando Bacani proved to be a very capable leader. The people were willing to work hard and to sacrifice, and so there was really no need for the Missionary Board to become involved officially. However, it did not violate the concept of indigeneity to encourage and assist from time to time. Financial grants were also in order. But this aid did not make the people of the congregations dependent upon the Church in America.

During World War II Japan conquered **Guam,** a small island in the southwest Pacific. Three years later, William Rife landed with the United States Marines under heavy gunfire. Rife's buddies fell all around him as the invasion force waded ashore and dug foxholes in the sandy beach. He felt his life had been spared for a purpose under God. I have stood with Bill on that beach and have heard him tell the story with tears running down his cheeks. It is not surprising, then, that in 1955 William Rife returned with his family to Guam to preach the gospel. He also taught school in order to earn a living. Rife and his family were met by Denny Armey, a member of the armed forces with whom contact had been made through the *Gospel Trumpet,* now *Vital Christianity.* The Rifes began a work among the Filipinos who had been hired by American contractors building for the United States Air Force and Navy. By this time Guam was a possession of America. Guamanians were American citizens, but without the right to vote. The population was 96 percent Catholic. At first, groups of interested persons met in a camp where the Filipinos were billeted. By 1958 the group of believers was large enough that property was purchased in Barrigada just outside the town of Agana. The First Church of God was incorporated in Guam to hold property. Tropical storms played havoc with the wood frame building, and so in 1963 a new steel-framed building was erected. A minister by the name of Wilbur Miller, who was from the Northwest, flew to Guam with his family to assist in the work. To support himself he operated the A & W Root Beer franchise on Guam. It was about this time that Rife left his teaching at the local high school to begin giving full time to the ministry, and the one congregation flourished.

On the island of **Hawaii** in 1955 Curt and Carole Loewen went to Honolulu from Pacific Bible College, now Warner Pacific College, and enrolled in the University of Hawaii. They soon met other Church of God people from the mainland, such as William and Dolores Wright, and house meetings were conducted in their homes. The group soon grew to about twenty persons and Carl Riley responded to their plea for a pastor. Regular services were first held in Kenneth Smith's residence and then in the M's Ranch Restaurant in the Aina Haina District of Honolulu. Soon there were about eighty attending. There were Japanese, Chinese, Filipinos, and mainlanders, including a few from the armed forces.

When Carl Riley resigned, my parents were taken out of retirement again and sent by the Missionary Board to Hawaii for two years. Since there was quite a turnover of persons in the congregation because of changes in military personnel and people going and coming from the mainland, it was thought good for the Missionary Board to assume responsibility for the work for a few years. In 1959 Hawaii became a state of the United States of America. Some conversation began with the Board of Church Extension and Home Missions to see if it would be interested in assuming responsibility for the work in the new state. Later you will read what happened. The following year a large residence was purchased on Mona Street in Aina Haina, and one part was remodeled for use as a small sanctuary.

After the Croses returned to the mainland, two pastors served for brief periods of time. Then Proctor and Virginia Barber began a four-year ministry, during which time the church was strengthened. During the Croses' ministry a number of Hawaiians of Oriental background were converted from non-Christian faiths.

Even though **Australia** is a separate continent from Asia, I am arbitrarily including it in the East Asia orbit of the Church of God. As you read in Chapter 2, contacts with E. P. May were broken in 1924, and the Church of God ceased to exist in Australia as a Reformation Movement until 1958 when Carl and Lova Swart reached Sidney as independent missionaries but with the Missionary Board's blessing. It was a venture of faith, and God rewarded their efforts. After purchasing a car and a small trailer the Swart family spent the first couple of months touring the eastern part of the continent to discover the best place to begin. During their travels they discovered some Church of God people from Germany, the Hermann Siebert family, who had settled in Warners Bay and had started a small congregation. The greater Sidney area was chosen by Swart as a starting point. The first meeting was convened in mid-1959 in the Masonic Hall in Canley Vale. Soon land was purchased in Canley Heights and a small house on it was renovated. By 1961 a new brick sanctuary was built. Annual camp meetings were conducted on the large grounds.

Not too long after meetings were started at Canley Heights the Swarts discovered the Harold Chilvers family, who had remained loyal to the Reformation Movement from the days of E. P. May. Chilvers and his married son, Lloyd, were successful dairy men. Both Harold and Lloyd Chilvers and their families were real assets to the Church of God as it was growing again in Australia. It was not long before Lloyd and Ruth Chilvers moved to Canley Heights and they became vitally involved in the work. God called him to the ministry and he began to pastor. Several persons arrived from the United States to assist the Swarts, and most of them were self-supporting through teaching school. It was about this time that E. P. May was discovered and by invitation attended one of the large camp meetings at Canley Heights.

Another congregation was started at Green Valley, a new and growing subdivision. Then God led the Swarts to the state of Queensland where land was purchased on the Isle of Capri in Surfers Paradise. But it was to be a few years before the first Sunday school was conducted. Edward and Leona Schweikert from Michigan and Gilbert Swart and his wife from Ohio, both couples being experienced pastors, were valuable self-supporting additions. By 1965 the leaders of the Church of God had organized, and the Association of the Church of God of Australia was legally formed. All church properties were held by the association.

Special Events and Significant Landmarks

World Missions Conventions. This was a period of increased interest on the part of the Church of God in missions. The National Woman's Missionary Society, the Board of Church Extension and Home Missions, and the Missionary Board of the Church of God were working together in missions education to assist the church in its desire to learn more about and to do more for the cause of missions. One of these attempts to inform was through World Missions Conventions. Guest leaders presented challenging messages, missionaries on furlough conducted conferences, and displays provided colorful information. Here is where the first three were held: Dayton, Ohio in September 1955; Wichita, Kansas in September 1957; Oakland, California in August 1959.

Following the third convention a careful evaluation was done. Concern was expressed at the point of effectiveness. The same group of convention goers in the Church of God were being reached at each convention. Little helpful information was getting back to the local congregations. It was then decided to attempt to take these meetings to more people by having several conventions about the same time. Therefore, the fourth World Missions Convention in 1961 was conducted in three cities in the East and three cities in the West. The fifth convention was held in Anderson, Indiana, in 1963 in the new Warner Auditorium. A final attempt at this kind of convention was to conduct almost simultaneous meetings in eight cities: Atlanta, Georgia; Sikeston, Missouri; Detroit, Michigan; Pasadena, Texas; Denver, Colorado; Walla Walla, Washington; Edmonton, Alberta; and Pomona, California. From that time forward better methods were employed in missions education within the church.

World Conferences of the Church of God. By the mid-fifties the time was ripe on the international level for bringing world representatives of the Church of God together for fellowship and sharing. Sponsorship at first was by the Board of Christian Education in America and was soon broadened to include the Missionary Board and the Executive Council of the General Assembly in America. Ultimately, representatives from the Church of God in other countries were brought into the World Conference Planning Committee. Following is where these important meetings have convened, even to the present: Fritzlar, Germany in 1955; Essen, Germany in 1959; Bochum, Germany in 1963; Zurich, Switzerland in 1967; Oaxtepec, Mexico in 1971; Beirut, Lebanon in 1975 (canceled due to civil war); Anderson, Indiana in 1980.

Through these very productive efforts world leaders of the Movement became acquainted with one another, discussed important issues, and shared valuable information from around the world. These conferences have remained strictly nonlegislative. They have not been considered a world General Assembly for the Church of God. Multiple and valuable blessings have come out of each one of these World Conferences. They caused people to think in terms of the Church of God all around the world.

Inter-American Conferences. A growing interest on the part of the church in America in Central and South America prompted W. E. Reed, the executive secretary of the Board of Church Extension and Home Missions, and me to visit almost every one of the Spanish-speaking areas where the Church of God was extant. So in mid-1960 we stopped in Miami, Florida, on our way south to determine the possibilities for ministry among the Cuban refugees. Then we went on to Cuba where we heard firsthand how the church was being affected by the revolution. In fact, Dr. Reed and I just got out of Havana in the nick of time. Then we met with churches and their leaders in Panama, Costa Rica, Guatemala, Mexico, and those involved in the Spanish-speaking work in Texas.

We picked up four definite recommendations that became the combined concern for both the "home" and the "overseas" boards. Leadership training and skills were number one. The drastic need for more literature in the Spanish language was the second recommendation. Because of that need a Spanish publication committee emerged. Number three was evangelism. And finally everywhere we went we were urged to initiate some kind of annual meeting for the entire area that could provide opportunity for sharing and encouragement. Out of this last expressed desire came the Inter-American Conference, to be conducted every other year. The two Boards assumed responsibility at first for these biennial meetings, but now the gatherings are entirely in Latin hands. Following are the places where the Inter-American Conferences have convened: Mexico City, Mexico in 1962; Guatemala City, Guatemala in 1964; Mexico City, Mexico in 1966; Guatemala City, Guatemala in 1968; Mexico City, Mexico in 1971 (back-to-back with World Conference in Oaxtepec); San José, Costa Rica in 1973; Panama City, Panama in 1975; Caguas, Puerto Rico in 1977; Curitiba, Brazil in 1980.

The Church of God throughout Latin America has been greatly strengthened as a result of these times of fellowship and inspiration enjoyed by both nationals and missionaries.

Fiftieth Anniversary of the Missionary Board of the Church of God. A golden anniversary is always a time for celebration. The Missionary Board was fifty years old in 1959 and appropriate expressions of gratitude were provided. A dramatic presentation entitled *Fifty Years of Missions* was presented during the International Convention in Anderson. A special banquet for the Missionary Board was prepared at each of the six regional ministers' meetings in America. A large fiftieth anniversary cake was served and appropriate speeches given. Weekend celebrations were conducted for clusters of congregations across the United States. The National Woman's Missionary Society promoted "Greenleaf" teas among local societies. A very well-done brochure was prepared that described the fifty years of service the Board had given on behalf of the church.

Lastly, the Missionary Board launched a special project, having cleared it through World Service, to raise one hundred thousand dollars for some special needs on the mission field. The theme for the entire celebration was *Because We Care.* And because the people of the church did care, the goal was reached. Twenty thousand dollars was designated to Japan to be used in helping to build small church buildings; thirty thousand dollars was given to Korea to help in the building program at the Seoul Bible Institute and to place a resident missionary in that country; and twenty thousand was earmarked for Kenya to help establish the new Kisii station, with an additional thirty thousand dollars set aside to add a maternity wing to the hospital at Mwihila as well as to build a kitchen and dining hall. Finally, it should be reported that the Missionary Board was making plans for advance during the decade of the 1960s and prepared a film entitled *Our Mission for the Sixties* for missionary education.

Missionary Education Committee. Very early in the 1960s an *ad hoc* committee was formed by the leaders of the National Woman's Missionary Society, the Board of Church Extension and Home Missions, and the Missionary Board of the Church of God, to include persons from each agency responsible for promotion. It was named the Missionary Education Committee and quickly became the focal point through which cooperative efforts were made by the three agencies to place before the church in America informative, educational, and inspirational material related to the mission of the church. It published the monthly *Church of God Missions* magazine and prepared various kinds of study materials. It introduced the concept of *schools of missions,* which later on were simply called *missionary conventions.* The MEC has continued through the years in a most effective manner, making a tremendous contribution to the missionary cause of the movement.

All-Board Congress. As America entered the decade of the sixties, revolutionary changes were taking place within its society. In fact, the entire world was being shaken with radical social, economic, political, and cultural upheaval. It was a new era that forced the Church of God in America to take a hard look at the situation and reach some conclusions as to how the church might fulfill its obligation to the peoples of the world. Therefore, members of all Church of God national boards and agencies, along with representative ministers from across America, came together in Anderson for four days in 1963 to think and pray about certain objectives. Specific goals emerged for the Missionary Board: (1) to develop a dynamic program to further the church in other lands; (2) to take advantage of specific missionary opportunities in the 1960s, such as in major urban areas of the world and among the unreached primitive peoples wherever found; and (3) to develop a "new breed" of missionaries to carry out the responsibility of the sending church as well as to prepare better missionary education materials and methods for use by the church at large. By involving many leading pastors from across the country, stimulating feedback to the boards and agencies was achieved.

Living Link Program. J. Edgar Smith, assistant secretary for the Missionary Board for many years, began work immediately following the All-Board Congress to bring together in a more personal way the church in America and the missionaries it was supporting. Merely giving to a missionary budget seemed quite impersonal and left many donors cold regarding how their contributions were being used. The result was the Living Link Program, whereby a congregation could take one or more missionaries to support and have direct contact with those missionaries. It was possible to support a missionary totally or only in part. Rules were drawn up, the concept was cleared by World Service as a valid way in which to raise funds in the church, and numerous pastors were approached for their reaction to possible involvement of their congregations. At the very beginning eighty congregations signed up and the program has been a success ever since. It has gone through several revisions, all for the good, and it now includes the partial support of national pastors wherever Grant-In-Aid funds are sent for that purpose. There is even greater interest today with over two hundred congregations involved.

Growth in Number of Missionaries. At this juncture it is of interest to note the manner in which the number of missionaries under appointment of the Missionary Board increased, for it was in 1964 that the number reached the maximum. The following statistics present the growth:

Year	Number of missionaries
1909	19 plus 8 evangelists in Europe
1920	32
1930	41
1945	60
1953	73
1964	96

Following 1964 the number of missionaries sent out by the Missionary Board declined to the low eighties and the high seventies. The reasons for this will be presented in the next chapter. It must always be remembered that the quality and extent of the missionary movement of any group is not measured simply by the number of its missionaries. More important factors enter in. The "numbers game" is important only within Western culture.

Theological Education. In a country such as Kenya where secular education was being upgraded so rapidly and made available to almost all children, it was only natural that within a few years Kima Bible School would be upgraded to Kima Theological College with entry requirements becoming gradually more demanding. As more young people with a secondary education were available in the Church of God in the Caribbean area, both Jamaica Bible Institute in Jamaica and the West Indies Bible Institute in Trinidad were upgraded. The Seminary House in Japan changed only slightly in how it functioned to facilitate Japanese young men in their quest for theological education. The Bible Institute in Korea maintained a level of education commensurate with the needs of those training for the ministry. La Buena Tierra in Mexico served the church's youth well. The Church of God in Germany continued to upgrade the courses offered by the Fritzlar Bible School. And in India any young person desiring to be trained for the ministry was being encouraged to attend Union Biblical Seminary if they were academically prepared.

But there remained the need for training at the post-secondary level. The Missionary Board felt that theological education was one very important contribution it could make, even in countries that were becoming self-reliant. Also in response to this need, the National Woman's Missionary Society made available a limited number of scholarships to worthy students recommended by their respective responsible church bodies, feeling it was much better to train students in their own country rather than to bring them to America.

Chapter 6

The Third World Church in Developing Nations

(1965-1975)

THE CHURCH OF GOD reformation movement wherever extant throughout the developing nations continued its growth during the decade beginning with 1965. This was in spite of continued unrest at home and abroad. In America student demonstrations on numerous college and university campuses many times ended in violence. There were marches of many descriptions. Feelings of revolt against institutions had an adverse effect even on the institutional church. And around the world numerous factors were casting their influence on the missionary scene: population explosion in many countries, continued rabid nationalism, violent revolution, resurgence of ancient world religions, new theologies within the Christian church at large, and sudden social and political developments with the balance of power shifting from the so-called white world to other people.

These general characteristics of the sixties made it imperative to discover fresh and meaningful guidelines for determining the missionary response to the world's life and the church's life held in tension. These would take us beyond the traditional in missions to more dynamic and effective ways of bringing to bear upon human need the fact of redemption through Jesus Christ. The Missionary Board was faced with the ever-present problem of determining priorities. Strategy in the midst of contemporary events demanded an unusually careful deployment of personnel and funds to demonstrate good stewardship. Policy required that somewhere between the reactionary right and the revolutionary left the Board must maintain a radical middle of vital conservative evangelical thought and action, emphasizing both the evangelization of individuals through the proclamation of the gospel and the expressions of social concern through service.

I emphasized that throughout all our missionary endeavors we must maintain a consistent historical perspective. The year-to-year political vicissitudes are not the criteria by which we judge success or failure in missions. Doors close and doors open; so we roll with the punches, maintaining long-range planning and strategy with a flexibility to meet the necessity for adjustments. It was also my simple thesis that regardless of methods used and policies followed, the theological imperative of the irreplaceable task of evangelism must remain uppermost. Our missionary efforts must be found in the right location within the magnetic field between the two forces of revolution and reconciliation.

Through all of the previously described situations my feeling was that the cause of missions should always serve with a practical extension of Christian love and compassion performed with responsibility and integrity. However, the missionary work of the Church of God is, I declared, a movement, not an establishment. It is and always will be the work of the Holy Spirit working through consecrated persons but not the work of people alone. Therefore, great things continued to happen. There were challenging developments during this period of time, as we shall now observe.

Proliferation of independency. For a period of more than fifty years the Reformation Movement in America had been looking to the Missionary Board as the focal point to give expression and direction to its missionary outreach into other countries. The Board had been formed by the Ministerial Assembly in 1909 to provide purpose, meaning, and coordination to former independent expressions of missionary activity. This mandate from the responsible body of the Movement was taken seriously by both the Board and the entire church body. But now, in the mid-sixties, there began to appear again an increasing proliferation of missionary independence. This well represented the mood of the times in America. And it was not all bad, although it did generate some situations requiring careful thought and cooperative effort for solution. Individual volunteerism, independent crusades, work camps, and para-missionary organizations became active, involving within a few years hundreds of missionary-minded persons from scores of local congregations across America.

There was still another situation that seemed to lend credence to this growing missionary independency overseas. The Missionary Board was one of the general agencies in World Service, the national united fund of the Movement for the support of the work of the agencies. As such, the Board was committed to operate within its budget approved by the General Assembly. It could not go to the church and promote nonbudgetary projects or solicit nonbudgetary funds. As a result, the Missionary Board was experiencing great difficutly at that time in enlarging its missionary outreach, even though there was increasing demand from the church to do so because of numerous opportunities in other countries. Through missions conventions being conducted in an increasing number of local congregations there was a growing desire on the part of numerous individuals to engage in some form of missionary service. Consequently, if the Missionary Board could not send them, some of these who felt led by the Holy Spirit went about raising their own support from one or more local churches and departed on their own to serve in a country where they felt there was need. Sometimes these persons partially supported themselves. It is true that many times these individuals would review their plans with the Missionary Board, seeking its blessing.

Independent ventures of faith appeared in Guam, Australia, Peru, Puerto Rico, and Tanzania. There were attempts on the part of some to provide special services of one kind or another in the Philippines and Guatemala where the church was maintained on an indigenous basis from its beginning. Para-missionary organizations became active within the Movement. Two such organizations were Vacation Samaritans headquartered in San Diego, California, and Project Partner with Christ, headquartered in Wichita, Kansas (now in Middletown, Ohio). There were those who considered the National Woman's Missionary Society and Church of God Men, International, as para-missionary organizations, but that was not quite correct. Both of those organizations have always been considered to be auxiliaries to the work of missions, for they have not sent out missionaries or engaged in any form of administration in missionary outreach. Some have thought that the Tri-S (Student Summer Service) Program at Anderson College was para-missionary. But it was primarily an academic activity with a strong emphasis in contacting and serving in areas of need in other countries. Whenever a group of students completed a project related to the Church of God in another country that was it. There were no sustained relations with the church.

The result of all this was much the same as that that led up to the appointing of the Missionary Board in 1909. Many church leaders in America began to wonder what kind of a church was being developed in countries where it was being started by independent individuals. The fragmentation of financial support was seen as a hindrance to any united effort to promote the missionary cause. By 1970 there was a general call for a clarification of relationships. During the 1974 General Assembly, action was taken to coordinate all independent activities with those of the Missionary Board. A Missions Study Committee was appointed, and the following year it submitted its report with an outline of helpful expectancies. The trend was and still is to bring these independent efforts within a working relationship with the Missionary Board, recognizing as valid the mandate given to the Board by the Ministerial Assembly in 1909.

World relief. The specter of world hunger was brought to the attention of Americans, especially Christian Americans, when in 1966 India suffered the worst drought in seventy years, resulting in 80-100 percent crop failure. Millions of people faced starvation unless immediate assistance reached them. The Missionary Board and the General Assembly passed resolutions that year calling upon the Movement's people to cooperate with efforts to alleviate world hunger. Contributions for world relief were sent to the Missionary Board and distribution was made immediately through Church of God missionaries involved in relief or through Church World Service. Compassionate Christians responded immediately. Thousands of dollars were distributed effectively. By the following year a real concern for refugees was developing around the world. By the beginning of the seventies when all of our brothers and sisters in Christ in East Pakistan suddenly found themselves as refugees in northeast India, it was not difficult for people of the Church of God in America to contribute several thousand dollars. That kept our fellow Christians alive in refugee camps and assisted in their repatriation and rehabilitation in what became known as Bangladesh. In 1973 our people were again moved to respond to the tragic famine in the Sahil region of sub-Sahara Africa. They were encouraged to give through Church World Service or through the World Relief Commission. In 1974 a Disaster Fund became a part of the World Service budget, providing funds for suffering resulting from natural disasters as well as from starvation. Later, in 1975, the Church of God in America became more serious in meeting world needs as a result of a resolution sponsored by the Missionary Board and passed in the General Assembly, placing one hundred thousand dollars in the World Service Disaster Fund. This provided funds for immediate use in time of need, without having to wait for funds to be sent in.

Continued progress by Third World churches toward self-reliance. The *Third World* is generally known as those countries that are developing in every aspect of their lives. So it was with the Church of God reformation movement in countries where missions from America had been working for several years. There was a growing consciousness on the part of the people in congregations that they were the church. A trend was observed in the change from a "mission complex" to that of "church consciousness." With the obvious devolution of our American missions in a number of countries, the Missionary Board became particularly sensitive to what the indigenous church in those countries was saying. The integrity of the church was recognized, along with the responsibility that it carried as a body with a unique identity. For instance, it was found necessary to work with the responsible body of the church relative to American missionaries. What missionaries did the church want, for what use, and where were they to be placed?

The word *flexibility* was in vogue among missionaries, recognizing the fact that they might well be asked by the church to serve in some capacity other than that for which they had been assigned when sent to the field. *Redeployment* became another word well understood among missionaries when their services were no long needed in one country and they would work with the Missionary Board in finding another field in which to offer their services. There were some countries wherein the number of our missionaries was decreased, such as in India, Kenya, and Jamaica. But there were other countries in which the number of missionaries remained constant, such as in Japan.

It is important to observe that relationships were never broken between the Western churches of the Movement and the new self-reliant churches in the Third World. Everyone within the fellowship felt they were a part of the worldwide Church of God reformation movement. And it became apparent that the "developing churches" and the "developed churches" must cooperate as partners on equal terms. This was especially true when the Church of God around the world was faced with the evangelization of the *Fourth World*. This was a new term to denote the peoples in the world who had never heard of Jesus Christ as Savior. All signs pointed to a time in the near future when self-reliant churches of the Movement around the world would be cooperating in Kingdom work.

In this connection recognition of Church of God congregations in several Third World countries was accorded. These groups, such as in Guam, Australia, Peru, Bolivia, Uruguay, Nicaragua, and Tanzania, had been established through some form of independent effort. Now it was time to acknowledge these Christians as part of the worldwide fellowship of the Reformation Movement.

Integration of the two Missionary Boards. The presence of two missionary boards of the Church of God was first brought to my attention by students attending the West Indies Bible Institute in Trinidad. They had become aware of the existence of the Missionary Board of the Church of God with offices in Anderson, Indiana, and the Foreign Missionary Board of the National Association of the Church of God with headquarters at West Middlesex, Pennsylvania. They wondered why there was a "white" board and "black" board. Also the Study Commission on Race Relations set up by the Executive Council of the Church of God in America suggested that where there might be duplication of boards of the Church of God on a racial basis an attempt should be made to effect integration. This was another reflection of the mood of the times in America.

During this time I had numerous conversations with Evans B. Marshall, chairman of the Foreign Missionary Board. Beginning in the mid-1960s a total of five joint meetings were convened in which official representatives of the two missionary boards reviewed the situation, agreed that something should be done about it, and came up with a schedule pointing toward the time when the two boards could be integrated. Missionaries working in the missions of the National Association on the islands of Bermuda, Antigua, St. Kitts, and Curacao were given the opportunity to discuss the proposed integration. A joint visitation to these islands was conducted by Evans Marshall and his wife; the Butlers, a leading black couple from Toledo, Ohio; Adam W. Miller; and me.

Upon the approval given by the General Ministerial Assembly of the National Association of the Church of God and the Missionary Board of the Church of God, the merger of the two boards took place by the signing of an official agreement on June 21, 1967. This agreement called for only one board, the Missionary Board of the Church of God. The Missionary Board would assume all administrative, financial, and church-related oversight of the work of the Church of God (Anderson, Indiana) then existing on the islands of Bermuda, Antigua, St. Kitts, and Curacao. The three missionaries who had been serving under the National Association, Wilhelmina Fraser in St. Kitts and Carl and Mayme Flewellen in Bermuda, were appointed by the Missionary Board to continue their services under its auspices. The agreement also provided for at least a second black member on the Missionary Board, with the possibility of a third. All of this was looked upon with great favor by the church in general across America and wherever the black church existed in other countries. But this was not the end of the race problem facing the Missionary Board.

Confrontation with black/white issues. The Executive Council of the Church of God in America convened a consultation in May 1968 to have discussion between twelve black leaders, generally known as the Black Caucus, and the executives of the national boards and agencies of the church. This provided opportunity for the black representatives to present their convictions relative to race relations within the Church of God and how to bring about improvements. Feelings ran high, but the grace of God prevailed. It was obvious some changes within the boards and agencies were appropriate. A resolution was presented requesting that the Church of God be made a fully integrated and equal opportunity church through the appointment of men and women from various ethnic groups to several executive positions in the national agencies, plus a more equitable policy for hiring agency employees.

By request, one of the black representatives presented the main burden of the Black Caucus to the annual meeting of the Missionary Board in June. The Board took the matter seriously and by a resolution adopted a position paper that promised specific action in three areas: (1) to include more black representation in Board membership; (2) to put forth every effort to consider persons of competence from the black constituency of the church for possible addition to administrative and office staff; and (3) to continue what is both proper and urgent in the appointment of missionaries representing the whole church. The result? By 1970 there were three black members of the Missionary Board: Leonard Roache, Donald Williams, and C. T. Boyd. In 1973 the minutes of one of the meetings of the board of directors included this statement: "It was observed that the new associate secretary or the fifth staff member, if hired, should be a black person if possible." When the second associate secretary was appointed by the Missionary Board it was a black brother, Thomas Sawyer. Perfect solutions to all the race relations problems found within the Church of God in America have not as yet been achieved. But the Missionary Board endeavors honestly to cope adequately with situations within its jurisdiction through which racial equality in all aspects of its work can be maintained.

Administrative transfer of the Mexico mission and the Hawaii mission. Over the years the Board of Church Extension and Home Missions and the Missionary Board of the Church of God have cooperated well in assisting the church in its missionary endeavors at home and abroad. During the decade following the visit of W. E. Reed, executive secretary of the Home Missions Board, and me to several Latin American countries in 1960, the two Boards worked together in those countries in the areas of education of leadership, literature production, evangelism development, the use of national and missionary personnel, and the Inter-American Conferences. Since the Missionary Board was planning a major missionary thrust into Latin America during the decade of the 1970s, and since both Boards were committed to good stewardship of leadership and finance in the total mission to Latin America, and as a result of preliminary discussions between the executive staffs of the Home Missions Board and the Missionary Board, the Board of Church Extension and Home Missions by a resolution adopted in its April 1969 meeting proposed to the Missionary Board that the work of the Mexico mission be placed under the administrative responsibility of the Missionary Board. This would have the effect of making the work of the Church of God in Mexico a part of the total mission to Latin America. The Missionary Board, during its annual meeting in June, agreed to assume that responsibility. This agreed-upon administrative transfer for the work of the Church of God in Mexico was favorably considered by the Executive Council of the Church of God and given enthusiastic approval by the General Assembly of the Church of God that same year. Missionaries who were serving in Mexico and involved in this transfer were Albert and Irene Bentley, Maurice and Dondeena Caldwell, George and Marie Geiwitz, Luz and Carol Gonzales, Ronald and Ruth Shotton, and Amelia Valdez. This was the first of two vivid illustrations of how the two missionary boards cooperated in sincere attempts to maintain the kind of unity required to allow the work of the church to go forward.

The following year another transfer between the two Boards took place involving Hawaii, which had recently become a state of the United States of America. It appeared to the administrative staff of both Boards that since Hawaii was now a state it should more logically be under the administrative responsibility of the Home Missions Board. The development of the work of the Church of God among people of Oriental heritage and an ever-increasing number from the mainland commended itself to the program of Home Missions. Conclusive exploratory work was accomplished between staff members of both Boards. Therefore, during its April 1970 meeting the Board of Church Extension and Home Missions voted to accept the transfer of the work in Hawaii from the Missionary Board of the Church of God. Subsequently, in its annual meeting in June 1970, the Missionary Board passed a resolution transferring the administrative responsibility for the work of the Church of God in Hawaii to the Board of Church Extension and Home Missions. This was favorably received by the Executive Council of the Church of God and enthusiastically approved by the General Assembly. The transfer involved one missionary family, Brice and Nancy Casey.

In both of these changes there were numerous considerations requiring appropriate solution. One was the holding of nonmovable properties. Another was adequate budgeting so that the work could continue growth uninterrupted. Personnel had to be informed and consent gained from them. This included both missionaries and national leadership of the churches. In fact, the responsible bodies of the church in each place had to be consulted. But no problem is unsurmountable when leaders are totally committed to the well-being of the church, which was the case in both of these transfers.

Missionary Board of the Church of God reorganized. An obvious and urgent need was seen for a major revision of the bylaws of the Missionary Board. This was to update the relationships and work of its officers and Executive Committee. The size of the Board and the time and place for its annual meetings required review. Further study was needed to determine whether or not the Board's Articles of Incorporation should be revised to conform with the Indiana General Not-For-Profit Corporation Act passed in 1935 by the Indiana General Assembly. This act had superseded the Act of 1901 under which the Missionary Board was originally incorporated in 1914. If any revisions were to be made of its Articles of Incorporation they would of necessity be made in conformity with the Act of 1935.

A committee under the leadership of Adam W. Miller was appointed to study the matter and to report at intervals to the Executive Committee and to the entire Board for guidance. Something of this importance required and benefited from legal advice. The final draft of the committee's work was presented to the Missionary Board during its annual meeting in 1970. The Articles of Reorganization were adopted by the Board and subsequently obtained the consent of the General Assembly. The bylaws were adopted that contained the provisions for the regulation and management of the affairs of the Missionary Board of the Church of God under its newly adopted Articles of Reorganization. To some this item of business may seem somewhat irrelevant to the task of missions. But on the contrary, the Missionary Board was in need of updating the rules and regulations that governed its effective operation in a considerably different world from that in which it was originally incorporated.

1970 Consultation of the Church of God. One hundred seventy-two delegates convened in Anderson at the invitation of the Executive Council of the Church of God to sense the times and to determine God's will for the movement during the 1970s. Roughly half of the delegates were state representatives with the remaining number being representatives from each of the national boards and agencies. The purpose was to consider projections or goals that would help give guidance to each of the general agencies. Consequently, there was much thinking and praying together. It is always good for the Missionary Board to have this form of close relationship with the Movement across America. One of the six groupings considered *missions* and it was broken down into three work groups. The results were brought together in the form of missions projections and reflections. I was pleasantly surprised that most of the projections were an affirmation of what the Missionary Board was already endeavoring to do. But there were suggestions about how to get the church in America to respond knowledgeably, concertedly, and adequately. The delegates also considered how to capture individual initiative and interest while at the same time uniting instead of fragmenting the work in lands of other culture. Emphasis was given to short-term missionaries going on specific assignments, and to reeducating the church as to the meaning of missions. All of this and more served as a point of reference for several years.

World economic forces provide challenge to missions. Especially during the period of time covered by this chapter (1965-1975), unanticipated situations presented grave obstacles to be overcome by missionaries and the Missionary Board. On the one hand, the American church was experiencing a fresh awakening to its missionary obligation, with a decade of advance in Latin America coming into focus. Also, the Missionary Board was assuming additional responsibility for missions in Puerto Rico, London, Hong Kong, Peru. Tanzania, Mexico, Bermuda, St. Kitts, Antigua, and Curacao. On the other hand, however, the devaluation of the dollar on the world market resulted in a growing loss on exchange when remittances were changed into local currencies. In addition, inflation was rampant in many countries, causing a very rapid rise in the cost of living. This meant missionaries were receiving less local currency when more of it was required to overcome inflation. Pastors of supporting churches in America insisted on sizable increases in a missionary's personal allowances. The Missionary Board promised missionaries that their personal allowances would be adjusted to maintain reasonable buying power. But these steps became necessary regarding other allowances. All unnecessary expenses had to be eliminated. If that did not balance the budget, program would have to be reduced. That was more difficult. If neither of these brought the desired results, the number of missionaries would have to be cut. There was excellent cooperation on the part of the missionary personnel.

Fortunately, an increasing number of American pastors were conducting annual missionary conventions in their local congregations along with a Faith Promise emphasis. Many wanted to support specific missionaries through the Living Link Program. Many requested that their support of the Missionary Board budget be nonleveled on the World Service budget. This gained such wide acceptance that it ultimately had to be regularized. But it did provide more dollars to offset the world situation described previously.

Mission to Latin America during the decade of the 1970s. It was an annual occurrence, but something very unusual happened in February 1968 when I went before the Budget Committee of the Executive Council of the Church of God to present the budget asking of the Missionary Board for the 1968-69 fiscal year of World Service. Going back a little, most Americans had considered Middle and South America in terms of revolution and threats. But during more recent years those same Americans had increasingly understood that there was a great continent to the south of us that demanded our best attention. The Alliance for Progress initiated by President John F. Kennedy did much to stimulate the notion that the United States could be of help without being motivated by colonial overtones.

This aroused enthusiastic interest in Latin America on the parts of numerous pastors of the Movement in the United States, who in turn sparked a strong desire within their congregations to do something worthwhile for God especially in South America. Traditionally the Church of God reformation movement had never been very deeply involved in that continent. And we knew very little about the few Church of God congregations located there. Some of the previously mentioned pastors had made trips on their own into some of the Latin American countries. I began to feel the gentle but ever-increasing pressure to discover ways and means to initiate a viable outreach of some magnitude into that vast area south of our American border. This brings me back to my meeting with the Budget Committee.

Beyond the asking budget requested for the Missionary Board, the main burden of my heart was presented to the committee. All five members appeared sympathetic with my feeling that then was the appropriate moment to lead the Movement in America in a special emphasis toward developing a mission to Latin America. This would require a special project to raise anticipated capital fund needs. Almost before I knew what was taking place I had outlined to the committee what I considered those needs to be. The committee then agreed to recommend to the Executive Council meeting the following week and then to the General Assembly convening in June 1968 that the Missionary Board be provided a special project through the World Service budget to raise $150,000 over two budget years beginning July 1, 1969. This would give the Missionary Board time to make necessary preparations.

During its annual meeting in June 1968 the Board voted to launch a special emphasis called Mission Latin America during the decade of the 1970s, including a special project to raise $150,000 in capital funds. The Board further authorized a survey team to visit Middle and South America during the first six weeks of 1969. Donald Johnson, David Lawson (representing World Service), and I visited Guatemala, El Salvador, Costa Rica, Panama, the Canal Zone, San Blas Islands, Colombia, Peru, Uruguay, Argentina, Brazil, Guyana, and Puerto Rico with our eyes, ears, and minds open to what work the Movement already had and what the opportunities were. Studied evaluations and recommendations were presented to the Missionary Board and in June 1969 it authorized its Executive Committee to proceed with Mission Latin America during the 1970s. The special project was increased to $165,000. Leadership training, literature development, planting churches in strategic centers, and providing limited missionary personnel when necessary became priorities. As promotion for Mission Latin America began among American congregations, it stirred again the fires of evangelism within the church to give expression in cross-cultural missionary effort. Further on in this chapter and in the final chapter you will observe the results of this decade of advance in Latin America.

But I will now turn to a review of what was transpiring in the Third World church of the Reformation Movement found in rapidly developing nations of the world. Attention will be focused on progress toward self-reliance being made by many of the Third World churches as well as on some exciting expansion in the American Movement's missionary outreach, especially as Mission Latin America got under way in the first half of the 1970s.

The Caribbean Orbit of Influence

Even though it required a number of years to reach the goal, the Church of God reformation movement in **Jamaica** became self-reliant. Relationships between the church, the missionaries, and the Missionary Board always remained at a high level in spite of some difficult situations to work through. A revision of the bylaws for Ardenne High School and the Jamaica School of Theology provided administrative authority to rest with the church and not with the mission. For the first time there was a full-time Jamaican instructor, Eugenia Campbell, at JST. Legal changes were made so that the mission secretary-treasurer would no longer be the attorney for the Society of the Church of God in Jamaica. A Jamaican would now hold that very important position. There was a noticeable effort on the part of the smaller mission staff to become thoroughly integrated into the Jamaican church program.

Staffing problems plagued Jamaica School of Theology. Since they could not return to Korea, Kenneth and Sue Jo Good were redeployed to Jamaica for a term to assist at JST. George and Eva Buck, assigned to theological education, replaced Tom and Dorothy Pickens as they transferred to England to give pastoral care to the new venture in London. Mary Olson resigned as headmistress of Ardenne High School in 1969 and a highly qualified Jamaican named Claire Gayle assumed that position. A review of the vocational department of Jamaica School of Theology indicated it was no longer needed for the self-support of students of that institution, and so it was given to Ardenne High School to provide vocational training for boys in that school. Therefore, Ralph and Helen Little soon left Jamaica, since their services were no longer needed in the vocational department. Plans were indeed in their final stages to close out the American mission in Jamaica.

The Movement in Jamaica appointed its first full-time executive secretary, Rupert Lawrence, for the Executive Council of the Church of God. He and his family lived in a former missionary residence at 35A Hope Road. During this time the opportunity presented itself for the church in Jamaica to begin a missionary outreach of its own in Haiti. A new work of the Church of God was needing guidance and help, and the church in Jamaica was seeking some form of missionary outreach. One of the Haitian leaders, Jean Surin, and his wife came to Jamaica to study in the Jamaica School of Theology. Through strong efforts to educate the people of the Jamaican church in stewardship, the finances were such that very few funds were required from America. But guest speakers, Tri-S programs, and Project Partner work camps were of great encouragement.

Two situations had been under advisement for a number of months, the first of which gave considerable concern to both the General Assembly of the Church of God in

Jamaica and to the Missionary Board. This was related to theological education for Church of God leadership on the island. For some time the trend had been toward "buying in" at the United Theological College of the West Indies University in Kingston, allowing the existing Jamaica School of Theology to be the base under the supervision of one or two missionaries for feeding students into UTC. After much study and discussion by the church, the Executive Council of the Church of God voted to cooperate with UTC in the training of its ministry. This appeared to be best for the church and was approved by the Missionary Board. The second situation had to do with the church's membership in the Jamaica Christian Council. Many years before, under the guidance of George Olson, the Church of God in Jamaica had become a charter member of JCC and had made a considerable contribution to the council in many ways as well as having profited much through this relationship with the total Christian community on the island. But now there was an element within the Movement's congregations, especially those located outside the Kingston corporate area, that was bent on withdrawing the Church of God from the council. In 1971 the General Assembly elected a very conservative Executive Council, which immediately reversed the earlier decision to cooperate with the United Theological College and voted to withdraw from the Jamaica Christian Council.

The decision had already been made for George and Eva Buck to be transferred to Trinidad, leaving no missionary in Jamaica. In light of this decision Jamaica School of Theology closed its doors, since there were no missionaries to carry it on and the church was unable to staff it. That was a serious blow. Until the church could find some way to reopen the school, Jamaican students would be attending an evangelical seminary nearby.

But there were other signs more encouraging. That same year a home for the aged was opened in Kingston, primarily by the Woman's Missionary Society in Jamaica. Church of God Men, International, organized in Jamaica. When the World Conference of the Church of God convened in Mexico there were thirty-five delegates from Jamaica. The Executive Council sent an official request to the Missionary Board for a missionary couple who were specialized in the field of Christian education and who were willing to serve one three-year term. Within a few months Alva and Bernadean Dean were working well under the direction of the church. And finally, Jamaica's first missionary, Phyllis Newby, was appointed to Haiti. This also was primarily at the request of the Woman's Missionary Society.

By 1965 the work on the **Cayman Islands** was requiring more and more American personnel, for the congregations were not producing their own leadership. The Missionary Board maintained one missionary couple in Grand Cayman until 1970. Dewey and Thelma Johnson from Canada were the last missionaries. After that the General Assembly of the church was responsible—not the mission. Each congregation supported its own pastor, although it was not easy to find American pastors who could live on what was received. A five-year Grant-In-Aid was arranged by the Missionary Board to provide some additional finances. Triple C School became an institution responsible to the church and was soon self-supporting. In the early seventies the leadership situation became desperate, but the Missionary Board was able to assist without taking over. Other kinds of assistance continued from America. For instance, in 1975 seventeen men and women from the Pennway Church of God in Lansing, Michigan, converged on the little island of Cayman Brac to build a parsonage.

Across the Caribbean to the southeast the General Assembly of the Church of God in **Barbados** was finding its answer to a difficult question: To what extent is a missionary subject to the General Assembly in Barbados? They were not the first assembly to wrestle with the problem. Does the missionary do what the Missionary Board directs or what the General Assembly says, especially at the point of where and how he or she will serve? LaVern and Darlene Root were missionaries in Barbados at the time, and they were very open to the feelings of the church. But, like many other missionaries of that period of time, they also felt they had some responsibility to their sending and supporting church. The church in Barbados desperately wanted to be independent, but at the same time it was in many ways dependent upon the mission. Following the Roots, Ron and Marcia Howland spent a three-year term, and even though they had some frustrations their enthusiasm was contagious. As part of their program they introduced the Faith Promise concept to aid the people of the churches in supporting the work more adequately. But when the Howlands left Barbados in 1970 there was no missionary replacement, and the scheduled Grant-In-Aid scheme was soon to be completed, making the Church of God in Barbados self-reliant. The church also maintained its missionary outreach to the island of St. Vincent.

The year 1965 was the beginning of a new era in **Trinidad** from the perspective of mission-church relationships. Progress was being made toward the incorporation of the General Assembly of the Church of God in Trinidad to make possible the transfer of church properties from the Missionary Board to the church. That legal and public transfer did take place in a special meeting in the Port of Spain church, and I was present to do what was needed on behalf of the Board. All Grant-In-Aid funds were now to be sent directly to the treasurer of the General Assembly. Also, all correspondence about the church was to be between the secretaries of the General Assembly and the Missionary Board. This eliminated the strategic position of the mission secretary in Trinidad.

The constitution and bylaws of the West Indies Bible Institute were revised, making it responsible to and under the control of a board of trustees representing the churches in the southern Caribbean area rather than the Missionary Board. Walter and Margaret Tiesel (Walter had been missionary secretary-treasurer) retired from the field in 1966 and Oakley and Veryl Miller (Oakley had been director of the vocational department of WIBI) left in 1967. To better the financial situation of WIBI one of the Trinidadian pastors became its manager, and soon afterwards its vocational department formed its own registered company called Master-bilt Products. Unfortunately, the company experienced financial difficulties within two or three years.

Tragedy struck the Trinidad mission in January 1967. A telephone call from Trinidad was received one night by the Coolidges in Georgetown, Guyana, informing them that William Fleenor had been killed in an automobile accident. At the time, I was speaking in a youth rally during a Church of God convention in Guyana. I learned the sad news immediately following the meeting and made arrangements to fly to Trinidad the next morning in time for the funeral in San Fernando the following day. I delivered the funeral sermon, which was a personal privilege, for I had known Bill over the years since 1930. He had accidentally stepped off a curb without looking and was struck by a taxi, living only a few hours afterward. No charges were filed, for it was obviously Bill's error. Emilia soon returned to America.

When the Millers left Trinidad that summer there was no longer a mission *per se* from America. However, the church was continuing in its attempt to get off dead center and requested a missionary to come to assist in evangelistic outreach. Tom and Jean McCracken were sent, arriving in mid-1967. They stirred the fires of evangelism, and things began to happen. George and Eva Buck came from Jamaica to help while the McCrackens were on furlough in 1972. By 1974 the McCrackens were redeployed to Brazil, leaving the self-reliant Church of God in Trinidad on its own. However, Eugene and Margaret Fehr were sent as area missionaries to the southern Caribbean, making Port of Spain, Trinidad, their place of residence.

It was an honor for me to be present in **British Guiana** in 1965 when the Church of God celebrated its fiftieth anniversary. The following year the colony received its political independence from Great Britain and became known as **Guyana,** an old Amerindian word meaning "land of waters." Guyana was the first South American country to become independent since Venezuela in 1830. The Union Jack had waved over the colony for 152 years, and so the celebration was nationwide. There was almost immediate "Guyanization" at every level. New missionaries were prevented from entering, and it was with great difficulty that a visa was secured for Paul and Noreda Kirkpatrick to enter in 1970 when Ralph and Ruth Coolidge retired from missionary service.

Guyana was rich in natural resources, but the masses of people in the few cities and towns were extremely poor. Hence there was little financial potential for the church, and it suffered greatly from a serious lack of leadership. As many of the young men and women returned from training at West Indies Bible Institute in Trinidad, they soon left Guyana for Canada or the United States. The work of the movement entered a holding situation. However, there was a move toward the incorporation of the Church of God in Guyana so that church properties could be transferred, with the belief they would be more secure when owned by a local corporation instead of an alien organization like the Missionary Board. The Kirkpatricks ran into visa problems and were redeployed ultimately to Peru. Tom McCracken made frequent visits of encouragement from Trinidad. When Eugene Fehr became the area missionary he also made regular visits to Guyana, but there were no resident missionaries in Guyana. The church was on its own, and the struggle for survival was not easy, in spite of valiant efforts on the part of several national leaders of the church.

As a result of the merger of the two missionary boards as described earlier in this chapter, the transfer of administrative responsibility to the Missionary Board had been accomplished quite well, but much remained to be done to lead the churches on the islands of **Bermuda, St. Kitts, Antigua,** and **Curacao** toward self-reliance. Fortunately the

211

potential was there. In 1969 Wilhelmina Fraser retired from St. Kitts, and Allen and Clovis Turner were sent as replacements with the specific assignment to develop indigenous leadership on the island. The following year Carl and Mayme Flewellen completed their term of service in Bermuda, and they were replaced by Raymond and Noreen Chin. It is of interest to note that Raymond came originally from Jamaica. In Antigua, where there were no resident missionaries, Monroe and Bernice Spencer had emerged several years before as the strong national leaders.

In Curacao repeated efforts continued to encourage intercommunication between the two groups of the Church of God, one led by the Lindos and the other by the Wades. Their united witness was being hampered by their unwillingness to work together on that small but oil-wealthy island of the Netherland West Indies. The work of the movement on the island of **Grenada** not too far from Trinidad had been cared for by the Trinidad mission. However, it was now being encouraged to form its own General Assembly and to receive its own Grant-In-Aid. Both missionaries and church leaders from Trinidad continued to visit, giving guidance and encouragement.

The Latin American Orbit of Influence

From what was said earlier about the emphasis on Mission Latin America during the decade of the 1970s and the special project to raise capital funds beginning in mid-1969, it should surprise no one that there was marked growth in the American church's interest and activity in the Latin world to the south of it. The special project had a goal of $165,000 and $216,000 was contributed! The Woman's Missionary Society continued to give further grants such as $15,000 for expansion into Amazonia. Also, thousands of bequest dollars made available to the Missionary Board were designated to Mission Latin America.

For some time there had been increasing interest in starting a work of the Church of God reformation movement in **Puerto Rico.** By 1966 Earl and Freda Carver, former missionaries to Cuba, were reappointed as missionaries to Puerto Rico, and they began by working closely with the Evangelical Council of that country to determine the area on the island where the Movement could make its greatest contribution. Turabo Gardens, a new urbanization project in Caguas just south of San Juan, was chosen. The following year a missionary residence was purchased, along with a nearby strategically located lot for future church facilities. A carport ministry was started immediately at the residence. A Sunday school and a daily vacation Bible school brought in many children and provided contacts with their parents.

The group grew so rapidly that within a year another residence had to be rented across the street to provide acequate facilities. By 1969 a new church facility had been erected on the land originally purchased. In addition to regular services, a nursery school was provided for the community. Growth continued among these middle-class people, and it demonstrated what could be accomplished in Latin American urban areas. A strong emphasis was placed on literature, and Carver purchased a Davidson press to make quantities of Spanish language materials possible.

Early in the seventies the congregation at Turabo Gardens was looking for its own pastor. Marciano Yates, originally one of the young men in Cuba the Carvers helped train for the ministry, was chosen to serve. Due to growth, adjoining lots were purchased at the church site until the entire cul-de-sac was owned. This provided opportunities for expansion. A kindergarten and then a first grade were started, and today the *Academia Cristiana* is a thriving elementary school. The church grew also. Laypeople held prayer meetings in homes, and a Bible class was started in the community center. By 1974 a new work was started in Mariolga, another urbanization development. In another year a third group was being established in Tomas de Castro.

Throughout the 1960s very little was known about what was happening in **Cuba.** The Missionary Board was able to send about eight thousand dollars a year through the World Council of Churches in Geneva and on through the Swiss Embassy in Havana, Cuba. This was part of a joint effort on the part of several church groups in America to send funds to their respective church bodies in that communist-controlled country. Sometimes this worked, but not always. By the early 1970s we began to have infrequent correspondence with Jaime Greene, the main Church of God leader, and by 1974 it was possible for Canadians to visit Cuba. Gordon Schieck, former missionary to India and now member of the Missionary Board, and A. D. Semrau, administrative director of the Canadian Board of Missions, were able to visit the Church of God in Cuba and observed that it had survived the Castro regime quite well. They attended a convention in the Finlay Church of God in Havana and meetings in all three of the Havana congregations but were unable to visit the two congregations in Matanzas, the one in Camaguay, one in Oriente, and one on the Isle of Pines. Schieck and Semrau found five ordained ministers serving 193 baptized persons over twelve years old. The regular attendance in the eight congregations was 380, and all services were conducted in the Spanish language. In spite of many obstacles the children of God had remained faithful. This provided a good example of what could happen in a communist country.

As the Missionary Board assumed administrative responsibility for the work of the Church of God in **Mexico,** it was observed that Mexican leadership wanted to carry more direct responsibility. But the relationship of the missionaries was still quite paternal. This was not a negative reflection on the missionaries, but rather on the current structure of the mission. In fact, there was a sincere attempt on the part of both national leadership and missionaries to determine and carry out proper church-

214

mission relationships. La Buena Tierra, the training school located at Saltillo, was being upgraded. A change in leadership brought in Eliu Arevalo as the school's new director, the first Mexican to hold that position. Juan Cepeda became director of CBH Spanish and the Spanish literature department. There remained the need to bring the Movement's activities in Baja California and Central Mexico more closely together. The Church of God in Mexico had the honor of hosting the first World Conference of the Church of God held in the Western Hemisphere. It convened in Oaxtepec just south of Mexico City in 1971. All of these contacts with the church in other countries provided the Mexican church leaders with a better understanding of what it was to be a self-reliant church.

Because there was the attempt to allow the growing work in **Guatemala** to be indigenous from the very beginning, it provided opportunity for numerous unilateral contacts from the American church. And not always were Americans understanding and sympathetic with Latin culture. As a result, some questions began to be raised regarding the activities and methodology of Isai Calderon as he gave leadership to the development of the congregations. Raymond Hastings from Houston, Texas, and I were requested to make a special trip to Guatemala to determine the exact nature of the situation. We found Calderon to be functioning well within the bounds of Christian ethics as interpreted within Latin culture, which is a perfectly normal procedure as the gospel is planted in country after country. In this situation that interpretation was not being controlled by a resident missionary.

I use this as a classic example of what can happen at times when sharp differences in cultural patterns are not taken into consideration and leaders from different cultures find themselves at odds over some question of ethics. But it was suggested to Calderon that a stronger group consciousness, loyalty, and involvement should be promoted within the Movement's existence in Guatemala. In the late 1960s considerable growth was noticed as the church reached out as far as Quetzaltenango as well as to the Cackchiquel Indians. Also, an Inter-American Conference convened in Guatemala City helped give more stability to the church in that country.

Just to the south of Guatemala is the little country of **El Salvador.** In 1969 a group of Christians made contact with Isai Calderon in Guatemala and expressed desire to become affiliated with the Church of God reformation movement. Over the next few years numerous contacts were made with those congregations. An independent effort on the part of Joe Salinas helped to solidify relationships. This work was followed by the combined efforts of Luz Gonzales and Harry Nachtigall, who were conducting institutes for leadership training in Costa Rica. There were six congregations.

When a devastating earthquake hit Managua, **Nicaragua,** in 1972, Project Partner hastened to the rescue with relief for the suffering. As assistance was given in a rehabilitation program, contact was made with an evangelical group under the leadership of Misael and Amina Lopez. This was the beginning of a growing relationship with the Church of God. Now there are twenty-four congregations with some two thousand members affiliated with the Movement. This is another group that was indigenous from the very beginning.

As a result of interest shown by some brethren in Florida, something new was developing in **Honduras.** On Roatan, a little island off the coast, a Christian by the name of Philip Allen began a work of the Church of God in 1972. Meetings were conducted under the trees and in his small home. Now there are three congregations with three pastors. Regular contacts are maintained with this group of believers. Honduras, like El Salvador and Nicaragua, was entered as a result of the growing interest in Latin America by Christians in North America.

What was taking place in **Costa Rica**? After the Planks left, a young Costa Rican woman named Millicent McLaren, a Christian education graduate from West Indies

Bible Institute in Trinidad, gave tremendous assistance to the group of Christians in San José. She supported herself through a good job in the same city. To strengthen this congregation in the capital city a pastor, Rafael Campos, was employed. He resigned, however, in 1967. In addition, Sidney Bennet resigned at Cimarrones and Siquirres, and Leroy Nicholls resigned at Puerto Limon. Those three resignations were devastating. Even though Jorge Moffat, a young Costa Rican who had just completed his training at La Buena Tierra in Mexico, was returning to his homeland to work for God, the church sent a despearte message to the Missionary Board requesting a missionary immediately to save the situation.

Edwin and Carol Anderson were sent but remained for only one term of three years. They were new missionaries finding their way, and the complexity of the situation only frustrated their efforts. Another attempt was made to give assistance by redeploying Luz and Carol Gonzales from Mexico to Costa Rica. Luz, a dynamic personality, had the tendency to take over everything. That did not prove to be good for the situation, for it was not in any manner developing national leadership for the congregations. Harry and Jene Nachtigall assisted for a longer period.

All through these few years a location was being sought upon which a Christian center could be constructed to provide facilities for the potential development in San José. Through all this time of uncertainty there remained the hope that something good would emerge. The Gonzaleses left in 1974, and the San José Christian Center was completed in 1975. The fact that this entire episode covered a decade of time vividly illustrates that there are occasions when the best of plans, seemingly God directed, simply do not work out.

Quite another situation was in progress in **Panama** and the **Canal Zone.** Throughout the mid 1960s there was phenomenal growth. A strong new congregation came into being in Villa Guadalupe, a large urbanization project on the edge of Panama City. A new church building was

217

erected in Colon, and a missionary residence was constructed in the Canal Zone. Rapid expansion took place among the Cuna Indians on the San Blas Islands and a leadership training center was established at New Providence. More and more emphasis was placed upon Spanish-speaking work. Other primitive peoples were being reached up the Indio River. The emerging leadership of the church felt itself capable of administering the affairs of the movement. Dean Flora began to experience major difficulties in maintaining *Pap Igar Ulu* (The Word of God Boat), the boat being used in the work among the San Blas Islands.

Other administrative and relational problems existed. Harry and Jene Nachtigall were transferred from Costa Rica for a year to assist in the situation. By 1975 Dean and Nina Flora left Panama after sixteen years of dedicated and helpful service. Local church properties were transferred to the Church of God in that country. Mission Latin America funds were being used to assist such projects as the building of the church edifice at Villa Guadalupe. Ronald and Ruth Shotton moved from Mexico, where they had given twelve years of service, to guide the church in Panama on toward complete self-reliance. That was a big assignment, but the church was ready for it.

As Paul Butz left his employment with the Zachry Construction Company to give full time to the work of God, trusting God for support through interested congregations and friends in America, he and his wife, Mary, devoted themselves unstintingly to starting a work of the Church of God in **Peru.** Their modest home at Campo Verde was the place of beginning. The need for leadership training was recognized, and La Buena Tierra Peruana was started. This project was greatly assisted by Tri-S work camps from Anderson College as students helped to develop the campus by erecting several buildings over several summers. By 1967 the first General Assembly of the Church of God in Peru convened, and plans were under way to incorporate the Church of God in that country. Paul and

Mary Butz had, as independent missionaries, started a very good work. But by 1969 they began to feel the need for being a part of a larger organization for guidance and support, especially since a major thrust into Latin America appeared eminent. The following year they were appointed missionaries by the Missionary Board, coming under its administration and support.

The first graduating class came out of La Buena Tierra in 1971, providing some leadership for expansion into other small communities surrounding Pucallpa, the main city on the eastern side of the Andes. Paul and Noreda Kirkpatrick, after spending time in language school in Costa Rica, arrived to give full time on the campus of La Buena Tierra. "Christian Brotherhood Hour" Spanish was being heard over one station in Peru. Part of the emphasis in Latin America during the 1970s was to develop appropriate outreach in major urban areas. An urbanization project in Zarate outside of Lima, the capital of Peru, caught the attention of Salomon Cabanillas. Therefore, a lot was purchased with funds from the special project and plans were prepared for a building. Robert and Jo Ann Tate gave para-missionary service at La Buena Tierra.

An opportunity to enter **Bolivia** came in an unexpected manner. Independent missionaries Homer and Elvira Firestone had been working for over twenty years among the Aymara and Quechua Indians. They would make regular trips to America, and during that time Homer would teach in some college to earn their support. During several of these visits in southern California the Firestones became acquainted with the Church of God and discovered commonality in beliefs and practice. The Missionary Board was approached by some of our pastors in southern California requesting the Board to study the possibility of accepting the Firestones as missionaries. The Firestones, in turn, approached the over ninety congregations and their leaders in Bolivia to secure their favorable reaction to being associated with a larger group. By 1974 this Bolivian work of God became associated with the Missionary

Board. This included Homer and Elvira Firestone's appointment as missionaries by the Board as well as that of their son Ronald and his wife, Violet. Ronald, a medical doctor, was carrying on clinical work in La Paz. This rather large group of approximately seven thousand Christians was indigenous from the beginning, and remains so even today. The Holy Spirit leads about seventy pastors and leaders, encouraged by missionaries and the backing of the church in America.

As mentioned earlier in this chapter the church in America became vitally interested in reaching out to Latin America during the 1970s. Wherein the Church of God in Germany through its Missionswerk was assisting the work in Brazil and Argentina, the Missionary Board desired to give further help only in areas not covered by Missionswerk. By 1970 there were twenty congregations of the Church of God in **Argentina,** mostly in Misiones Province to the north. Most of the work was among German immigrants who were pioneers in developing the country.

Floreal Lopez began a group of Spanish-speaking persons in the 1950s. The Missionary Board used Mission Latin America funds to help complete the church building in Alem for this Spanish-speaking congregation. Many of the young people were three generations removed from Germany, and they had been educated in Spanish. Therefore, there was a definite trend toward using the Spanish language in the church, including reaching out beyond the German community. By request from the Assembly in Argentina the Missionary Board in 1973 redeployed Albert and Irene Bentley from Mexico to develop Theological Education by Extension, thus setting up a leadership training program.

Over several years evangelistic meetings were conducted across the Parana River into **Paraguay.** In 1974 a lot was purchased in Colonia Obligado as house meetings were being established. As can be seen, the work of the Church of God in Paraguay really started as a missionary outreach by the church in Argentina.

By 1970 some thirty-five congregations had been established in **Brazil** by the German work headquartered in York, Nebraska. Now the Assembly of the Church of God in Brazil requested the Missionary Board to assist them at two main points: leadership development and literature. Brazil is the only South American country to use the Portuguese language; so in breaking away from the German-speaking community, Portuguese had to be used.

In 1970 Maurice and Dondeena Caldwell were transferred from Mexico to Brazil. They spent time in language school to shift from Spanish to Portuguese. Then they took up residence in Curitiba. Construction of a Bible school began in nearby Guarituba, and in 1972 the Caldwells were requested to assume the leadership of *Instituto Biblico Boa Terra*. Since Maurice Caldwell had been editor of *La Trompeta*, the Spanish *Gospel Trumpet*, he was asked to be editor of *Trombeta* in Portuguese. These two contributions helped to unify the Church of God in Brazil and to point toward its outreach beyond the German Community.

Farther to the north, in Amazonia, the Missionary Board cooperated with the church in establishing at Itaituba a bridgehead for a growing work in the great Amazon basin. In 1972 the Missionary Board sent William and Betty Mottinger to work at Itaituba following language study, and the church in Brazil sent missionaries from among the first graduates of the *Instituto Biblico Boa Terra* to Amazonia. In 1974 Thomas and Jean McCracken were ready in São Paulo to inspire the Church of God to launch an urbanization program to reach out into several districts of that tremendous metropolis of eleven million people.

Finally, one more opportunity opened in **Uruguay.** An independent Slavic Gospel Mission had been established in San Gregorio by Emma Spitzer. In the late 1960s she was in Canada and was invited by friends to attend the International Convention in Anderson. Emma was deeply impressed with what she saw and heard and decided to turn over her work in Uruguay to the Church of God. That took place in 1973. Short-term missionary service has been supplied through the Missionary Board with missionaries in Brazil giving some assistance.

The European Orbit of Influence

Major urban areas of the world were targets that the Missionary Board had in mind when considering expansion. There was a unique opportunity in London, **England.** The group of Church of God West Indian immigrants that had come together was requesting assistance. In 1965 plans were prepared for the London project, which was initiated the next summer following a Billy Graham crusade in London. Marvin Hartman, pastor of the church in St. Joseph, Michigan, agreed to spend a year in London. He was replaced that year in St. Joseph by Philip and Phyllis Kinley on furlough from Japan. Hartman made preparations for a Church of God campaign to be held in the town hall in the area of London where the church gathered in rented quarters. The speaker would be Dale Oldham. This generated considerable enthusiasm and set the stage for growth. Thomas and Dorothy Pickens were redeployed from Jamaica, having been chosen to pastor the congregation in London. They were not considered missionaries. That proved to be a good move.

The congregation was international and interracial in name and design, bringing in Church of God people from various countries of the British Commonwealth, but in reality it continued to be composed primarily of West Indians from the islands of the West Indies. In 1970 an old church building was purchased and a downpayment on a manse was made. There was a very rapid decrease in the temporary Grant-In-Aid that the Missionary Board had provided. When the Pickenses returned to America in 1972 the church chose Martin Goodridge, a member of the congregation, to be pastor. He had graduated from the West

Indies Institute in Trinidad some time back, and he and his wife originally came from Barbados.

In **Denmark** the movement was learning very well how to maintain itself as a self-reliant church. The people were no longer dependent upon the leadership of missionaries. But several contacts each year were maintained with the Church of God in Germany, and this helped make them feel a part of a larger group. In the late 1960s, however, there was one major disappointment. Two brothers, Jorgen and Kresten Norholm, had gone to America to train for the ministry in two of our church's schools. They married American girls and returned to their homeland of Denmark where they assumed pastoral responsibility in Church of God congregations. Their wives learned the language and made excellent adjustments to a new culture. But both Jorgen and Kresten became impatient with the slowness of growth in the Church of God in Denmark. They tried using methods in evangelism that they had learned in school in America, but those methods did not produce results in the Danish culture. I appealed to them as young Danes to be patient and discover under God methods based on New Testament teachings that would bring results. Unfortunately for the work in Europe, they returned to America with their families where they are serving well. This is not to discredit these fine young men, but is it to show how the proclamation of the gospel must be done in such a manner as to make its claims understandable within the culture of the hearers.

There is one more reflection on the work in Europe during this period, and it is a sad story. During the late sixties the small congregation in Belfast, **North Ireland,** tried another time to find pastoral leadership. A young man named Fred Murdock was chosen, but he remained for only two years. So again Sam Porter, a dedicated layman in the congregation, endeavored to give leadership. But the group was growing smaller and there was not one young person there. For some reason that I was never able to discover, the believers from several decades back had never been able to hold their young people. Consequently, when civil strife broke out in North Ireland it practically destroyed the existence of the Movement. Politically, the Catholics representing Ireland, and the Protestants representing North Ireland were at each other's throats. The Irish Republican Army, representing freedom for North Ireland, was fighting a guerrilla war with the British Army, which was presumably protecting the rights of the Protestants. Doers of evil took advantage of the perilous times, and loss of life and destruction of property were daily occurrences. Whole sections of downtown Belfast were burned and destroyed. During one visit I looked upon what was once our congregation's church property. It had been totally destroyed. Roadblocks were maintained and it was difficult to move about. There were no more meetings for our people. Sam Porter continued to visit the very few elderly persons. The work of the Church of God in North Ireland had, for all intents and purposes, ceased to exist. Yet there were a half-dozen persons still claiming loyalty to the Reformation Movement.

The Middle East Orbit of Influence

With only one missionary couple in **Egypt,** the mission was in a holding pattern. Ernest and Grace LaFont spent much time assisting in the work of the youth centers in Cairo and Alexandria, but as much as they tried, they did not feel their influence was doing much to help the Egyptian church. Time after time the LaFonts endeavored to bring to bear upon members of the General Assembly of the Church of God in Egypt the necessity of becoming self-reliant so that they would not be dependent upon the mission or the missionaries. An outstanding Greek named Christo Psiloinis, who had not as yet left Egypt, gave yeoman service. He had been reared in Egypt in a Church of God family, knew Arabic very well, and was a good leader in the Cairo Youth Center. For a time he was both vice-chairman and treasurer of the General Assembly. Unfortunately, he soon moved to Cyprus.

Then the 1967 War broke out between Egypt and Israel. The LaFonts had to evacuate and remain out of the country for some time. Upon their return they faced tremendous difficulties. Franco and Beatrice Santonocito were leaving the work in Alexandria to go to Italy, the move being necessitated by Franco's dangerous health situation. There were pressures on all American missionaries in Egypt. They were followed by secret service men. The reason? America was behind Israel, the enemy of Egypt. The Church of God in Egypt had broken relations with the Protestant body known as *Maglis-el-Milli,* which represented evangelicals before government. That was a miscalculation on the part of our people and was the cause of problems later on. The church's leadership had reached a stalemate in relationships.

Early in 1971 the Missionary Board encouraged Nasser Farag and his American wife to go to Egypt as laypersons to help the situation. Nasser was the son of the late Salib Farag and his American wife to go to Egypt as laypersons to help the situation. Nasser was the son of the late Salib Farag, the Church of God printer in Alexandria. The LaFonts decided to leave Egypt as the last resident missionaries, move to Beirut, and become missionaries for the eastern Mediterranean area. Farag's ministry, though not totally successful, highlighted some of the glaring difficulties that were hindering growth. In 1973 the Farag family left Egypt, being sent as missionaries to Kenya. That left the Egyptian church at a very low ebb. On occasion the LaFonts would give some encouragement through a brief visit. Also, Lebanese leaders tried to provide inspiration and guidance through infrequent visits.

Into the seventies the Church of God in **Lebanon** continued to prosper spiritually and materially. God was blessing the efforts of all the believers and they worked together to spread the gospel. Not only was there evangelistic outreach into other parts of Lebanon, including new districts of Beirut, but there was also missionary outreach into

225

other countries. Fouad Accad, now retired from a career with the United Bible Society and a second-generation member in the Movement, was encouraged to go as a missionary to Bahrain in the Persian Gulf to witness in his unique way to Muslims. Amol Boudy, another second-generation person in the church, went to Nabi Othman in the Arabian Gulf, supporting herself as a midwife. She built her own tent of palm leaves, and ministered both physically and spiritually to the women. These were encouraging signs of vitality. However, the people of Lebanon were about to enter an unprecedented time of suffering and trial. In the spring of 1975 civil war erupted that was so severe the leaders of the church in Lebanon recommended that the planned World Conference to convene in Beirut that summer be canceled. What followed takes us into the next chapter.

The future of the Reformation Movement in **Greece** was becoming uncertain. The relationship the Greek people of the Church of God in Chicago, Gary, and Detroit had to the work became somewhat nebulous. Savas and Olive Joannides felt a lack of cooperation as they endeavored to strengthen the congregation in Athens, feeling they would soon be leaving, which indeed they did in 1968. The Missionary Board was ready to phase out the work in Greece, selling the valuable property in Athens to perhaps the Oriental Missionary Society. But that did not work out. The Greeks in the American church objected vehemently. Nick and Rose Zazanis came out of retirement and arbitrarily returned to Athens. But there was little enthusiasm for the future. Failing health forced the Zazanises back to America within three years, having performed a holding position. The Missionary Board had second thoughts about selling the property and decided it might become a center in the eastern Mediterranean orbit, especially with the growing uncertainties developing in Lebanon. Consequently, Panayote Dendrinos and his wife were sent to Athens in 1973 to carry on. You may recall that they were the ones who followed the Zazanises in Cairo, caring for the Greek work until all the Greeks emigrated due to political pressures.

It was a sad time for Franco and Beatrice Santonocito when they left Egypt for **Italy** in 1968. Franco required surgery by a specialist in Rome. The future was uncertain. But God was merciful, having something more wonderful in store for the Santonocitos. During his convalescence Franco began to see God's hand leading them to begin a work of the Church of God reformation movement in Rome. By 1971 the possibilities were definite. As I was going to India that year I met with Franco and Beatrice at Rome's airport during an hour-and-a-half plane stop. On the basis of that conversation the Missionary Board decided to assist in making the project possible. Consequently, in October 1972, following careful study on where to begin, a start was made in Ostia, a suburb of Rome located by the sea. It was clear to all that this development was not to be a mission from America, but that it should grow naturally within Italian culture, using ways and means commensurate with the understanding of the Italian people. Success was almost immediate, and by the end of two years two young men had completed their training for the ministry and another suburb of Rome, Dragoncello, had been entered. You will note that even though Italy is really a part of Europe, as is Greece, it seemed appropriate to consider the work in these two countries a part of the eastern Mediterranean orbit of influence. However, this new development in Italy soon attracted the attention of Church of God leaders in Europe and lasting contacts were established.

The East African Orbit of Influence

Continued movement toward self-reliance was the pattern followed in **Kenya** during the last half of the sixties and the first half of the seventies. Kenya's president, Jomo

Kenyatta, declared that his government was "committed to support the churches and stand back of the work that they are doing." The concept of gradualism was no longer valid. Rapid Africanization had to take place, including the transfer of authority. For both the church and the mission this meant, as one leading African Christian said, a "flexible capacity for rapid change in the days ahead." And indeed there was great progress in the work during this period of time.

In spite of some observable weaknesses in church leadership and in the life and work of the church, the responsibility for the work in Kenya and its functions was actually passing from the mission to the church. All departments and committees now functioned under the General Assembly: evangelism, stewardship, radio publications, women's work, youth, education, religious instruction in schools, Christian education, and the boards of governors responsible for the four secondary schools, Kima Theological College, and the two hospitals. Almost all the department and committee chairpersons were Africans. The headmasters of the secondary schools were now Africans. And the chairman and the treasurer of the General Assembly also were Africans. The General Assembly had by 1970 a full-time African executive secretary, Byrum Makokha. And there was a phasing out of the short-term teaching program for secondary school teachers from America, for by this time Africans began to to return to Kenya, having earned their bachelor's degrees in education.

All of this required a review of the function of the mission and the role of its missionaries. What were the implications in mission-church relations? What, if any, redeployment of missionaries would be necessary? It became obvious that the large and powerful Church of God mission in Kenya should be phased out. It was also obvious there was a trend toward more specialized missionaries as might be required to assist the church. The General Assembly appointed an Overseas Personnel Recruitment and

Placement Committee (generally known as OPRPC) to work with the Missionary Board in the selection and placement of missionaries. The Assembly appointed two or three missionaires to the OPRPC. Missionaries were appointed or elected to committees and boards of the church not because they were missionaries but because of their individual skills and abilities, which Africans saw as desirable.

In place of a mission in Kenya, with all the negative overtones the word *mission* carried with it, there came into being the East African Ministries of the Missionary Board of the Church of God. The name was almost frightening. Usually "East African Ministries" was used. The former position of mission secretary-treasurer became that of coordinator. And to make it easier for the new African executive secretary to function with an office at Kima, the new coordinator's place of residence was moved from Kima to Nairobi. Instead of funds from America being sent through the mission, all Grant-In-Aid funds and special grants for the church were to be sent by the Missionary Board directly to the bank account of the General Assembly.

In 1966 the church in Kenya, the mission, and the Missionary Board grappled with a situation in the mission staff in Kenya that brought heartache to many. Lew and Wanda Goodrick, excellent missionaries with nine years of fruitful service behind them in Kenya, became enamored with and involved in the Charismatic movement. Since Lew was then principal of Kima Theological College, this became a real problem for the church's leadership. Missionaries on the field were disturbed, and as a result the Missionary Board had to deal with a public relations problem. Following considerable discussion in Kenya between the Goodricks and both African and American personnel, and after much frank and open correspondence between the Goodricks and the Missionary Board, the Goodricks gracefully resigned as missionaries to Kenya, seeing they could not accept the position generally held by the Church of God reformation movement relative to the Charismatic movement. This was the honorable way out of a delicate situation and left no permanent scars on the work of the church in Kenya.

As the educational and medical programs began to receive more and more government aid and the church was carrying administrative responsibility for those related institutions, the missionaries were giving more time to direct church-related work. Whatever the Missionary Board might do for Kima Theological College or even for the medical program would be through their respective boards of governors. The government was not interested in subsidizing KTC, and so the Missionary Board had considerable responsibility to see that KTC functioned well in providing leadership training for the African church.

During this period of time it was difficult to find medical personnel to serve. A Canadian physician named Larry Hoogeveen who, with his wife, Verna, served two years, and a Mennonite doctor named Ron Loewen was seconded for a brief time. They were followed by the first African doctor at the hospital, Geoffrey Ingari. African nurses began to be employed, although Caroline Ackerman remained by request as a missionary nurse. Clair and Retha Shultz were withdrawn in 1970 so that he could join the administrative staff of the Missionary Board. Shultz was replaced by Douglas Welch as coordinator. The publication work that had been assisted by Welch was now directed by Africans. Jewell Hall retired in 1972 and was not replaced. Irene Engst retired in 1974, and an African woman replaced her in women's work. Edgar and Lima Williams left the field in 1970, and the board of governors elected Dennis Habel to succeed Williams as principal of KTC. Vivian Woods served for one term. Nasser and Marilyn Farag arrived from Egypt and served in the Kisa, Idakho, and Butsotso areas by request of the church.

Two of our missionaries, with the church's approval, served for several years in strategic ecumenical positions. Aaron Kerr was seconded to be executive secretary of the

Protestant Churches Medical Association at a time when he could give much needed advice to our church's medical program. David Crippen was secónded to the Christian Churches' Educational Association with the specific assignment of working on the curriculum for religious education courses being taught in both elementary and secondary schools throughout Kenya. Both of these families lived in Nairobi. In February 1972 a great gathering convened at Kima to witness official ceremonies through which all nonmovable properties were transferred to the Church of God in Kenya. These properties included all missionary residences and all buildings of the institutions and were conservatively valued at $356,800. Certain valuable pieces of equipment found in the institutions were also given to the church. Government officials, numerous church leaders from various communions, and many friends made the occasion a memorable one. I was privileged to be the representative of the Missionary Board to sign the transfer documents. In the following chapter you will read how the church managed, having achieved indigeneity.

As mentioned in the last chapter, it had become the desire on the part of the independent missionaries serving in **Tanzania** under the auspices of the World Missionary Fellowship based in Canada to have the mission come under the administration of the Missionary Board of the Church of God. This was primarily to help the church in Tanzania to become a part of the Church of God fellowship in East Africa and to achieve indigeneity. It required over two years of working with the Executive Committee of the World Missionary Fellowship and the Canadian Board of Missions to arrive at a suitable agreement, which was signed by representatives of the three agencies in 1968. Four main points in the agreement were the following: (1) the entire mission and church in Tanzania (including evangelism, teaching in the two Bible schools, present and future lands and buildings and present and future missionaries) would immediately come under the administration and financial arrangements of the Missionary Board; (2) the World Missionary Fellowship would remain registered with the government so that properties could be held and visas and work permits could be secured for missionaries; (3) all properties would still be owned by the World Missionary Fellowship until such a time when the Church of God in Tanzania should become a legal entity to hold property, at which time properties would be transferred to the church; and (4) the present missionaries would become missionaries under the appointment of the Missionary Board.

The church was strengthened and a stronger national leadership was being developed. The church was reaching out with greater spiritual vitality. Simon and Mae Robinson gave a year of service, being transferred from Kenya. Roy and Magaline Hoops were also transferred from Kenya to work long term at Mirambo, an assignment that was cut short by Roy's sudden death during furlough in 1980. When the Farmers left Tanzania in 1973 after thirteen years of service they were replaced at Mbulu by Robert and Janet Edwards. By 1972 the church had organized its General Assembly with an executive secretary, Eleazar Mdobi. He began to have direct relationship with the Missionary Board. There were by then thirty-three congregations.

By the end of 1974 the Church of God in Tanzania had officially registered with the government and incorporated as a legal entity. The government, eager to Africanize the church as it became registered, automatically and unilaterally transferred all the properties from the World Missionary Fellowship to the Church of God in Tanzania and canceled the registration of the World Missionary Fellowship in that country. The government also understood that any missionaries coming in at the invitation of the church would be sponsored by the Missionary Board. The terms of the 1968 agreement had been fulfilled. This was not easily understood by the Fellowship, but the mission was now the church in Tanzania.

A number of Church of God Africans from Kenya had crossed the border into **Uganda** for employment. They began to come together in Jinja, Kampala, and two or three smaller places. The church in Kenya sent and supported as its missionary to Uganda, Jackson Amule and his family. Frank and Margaret LaFont were loaned by the Missionary Board to go to Kampala not to form a mission from America but to assist in establishing the work. In 1971 a political upheaval took place and all Kenyans were forced to leave Uganda. The LaFonts were evacuated, and the church in Kenya asked them to reside in Mombasa to assist in two church building projects. Jackson Amule remained for a while but ultimately had to leave. These events just about ended the presence of the Church of God in Uganda.

The South Asia Orbit of Influence

The Church of God Mission in **India** continued to experience difficulties in securing visas for American missionaries. This was also true for endorsements for Canadian missionaries. However, it was made possible for Canadians Bertram and Marian Steers to be sent to South India so that Bertram could, by request of the South Indian church, be administrator of the Church of God in that area. Another Canadian couple, Eugene and Margaret Fehr, accepted appointment to South India to reside in Trivandrum where opportunities were present for beginning a new work, especially among university students. On the minus side, however, Gordon and Wilhemina Schieck left India in 1967 after twelve years of service. In addition, the sudden and unexpected death of Marian Steers brought sorrow to those who had known her for only a brief time. She was buried in Nagercoil. Bertram completed a three-year term, after which he returned to Canada.

The All-India Assembly continued to meet annually, bringing the Movement's leaders together from the northern, central, and southern parts of India for fellowship, inspiration, and business. Outstanding Indian and American guest speakers provided helpful insights to assist in the strengthening of the church. During one of these annual meetings in Cuttack when groundbreaking ceremonies for a guest house took place, I brought gifts from the Woman's Missionary Society in Barbados and from the Church of God in Japan to assist in financing this project. Such a gesture reflected a good church-to-church relationship in those days. The Assembly annually reviewed the progress that was being made toward the registration of the Church of God Trust Society of India, which finally was incoporated in 1972. Then the amalgamation of the Missionary Board of the Church of God with the Church of God Trust Society provided the transfer of properties conservatively valued at around $250,000 to the church in India. That procedure had taken seventeen years!

The church in South India finally made the necessary adjustments and agreed to form its Coordinating Council with P.V. Jacob as chairman. Area assemblies were structured. The Church of God in India was now in a position to "go it alone." Eugene and Margaret Fehr left South India at the end of their five-year term. Clifton and Mary Morgan left their responsibilities in the state of Orissa after ten years of service. And Sidney and Jean Johnson left India in 1972, the last of our *resident* missionaries to leave. They had given seventeen years of their lives to India and were not ready to leave southern or southeast Asia, as we shall see later on. Church of God expansion was led by enthusiastic Indian leadership. Evangelistic outreach began afresh with results, especially in South India where the motto was "Double in a Decade." And they did! A radio program aired from Seychells Island in the Indian Ocean provided P. V. Jacob with thousands of contacts as the message went out in the Malayalam language. In view of this enthusiasm, the Missionary Board promised its continued interest in assisting and working with the Indian church in its endeavors to evangelize and to do missionary work.

Political disturbance in **East Pakistan** in 1965 required the sudden evacuation of Joseph and Ramona Spires and their children along with Nova Hutchins and her children. Paul Hutchins remained in a caretaker situation. The evacuation was to Manila. From there the Spires family went on to America and did not return to East Pakistan. Nova Hutchins remained in Manila until Paul could come to get her, and the family returned to East Pakistan. Since there was continued refusal to grant visas for new missionaries, more responsibility was carried by national leadership. The work in the Sylhet District grew. There were now Church of God congregations in seventeen of the sixty Khasi villages. The main church was at Lumpangad Pungee with B. Lyngdoh as pastor. Twenty-eight acres was purchased and named *Balang U Blei Lumdonbok* (Church of God "Hill of Good Fortune"), whereon several excellent projects were to develop. I will long remember the gathering on top of one of the hills on a very hot Sunday morning when the land and concept were dedicated to God.

Before Paul and Nova Hutchins left for furlough in 1970 they were able to assist the church through the process of developing bylaws for the Administrative Council of the Church of God in Rangpur District, outlining how the work of the church was to be carried on. These developments were most fortunate, for tragedy struck the inhabitants of Rangpur District while the Hutchins family was in America, preventing the Hutchinses' return to East Pakistan.

On Easter Sunday, 1971, the West Pakistan Army entered Lalmanirhat and the surrounding countryside. About 150 of our church people escaped, although a few were killed and a number of women molested. All the mission property in Lalmanirhat was taken over by the army. There was considerable destruction and damage.

The people fled across the nearby border into West Bengal of India and settled in a large refugee camp at Cooch Behar that was being operated by the World Lutheran Federation under the direction of a Norwegian doctor named Olav Hodne. Relief funds were immediately sent from America. Almost a year was required before our people could return to Lalmanirhat. East Pakistan had proclaimed its independence and was known as **Bangladesh.** Olav Hodne gave personal assistance in developing a tremendous rehabilitation program at Lalmanirhat. Property and buildings were repaired and our people's homes were reconstructed. Various kinds of work were provided to aid persons financially. Several thousand dollars was donated by the Movement in America and sent to make this relief project a success. Late in 1972 Paul Hutchins was able to visit Bangladesh for a brief period. That was a great encouragement. The younger leadership of the church had learned much through the tragedy and were now giving more adequate direction.

Something new and significant was happening in **Thailand.** During their year's furlough following their departure from India, Sidney (Mac) and Jean Johnson were seeking guidance for their next appointment. Inspiration came in the spring of 1973, and it was decided that they should live in Bangkok, Thailand, and be missionaries at large to serve the Movement's interests in India, Bangladesh, the Philippines, and Hong Kong. That fall they entered language school in Bangkok and made initial contacts in the area as well as with the Christian communions present in Thailand.

When I met Mac in Bangkok in January 1974 I spent an entire day with him working on his visa problems. At that time I also met Wichean Watakeecharoen for the first time. He held a responsible position with the Church of Christ in Thailand and was giving valuable assistance to the Johnson family. I was deeply impressed with him. The next time I met Mac was in January 1975 at the Calcutta airport. His enthusiasm was overwhelming as he shared in detail the information that Wichean Watakeecharoen was available to lead the beginning of a Church of God in Thailand. Space will not permit the recording of all the details that led up to this recommendation, but the Holy Spirit was obviously at work. The Board of Directors of the Missionary Board gave its approval to the plan and that June, with Watakeecharoen present, the Missionary Board voted to establish a work in Thailand with Watakeecharoen in charge in the hope that the work could be as self-reliant as possible from the beginning. Johnson and Watakeecharoen had developed a ten-year plan, setting goals along the way. It appeared practical and possible. So in August 1975 a new work of the Reformation was born in Thailand where 98 percent of the population is Buddhist. The area chosen for the New Life Center in Bangkok contained four hundred thousand persons who were without any Christian witness. Our missionaries were playing a supportive role.

The East Asia Orbit of Influence

With each visit made to **Japan** I was increasingly aware that the Church of God there seemed to know where it was headed and how it was going to achieve its goals. Missionaries and Japanese church leaders were working well together. They were constantly searching for new forms of ministry through which non-Christian persons could be reached with the gospel. Short-term Church of God teachers from America were being encouraged to teach English in various institutions while at the same time sharing their Christian witness. Arthur and Norma Eikamp started a "coffee house" approach, along with teaching English, in the Tarumi District of Kobe, a large city next to Osaka. Nathan and Ann Smith were in the process of developing a Christian center in Futsukaichi, not too far from Fukuoka. And not far away another congregation began in Saga. Orlo and Carol Kretlow were aiding in new developments at Nishi Kunitachi in the greater Tokyo area. My impression was and still is that the Church of God in Japan is a vital force, although relatively small, with which we must cooperate to evangelize East Asia.

Because the Japanese church had so few leaders it was unable to take advantage of opportunities it had in joint missionary efforts in Brazil, Taiwan, and Guam. The one experience it had in missionary endeavor in Okinawa was very successful, for by 1972 there was a strong and self-supporting congregation at Ameku, as well as several preaching points on the island. When America returned Okinawa to Japan it became a prefecture, and the church became integrated into the total work of the Movement in Japan.

By 1967 the Church of God in **Korea** had thirteen churches, two primary schools, two junior high schools, one high school, one Bible institute, and two orphanages. Unfortunately, its leaders had been influenced to join the International Council of Christian Churches headed by Carl McIntyre. Some of the reasons might be considered valid, but mercenary motivations were evident. At the end of Kenneth and Sue Jo Good's first furlough in America, the Missionary Board was advised by the Koreans not to return the Goods to their country but to send the church the money it took to support and maintain them on the field. The Board transferred them to Jamaica where their services were needed, requiring their total allowances. During the late sixties and early seventies I made several visits to Seoul. The door was also kept open through correspondence. It was not too long before the "middle generation" of Korean leaders (those who had received training in the Bible institute) became disillusioned with McIntyre because he was not producing all he had promised. A period of establishing cordial relations was entered. Hong Mook Yoo, a young man who was now president of the Korean General Assembly of the Church of God, made a visit to America, stopping in Anderson. The time would soon come when the Church of God in

Korea would again be united with the Movement around the world.

Hong Kong is always a place of opportunity. Even though originally the Missionary Board did not desire to add to the scores of evangelical missions working among the Chinese, Ethel Willard was sent in 1969 as a missionary to serve the Junk Bay Medical Relief Council as a private secretary while studying the Chinese language. After her first term she became secretary-treasurer and later business manager. She cast a spiritual influence through several opportunities in that British colony. In 1971 P. K. and Lovena Jenkins officially came under appointment of the Missionary Board. Growing pressure from government to nationalize all positions, brought about the retirement of Jenkins as medical superintendent. He was replaced by a Chinese Christian doctor, David Lum. The search was on to find a Chinese person to replace Willard. Considerable thought was being given in the mid-seventies about the kind of witness the Church of God could make in the rapidly growing sections of high-rise apartments by these Church of God missionaries who were qualified for the task.

By 1965 the sixth anniversary of the Church of God in the **Philippines** was celebrated. Eduardo Viray, the first graduate from the Pacific Bible Institute, started a new work in Tondo, an economically depressed area of Manila. About this time, Bacani's brother-in-law, Greg Federis, began to show signs of leadership. Contacts were maintained with the original work far to the north at Laoag. Year after year an additional grade was added to the elementary school at Valenzuela. A school was started at Tondo. In 1970 a General Assembly of the Church of God in the Philippines was organized by twenty-three delegates from four congregations. Later a Woman's Missionary Society was formed, generating missionary outreach by these four congregations. This particular self-reliant church overused, not always to its advantage, Western methodology and actively sought Western financial support.

In 1966 William and Frances Rife incorporated the Pacific Ocean Mission in **Guam** and established an interdenominational congregation at Barrigada. Wilbur Miller failed in the A & W Root Beer business and had to withdraw. Rife hoped to evangelize all the Trust Territory islands, but as an independent he could not gain permission. Phillipe Marioles, a Filipino who attended Gulf-Coast Bible College the same time as Rolando Bacani, married an American girl and arrived in Guam to start another congregation. But that effort failed. Finally in 1976 the Rifes resigned and returned to the mainland. The Missionary Board was then asked to send missionaries.

The first commissioned missionary pastors to **Hawaii** were Brice and Nancy Casey. While they were in Honolulu a second congregation was started at Waipahu pastored by Ernesto Babas. But it was discontinued after a couple of years. Also during the Caseys' time in Hawaii the administrative transfer took place from the Missionary Board to the Board of Church Extension and Home Missions. In **Australia** Austin and Nancy Sowers arrived to start the Australian Bible Training School. After ten years of work in that country the Church of God had produced only Lloyd and Ruth Chilvers as pastors. The work was still very much dependent upon American leadership. While visiting Australia in 1972 I endeavored to discover with the help of those in the work there exactly what plans could be employed in the future and what the role of the Missionary Board should be in assisting. The answer came later.

Chapter 7

Partnership in World Missions
(1975-1980)

BY NOW the disturbances of the 1960s in American society were almost a thing of the past. Within our Movement
people were ready to move out and discover afresh how to
work more closely together. Believers in the Third World
church were ready to act in taking the gospel to the Fourth
World. In the Missionary Board office a "changing of the
guard" was due. By action of the Missionary Board and
ratification by the General Assembly, Donald D. Johnson
became the new executive secretary-treasurer. He came to
the office in 1975 after six years of missionary service and
seven years as my associate secretary. For one year I
continued service as secretary of research and development and then was loaned to Anderson School of Theology to initiate the Department of Missions, developing and
activating a curriculum of studies leading to a Master of
Arts in Religion with emphasis in Christian missions. In
1977 I retired from the employ of the Missionary Board
after forty-four years of service. My second retirement
was from the School of Theology after two years of teaching. Douglas Welch, adequately qualified academically and
with fifteen years of missionary experience in Kenya, was

chosen as my successor. The transitions were accomplished with ease.

The coming of Donald Johnson as chief executive officer of the Missionary Board provided a new face-off in missions for the Movement, and several developments were forthcoming. He came in with a dynamic and ability that led the Board through some helpful situations and changes. Encouragement was given to the Board's Long-range Study Committee, which had been formed in 1973. By 1979 it had completed its assignment but not before it had grappled with the theology, philosophy, strategy, and methodology of missions. On the practical side, Johnson urged the building of the Crose Missionary Residences on Tenth Street in Anderson, Indiana. This project was designed to provide a condominium of six well-furnished apartments that would provide "a sense of dignity and well-being to our missionaries," showing that the church really cared for them as they at times lived in Anderson. The apartments were dedicated in 1977.

Picking up on what was mentioned about world relief in the last chapter, the Missionary Board was given more responsibility in administering disaster funds. Major relief and rehabilitation required $144,000 in Guatemala following a major earthquake in 1976. Fifty-five thousand dollars was sent to help our fellow Christians in Lebanon during the civil war. A small amount was given to Antigua following an earthquake that damaged some church buildings. Several thousand dollars was remitted to the Philippines after a severe fire in the Valenzuela church school badly burned a number of students. Eight thousand dollars was yet needed in Nicaragua for rehabilitation. Funds were sent to St. Vincent following the eruption of a volcano. In Jamaica severe flood damage required eleven thousand dollars in aid to our people. And in 1980, twenty-five thousand was sent to Southeast Asia to help care for Cambodian refugees. Also, one hundred Haitian and Cambodian refugees were settled in Church of God congregations in America through efforts administered by the Missionary Board offices.

In 1979 the Missionary Board adopted a revised missionary manual. You will recall the last manual was issued in 1947. Obviously a great deal of upgrading was required to bring regulations and policies up to date. Several new programs were developed through which individuals could perform some missionary service. Among them were VIM (Ventures in Mission) wherein groups could go to a specific country to perform some needed task, and Spot Missionaries, who would go to a country at their own expense where their particular skills were needed. During the 1977-78 fiscal year the Missionary Board for the first time received over two million dollars. But continued inflation of between 30 and 40 percent in most countries and the devaluation of the dollar continued to work havoc on the field and make it difficult to increase the number of missionaries. It was estimated that during the prior ten years the buying power of the American overseas missions dollar had been reduced by 128 percent! That is why in its 1980-81 budget the Board was spending $941,000, or 45 percent of its budget, for the support of seventy-eight missionaries.

Durings its seventy-first annual meeting in 1980 the Missionary Board made some major revisions in its operation. It enlarged the Board's membership from fifteen to twenty. The term of the executive secretary-treasurer was changed from three to five years beginning in 1981. A pilot experience was launched: the naming of Sidney Johnson as a Southeast Asia liaison, meaning he would represent the interests of the Missionary Board in that area wherever there were no resident missionaries. The Missionary Board agreed to assume administrative responsibility for the Church of God Refugee Program. A year earlier the Board passed a resolution honoring Hallie Patterson as she retired from its membership, having served thirty years, twenty-five as a member of the board of directors. Shortly after that Board meeting another valued member, David Gaulke, was lost by death.

Four Consultations on Missions Strategy

Covering two years, 1976-77, consultations were held in Michigan (September), California (November), Oklahoma (February), and Georgia (April). They were designed to listen to what the church was saying about missions as well as to challenge delegates with what was going on in other countries. Attention was given to methodology and strategy in the Movement's missionary enterprise. But inevitably some consideration had to be given to the theology and philosophy of missions. These consultations helped both the churches and the Missionary Board during the immediate years ahead.

Inter-American Publication Consultation

Serving under the direction of the Inter-American Conference, the Inter-American Publication Committee had been meeting each year during the 1970s to fulfill one of the objectives of Mission Latin America: more Spanish and Portuguese literature to aid in the advancement of the Movement as it reached out into new areas. To add impetus, an Inter-American Publication Consultation convened in Oaxtepec, Mexico, in 1978, representing not only members of the Inter-American Publication Committee but also delegates from the Board of Church Extension and Home Missions, Warner Press, Women of the Church of God, and the Missionary Board. This was to bring more cooperation and better coordination in literature publication. Throughout the decade thousands of tracts, books, and doctrinal booklets were published and distributed. *La Trompeta* (Spanish) and *Trombeta* (Portuguese) were widely used in evangelistic outreach and in keeping the Latin American churches informed. A Spanish Church of God hymnal with notes was a major publication funded by Warner Press.

Caribbean Consultations

Throughout the English-speaking West Indies the people of the Church of God reformation movement had moved from dependence to independence to interdependence in their relations with the Missionary Board. In twelve territories, as these island countries are called, there were 170 congregations in the Movement with around seven thousand believers. They had their own problems related to interterritorial cooperation. Throughout the transition from independence to interdependence the Movement in the entire area experienced difficulties related to theological education, suitable literature, capital funds, and ways of meeting socio-economic conditions. The West Indian church coveted the cooperation of the Missionary Board as they struggled against low wages, high inflation, and government pressures. Consequently, with a determination to press on, four consultations convened during the decade of the 1970s.

Consultation I met on the island of Antigua in 1971. The role of the Church of God in contemporary West Indian society was reviewed. Theological education was discussed. Relations between the churches and the Missionary Board were reviewed, with the Board expressing sincere willingness to be of service. Consultation II congregated on the island of Grenada in 1973. The emphasis was on stewardship and theological training. Helpful suggestions were presented on the first subject, but little cooperation was evidenced on the second. There was talk about drafting proposals for a regional body of some kind. Consultation III convened in Trinidad in 1975. Discussion took place on whether or not the Church of God in the Caribbean area should join the Caribbean Conference of Churches. A committee was appointed to work on a regional hymnal and a yearbook.

Unusual headway was made during Consultation IV when thirty-five Church of God leaders from eleven territories came together on the island of St. Kitts in 1979.

These delegates convened to do business. Only the delegate from Haiti could not be present. Four main issues were carefully presented and discussed: West Indies Theological College, missions, family life, and area organizations. The first three were dealt with quite adequately, but there was an organizational breakthrough relative to the fourth topic. It was thought that the entire area could be divided into three zones. Zone A would include Cayman Islands, Jamaica, Haiti, and Bermuda. Zone B would include St. Kitts-Nevis, Antigua, Barbados, and St. Vincent. And Zone C would include Trinidad-Tobago, Grenada, Guyana, and Curacao. It was recommended to the General Assemblies in each of the territories that a regional assembly be formed, having a full-time regional director. The organization would be called Caribbean-Atlantic Assembly of the Church of God. Delegates were to return to their respective territories seeking the approval of the General Assemblies. A *protem* director was elected, and the first meeting of this vital area Assembly was to meet in the near future. This was a great step forward, pointing toward a period in which greater witness and growth would be achieved through united efforts in the Caribbean.

Centennial of the Church of God Reformation Movement

It was a great celebration in Anderson, Indiana, June 20-29, 1980! More than thrity-five thousand of the Reformation Movement's believers came together from all over the world to give serious and joyful expression on the occasion of the one hundredth birthday of this Church of God reformation movement. It's heritage was celebrated and the future projected. This was all done during the ninety-first International Convention, convened in Anderson. The Missionary Board and church leaders in many countries of the world looked forward to this year of 1980, the centennial year, for some very specific reasons: (1) to celebrate the Decade of Advance in Latin America, (2) to launch a Decade of Special Emphasis in Asia, (3) to give thanks for what would be accomplished through the raising of the special project, Million for Missions, and (4) to be involved in the World Conference, especially with the possibility of developing a World Forum. These must now be considered in greater detail, for they represent important landmarks in the misisonary movement of the Church of God throughout the world.

The Decade of Advance in Latin America

The capital fund drive at the beginning of the 1970s provided Mission Latin America with finances to assist in building as the church in these countries began to expand. At the beginning of the decade the Missionary Board was involved in only six of the twenty-two countries of Middle and South America: Mexico, Guatemala, Costa Rica, Panama, Cuba, and Puerto Rico. Seventeen missionaries were involved. By 1980 eleven new countries had been entered as part of the Missionary Board's outreach for the American church: Honduras, El Salvador, Nicaragua, Colombia, Venezuela, Bolivia, Peru, Brazil, Uruguay, Argentina, and Paraguay. This made a total of seventeen countries in which thirty-four missionaries from America were involved, although American missionaries were not found in all of these countries. By 1977 the Missionary Board's budget for Latin American countries had multiplied five times since 1970. By the end of the decade the number of Bible schools had doubled, the two new ones being started in Brazil in 1972 and in Argentina in 1977. A radio ministry through CBH Spanish was being broadcast in several countries and CBH Portuguese was broadcast in Brazil. The first Christian Community Center was established in San José, Costa Rica. A strong urban emphasis was placed in such major cities as Mexico City, Guatemala

City, Panama City, Lima, São Paulo, and Buenos Aires. People had been reached with the Good News, and by 1980 there were twenty-two thousand believers in the Movement in Latin America gathering together in 340 congregations. All of this means that the work of the Church of God in that part of the world *doubled* in a decade! This was because of the Holy Spirit working through the lives of hundreds of God's children. Presently, leaders look forward to entering Chile and Ecuador.

Asia in the 1980s

As early as 1974 Sidney Johnson and I began to have dreams about a decade of special emphasis in South Asia and Southeast Asia immediately following the Decade of Advance in Latin America. This was later expanded to include East Asia. What a staggering thought! For that is where masses of people reside who have never heard of Jesus Christ. If you draw a line from Bombay to Peking, two-thirds of the world's population resides below it! One half of the world's people are Buddhist, Hindu, and Muslim, and most of them live in Asia! In Asia only 2 percent of the population is Christian, including Roman Catholics! The Asian countries are where most of the 2.7 billion people live who have never heard of salvation from sin through belief in a Savior. And that is where the population is growing faster than anywhere else in the world. Indeed, this is a difficult area in which to witness. But what a challenge it is to the Reformation Movement to become a viable part of the total missionary task force operating in Asia. By 1975 the Missionary Board had taken action to launch in Asia in 1980 a strong united evangelistic and missionary outreach by the Church of God.

To determine what plans the Missionary Board should make to become correctly involved during the decade of the 1980s, two consultations were conducted. The first was a five-day Consultation in Tokyo in July 1978. Twenty-seven long-term and short-term missionaries were present, along with nine delegates from America. This was primarily to hear what missionaries in Asia were thinking about the possibilities for outreach and what the Missionary Board's involvement should be. The second was a three-day Consultation in Bangkok convened in February 1979. Seven church leaders representing the Church of God in Korea, Japan, Taiwan, the Philippines, Thailand, Bangladesh, and India met with three persons from America to review what the Reformation Movement's believers in Asia considered to be the approach in evangelism and missions among non-Christians and what would be the most appropriate assistance from the Missionary Board. Later that same year the Missionary Board itself gave serious thought to recommendations coming out of both consultations.

It appeared a number of emphases would be most helpful, working with the Church of God extant in Asia. Here are some of the guildelines considered appropriate: (1) an Asian identity for the Movement to be created by fostering interrelationships between the churches extant in various countries, (2) specialized long-term missionaries to be invited to serve, (3) short-term missionaries to play an increasing role, (4) Missionary Board assistance in the training of leaders to be given, (5) literature to be produced in greater quantity, and (6) Board partnership in missionary outreach into new countries to be encouraged, the Board being at times the initiator and coordinator. All the way through the decade of the eighties the American church, being supportive, must recognize that results come slowly and not in great numbers. Such a concept is difficult to understand in American culture where immediate returns for investment made are almost demanded.

Million for Missions Special Project

Million for Missions was a joint project approved by the

General Assembly for the Missionary Board and the Board of Church Extension and Home Missions. The sum of $750,000 was to be raised for the Missionary Board and $250,000 for the Home Missions Board for a total of $1,000,000. This was a capital fund project to cover three budget years beginning July 1977. For the Missionary Board this was to provide nonbudgetary needs especially for Asia in the 1980s, although some vitally needed projects in other parts of the world would be included. By the end of the three years, approximately $750,000 had been raised, giving the Missionary Board about $560,000.

The project, now in its fourth year, is hoping to raise a total of at least $900,000, which would give the Missionary Board $675,000. This would mean a project curtailment, but certainly would meet many critical needs. For Asia, Million for Missions is providing an outreach program in Bangladesh; missionary outreach, leadership training, and contribution toward the relocation of Union Biblical Seminary in India; a new multipurpose church building at Tamagawa in Japan; facilities for the new development in Singapore; assistance in high school facilities in the Philippines; a Christian center in Taipei, Taiwan; and assistance in small church buildings and a new missionary outreach into Cambodia from Thailand. These and many other very important projects have and are being cared for through Million for Missions. The church in America has responded well.

Sixth World Conference of the Church of God

The Worldwide Strategy and Planning Consultation convened in Kenya in 1977 to plan for the joint meeting of the sixth World Conference and the International Convention to celebrate the centennial of the Church of God in 1980. This would be the first World Conference to meet in the United States of America. Plans for the World Conference were coordinated with the Centennial Celebration Committee and the International Convention Program Committee. The first three days of the joint meeting were designed for the World Conference. Co-chairmen were Willi Krenz from Germany and Carlton Cumberbatch from Trinidad. Leading speakers from nine different countries brought challenging messages. In addition, there were conferences, Bible study groups, prayer and testimony meetings, and plenty of time for fellowship and sharing. Many leaders became acquainted with each other for the first time. Names became faces! For the first time hundreds became aware of the great strength of the Church of God around the world and the tremendous task before it to present the Good News to the world.

World Forum of the Church of God

I was one of several who had been thinking for some years about the necessity for a kind of world gathering for Church of God leaders where more definite planning for the Church of God in mission could be done on a scale never before possible through the World Conferences. A World Forum was proposed during the Worldwide Strategy and Planning Consultation in 1977, to have its first meeting during the centennial celebration in 1980. The World Forum would not be administrative or legislative but rather consultative as world leaders would gather from time to time to consider topics of vital concern affecting the life and work of the Movement worldwide.

In June 1980 some fifty-five delegates gathered during two sessions of the first World Forum. Organizaitonal business was cared for. But the main topic for consideration was "International Partnership in Mission," an appropriate starting point due to the interest in missions on the part of the Third World church. Papers presented by Donald Johnson and Douglas Welch created discussion and considerable consensus regarding the future. Indigeneity is not achieved until the gospel takes root in the culture of the people where it is planted, or until a missionary outreach of the new church is established. The mission church must become a missionary church! Then and only then can there be real partnership in mission by the Church of God around the world. But that partnership must be based on mutuality. At this point some big words were introduced: *reciprocity, complimentarity,* and *interdependence.* But they were properly defined, and they added up to the concept of the *internationalization of missions.* Missions on a global scale will involve persons from the "developing churches" and from the "developed churches." A linkage system could be maintained through the World Forum.

The Church of God: A World Movement

During the immediate years preceding 1980 the Third World churches of the Movement continued to show signs of strength and growth and a determination to join with one another and First World churches to evangelize the Fourth World. This will be illustrated in the closing pages of this book. You will note that the need for missionaries from America remains, involving redeployment at times.

The Movement in **Jamaica, Barbados,** and **Trinidad** had come of age. West Indies Theological College was functioning well. Eleven out of fifteen pastors in Trinidad and Tobago were alumni. The school had incorporated in 1979 and properties were transferred. In **St. Kitts** Clarence and Bernice Glover replaced Allen and Clovis Turner. Vernon and Ruth Lambe had come to **Bermuda.** When Jamaica withdrew its missionary involvement in **Haiti** the work continued to grow with some assistance from America. There are now twenty congregations with fifteen hundred believers and three day schools, one clinic, and an orphanage.

When Warren and Devie Kinion completed a term of service in **Mexico,** Aaron and Kathryn Kerr were redeployed from Guam to serve in Baja California, and Nasser and Marilyn Farag were redeployed from Kenya to serve in northcentral Mexico. A rapid growth of the church in **Guatemala** took place after the severe earthquake and there were now more than sixty congregations. The Christian Center in **Costa Rica** provided a kindergarten, gymnasium, coffeehouse, library, and a place for the congregation to worship. Ronald and Ruth Shotton retired from **Panama** in 1979 and were replaced by Vernon and Cathy Allison. That same year Earl and Freda Carver retired from **Puerto Rico** and Joseph and Elva Mattox continued serving the Academy, which then had 193 students. Paul and Mickey Zoretic were redeployed from Peru to pastor the congregation at Turabo Gardens. Mendoza and Daisy Taylor in Panama heard the call from **Colombia** and responded. Within a brief time there were six congregations with pastors. Even with visa problems Thomas and Mary Lou Walls finally found themselves in Ciudad Guyana, **Venezuela,** beginning a work there. Albert and Irene Bentley left **Argentina** and Bill and Kay Konstantopoulos served a term there. Appointed to the Instituto Biblico Boa Terra in **Brazil** were Willi and Esther Kant. And the work in Amazonia expanded to Santarem and several settlements.

By 1980 the work in **Italy** was seven years old and there were two new groups, making a total of four congregations in the suburbs of Rome. An FM radio station was purchased and broadcasting began. Donald Johnson made contact with a work in **Poland,** bringing encouragement through the Missionary Board. More was learned about the fifty congregations of the Church of God in **Russia.** A consultation for leaders in the eastern Mediterranean convened in **Cyprus** in September 1980—the first expression of interdependence following the World Conference in June. Delegates strategized regarding evangelism among non-Christians and recognized the need for a place in the area where leaders could be trained. **Egypt** received new missionaries, James and Betty Albrecht, introducing a new era for the church. The Church of God in **Lebanon** had been under fire during five years of civil war. Thirty-five families had lost their source of income. But not one believer was killed, or did one pastor forsake the flock. Now almost all have been rehabilitated and the churches are self-supporting again. During this period of time Ernest and Grace LaFont terminated their services in the eastern Mediterranean.

Further south in **Kenya** Douglas and Ruth Welch terminated their services. His position as coordinator was not refilled. But George and Eva Buck were sent so that George could serve as administrative assistant to the executive secretary of the Church of God. By 1979 the missionaries present in Kenya reorganized so that they could care for missionary problems with which the church did not wish to bother. There was a strong outreach among the Masai in South Kenya. Eugene and Barbara VanAlstyne began service at Kima Theological College. Heidi Froemke went as a nurse to replace Edna Thimes, who retired in 1979. Robert and Evelyn Lindemuth spent two short terms assisting in the business of the church. David and Margaret Montague left the field. Church of God headquarters in **Tanzania** were established in Babati. New missionaries Stanley and Patricia Desjardine were stationed in Arusha, and Sherman and Kay Critser in Mirambo. The Emerald Avenue Church of God in Chicago had made several contacts with a group in **Ghana** and Donald Johnson and Paul Hutchins found this to be a viable work of the Church of God when they made a brief visit.

The movement in **India** remained in a period of growth in Kerala, Orissa, and Meghalaya. An Asian Bible college was opened to train workers to reach the villages in Kerala. Eighty-eight percent of the population of India lives in villages. Self-help projects continued to assist the people and the church. Indian music and the art of meditation enhanced worship services. The church in Meghalaya was longing for another expression of interdependence by joining with the Missionary Board in some missionary outreach into an Asian country. *Kinderhilfswork* from the Movement in Germany was assisting in schools and orphanages in both India and **Bangladesh.** For months the Missionary Board tried to secure visas for Raymond and Nina Martin to enter Bangladesh, but it was unsuccessful. However, more and more people were accepting Christ in non-Christian communities. The ten-year plan was right on target in **Thailand.** The New Life Center was opened in 1975 and the Gospel Training Center in 1976, both in Bangkok. Already young graduates from the training center have successfully established five new churches in the Buriram Province near the Cambodian border. In 1977 Marvin and Karen Helsel were sent to assist in the Bible school. And in 1979 a new work came into being in **Singapore** under the leadership of Neivelle Tan. It was incorporated as Asian Missionary Outreach, with a subtitle of The Church of God in Singapore.

Japan was enjoying the services of several short-term teachers who assisted the church. To show good faith in the reconciliation process in **Korea**, Nathan and Ann Smith were redeployed from Japan, and they were soon joined by David and Greta Reames. Following language study all four were assisting the movement in Korea, which had by then grown to twenty-seven congregations with fifty-five hundred believers. The missionaries in **Hong Kong** were still working on how to establish a Bible study center in a new high-rise apartment complex. The church in **Australia** had been reduced to three congregations. The Missionary Board assumed administrative responsibility by request and the three missionary couples, Kenneth and Sue Jo Good, Andrew and Rebecca New, and Jack and Bonnie Dunn were officially appointed by the Board. As mentioned earlier Aaron and Kathryn Kerr left **Guam** and were replaced by Steve and Maxine Igarta. And finally a new work developed in **Taiwan.** The first congregation, located in Taipei under the leadership of Thomas Lo, came with the Church of God in 1976. The second group, also in Taipei, came to the movement in 1977 under the leadership of Joseph Loh. Now they are hoping for a third congregation in southwest Taiwan.

The Missionary Board commissioned a sizable number of missionaries during its annual meeting in 1980: Will and Patsy Kline to Brazil, Charles and Evelyn Wilson to Kenya, Cova Ricketts (actually a Jamaican trained as a nurse in England) to Kenya, Mark and Sherrie deFelice on short-term assignment to Italy, David and Barbara Miller to Bolivia, and Keith and Gloria Plank to Costa Rica. A number of short-term teachers were also recommended to serve in Asian countries.

After Ninety Years of Missionary Activity

The Church of God reformation is now found in sixty countries with the Missionary Board carrying responsibility in forty-two of them. The sun never sets on Church of God missions! Growth has taken place and is indicative of sustained activity. In 1979 there were 177,736 members in the movement in America (including Canada) and 150,778 members in the sixty other countries. There were 2,308 congregations in America (including Canada) and 1,715 in the other countries. Since there is more rapid growth in the churches in the Third World it is believed that before the end of this present decade there will be more believers in the Movement in other countries than in America. The results in years to come will inevitably be much greater than now anticipated. Why? Because of the partnership now rapidly developing to hasten the bearing of the Good News to the millions in Asian countries who have never heard of God's love for them.

Passports are being issued not only to missionaries of the First World but also to an increasing number of Third

World missionaires. One very recent example is the sending by the Church of God in Meghalaya, India, of two of its members, Leaderwell and Rivulet Pohsgnap, as missionaries to Kenya where he will teach Old Testament in Kima Theological College and she, a nurse, will work in the Kima Maternity Hospital. Exciting opportunities await us just around the future's corner. China is one example. The instiutional church died during the ten-year Cultural Revolution under Mao Tse-tung and his little Red Book. But the resurrection came through the house-church movement involving some one million Christians. This should provide a unique opportunity for our Movement. It would not be the traditional entry of Western missionaries; instead it would happen as a result of Chinese and Southeast Asian Christians entering China as professionals for the purpose of witnessing. However, various forms of partnership will be required to cope adequately.

Unreached people remain a challenge to modern-day apostles from many countries to join together as contemporary pioneers of the Reformation Movement in cross-cultural missionary service. As the church's sons and daughters go out to proclaim Christ as Savior and Lord the statement of the Apostle Paul will continue to be a reality: "All over the world this gospel is producing fruit and growing" (Col. 1:6, NIV). We are indeed on the threshold of entry into an exhilarating missionary era as the Church of God reformation movement enters its second century.

Appendix A
Key to Countries

Antigua	AN	Ireland	IR
Argentina	AR	Italy	IT
Australia	AU	Jamaica	JM
Bangladesh	BA	Japan	JA
Barbados	BR	Kenya	KA
Bermuda	BM	Korea	KO
Bolivia	BO	Lebanon	LB
Brazil	BZ	Mexico	MX
British Guiana	BG	Norway	NO
British Isles	BI	Pakistan	PK
British West Indies	BWI	Panama	PA
Canal Zone	CZ	Peru	PE
China	CH	Puerto Rico	PR
Costa Rica	CR	Russia	RU
Cuba	CU	St. Kitts	SK
Denmark	DN	Scotland	SC
Egypt	EG	Southeast Asia	SA
England	EN	Sweden	SW
Germany	GM	Switzerland	SZ
Grand Cayman	GC	Syria	SY
Greece	GR	Tanzania	TZ
Guam	GU	Thailand	TH
Guyana	GY	Trinidad	TD
Hawaii	HA	Venezuela	VE
Holland	HO	West Indies	WI
Hong Kong	HK		
India	IN		

Missionaries to Countries Outside North America
(As of May 1980)

*Recommended but not commissioned, such as short-term teachers and other workers

ABERNATHY, Amos and Edith (IN: 05-10)
*ABRAMS, Alta (KA: 63-65)
*ACHOR, G. R. (EN: 1893-94)
ACKERMAN, Caroline (KA: 70-78)
ALBRECHT, James and Betty (EG: 78-   )

ALEXANDER, W. G. and Josie (JA: 09-20)
ALLAN, Adam and Mary (SC: 09-18/IR: 18-46)
ALLAN, Naomi (IR: 20-56)
ALLISON, Vernon and Cathy (PA: 79-)
ANDERSON, Edwin and Carol Ann (CR: 67-70)
ANDERSON, William and Beatrice (KA: 67-71)
ANDREWS, Harold and Ann (JM & GC: 24-41)
ARBEITER, Karl and Auguste (SZ: 12-20)
*AXUP, E. J. (EN: 08-10)

BAILEY, George and Mrs. (IN: 04-05)
BAILEY, Homer and Vivian (KA: 37-46)
BAILEY, William J. and Lilly (KA: 24-34)
BAKER, Mabel (KA: 14-53)
*BALES, Wilma Dean (KA: 67-70)
BANNISTER, Gladys *(KA: 65-68) (KA: 68-70)
BARBER, Proctor and Virginia (HA: 63-67)
*BARKMAN, William and Glynda (JA: 80-)
BARNETTE, Cornelia (KA: 67-73)
*BARTON, Bernard and Cheryl (JA: 76-79)
BARWICK, Burd (IN: 22-26)
BEACH, Glenn and Alice (IN: 60-63)
BEATY, Deloris (KA: 59-68)
BEATY, Esther (KA: 62-66)
BENTLEY, Albert and Irene (MX: 58-59, 68-73/BZ & AR: 73-75)
BENTLEY, Patricia (JA: 69-72)
BETTS, Samuel and Jane (KA: 58-63)
BILLINGS, Lovena (CH: 46-49/HK: 49-) (Married P.K. Jenkins
1949) (Independent 49-71)
BLASKOWSKY, Emilia (GC: 49-52/BR: 52-54/JM: 57/TD: 57-67)
(Married William Fleenor 1955)
BLEILER, E. L. and Martha (IN: 26-32)
*BLOCHER, Bert and Jeanne (JA: 77-80/KO: 80-)
*BLORE, F. C. and Eskell (IR: 24-26)
BLUMENBERG, Richard and Carol (TZ: 76-77)
BOLITHO, Axchie (JA: 21-26)
BOLLMEYER, Rosa (KA: 57-60)
BORDEN, Oscar and Norma (KA: 64-76)
BRAILLIER, Calvin and Martha (KA: 50-62)
BREWSTER, E. G. and Elizabeth (PA: 08-15 (Elizabeth, SK: 34-40)
BROOKOVER, W. L. and Opal (BWI: 16-38) (Opal died in 1934)
BROOKS, H. A. (IN: 07-08/BI: 19-20)
BRUCE, Roger and Margaret (KA: 69-73)
BRYANT, Leroy (BR: 16-19)
BUCK, George and Eva (JM: 67-71/TD: 71-72/KA: 75-)
BUETTNER, Milton and Eleanor (CH: 46-50)

*BURNS, Glenn and Francine (KA: 73-77)
 BUSCH, Edgar and Inez (GC: 47-48/HA: 63)
 BUTZ, Paul and Mary (PE: 58-   ) (Independent 58-70) (Mary died in 1977)

 CALDWELL, Maurice and Dondeena (MX: 54-62, 66-69/BZ: 70-76)
*CALDWELL, Timothy and Robin (JA: 78-   )
 CARVER, Earl and Freda (CU: 52-60/PR: 66-79)
 CASEY, Brice and Nancy (HA: 68-72)
 CHAMBERS, Zuda Lee (JA: 17-22)
 CHEATHAM, William and Anna (BI: 06-15)
 CHEW, Byron and Zella (BWI: 28-41)
 CHIN, Raymond and Noreen (BM: 70-75)
 CLARK, Robert and Frances (PK: 47-61)
 COLLINS, Ralph and Mary (PA: 45-46)
 CONKIS, William and Mrs. (EG: 33-36)
 COOLIDGE, Ralph and Ruth (TD: 46-56/GY 64-70)
 COPLIN, George and Maude (TD: 11-14/BR: 16-19)
 CRIPPEN, David and Karen (KA: 67-76)
 CRITSER, Sherman and Kay (TZ: 79-   )
 CROSE, John and Pearl (JA: 20-22/SY: 23-49/KO: 55-56/HA: 58-60)
 CROSE, Kenneth and Mabel (EG: 47-48)
 CROSE, Lester and Ruthe (LB & SY: 33-41/BR & TD: 41-45/LB & SY: 45-50/EG: 50-54)
*CUMMINS, Kay (KA: 69-75) (TZ: 79-   ) (Married Sherman Critser 1978)

 DALLAS, Daniel and Aleta (GR: 58-62)
 DALLAS, George and Mrs. (EG: 33-38)
 DAUGHERTY, John (EN: 1893-95)
*DAVIS, Doris (CU: 47-48)
 DAVIS, Willa (SK: 48-50)
 DAZLEY, Janet (KA: 68-72)
 DEAN, Alva and Bernadean (JM: 72-75)
*deFELICE, Mark and Sherrie (IT: 80-   )
 DEITZ, Margaret (KA: 70-74)
 DESJARDINE, Stanley and Patricia (TZ: 77-   )
 DETWILER, Darlene (KA: 60-70, 73-74, 76-77)
 DIEZEL, Katie (BR & TD: 13-14)
 DOEBERT, Otto and Gertrude (GM: 07-13/SZ & GM & RU: 14-26)
 DONOHEW, Wick and Grace (GM: 46-51/KA: 51-62)
*DORTMUND, Janet (JA: 77-79)
 DUNCAN, Noah and Myrtle (TD: 06, 08, 19-20)
*DUNHAM, Barbara (KA: 67-70)
 DUNN, Jack and Bonnie (AU: 76-   )

EBEL, William and Anna (GM & RU: 10-19)
*EDWARDS, Robert and Janet (KA: 67-69) (TZ: 72-)
EIKAMP, Arthur and Norma (JA: 49-)
ELLIOT, B. F. (MX: 1891-1910)
ENGST, Irene (KA: 47-74)
ERICKSON, Gerald and Helen (GC: 45-47)
EVANS, Karen (JA: 65-69)

FAIR, James and Esther (DN: 57-62)
FARAG, Nasser and Marilyn (KA: 73-78/MX: 79-)
FARMER, Ralph and Gertrude (TZ: 59-73) (Independent 59-68)
*FATZINGER, Steve and Connie (TD: 76-77)
FEHR, Eugene and Margaret (IN: 65-70/TD: 74-78/BR: 78-)
FIRESTONE, Homer and Elvira (BO: 74-)
FIRESTONE, Ronald and Violet (BO: 74-78)
FISCUS, Olive (KA: 56-58/GR: 63-68) (Married Savas Joannides 1958)
FISHER, Ruth (KA: 22-40) (Married James Murrary 1925)
FLEENOR, William and Vada (SY: 30-32/EG: 32-34, 45-46, 51-56/JM: 57/TD: 57-67) (Vada died 1950) (Married Emilia Blaskowsky 1955)
FLEWELLEN, Carl and Mayme (BM: 64-70)
FLORA, Dean and Nina (PA: 59-75)
FORSBERG, Carl and Laura (SW & DN: 14-18/SW: 20-27)
FRASER, Wilhelmina (AN: 40/SK: 41-69)
FROEMKE, Heidi (KA: 78-)
*FULLER, Douglas and Dontie (KA: 72-74)

*GARD, Diana (KA: 69)
GAULKE, David and Elsie (CH: 46-50/KA: 53-58)
GEIWITZ, George and Marie (MX: 69-77)
GLASSMAN, Caroline (GC: 42-51)
GLOVER, Clarence and Bernice (SK: 79-)
GOENS, Donald and Arlene (JA: 54-63)
GONZALES, Luz and Carol (MX: 67-70/CR: 70-74)
GOOD, Kenneth and Sue Jo (KO: 61-66/JM: 67-70/AU: 72-) (Independent 72-77)
GOODRICK, Lew and Wanda (KA: 57-66)
GOODWIN, Eva (IN: 20-26)
GREER, Hester (CU: 34-46)

HABEL, Dennis and Elaine (KA: 65-75)
HALE, Alice (IN: 07-12)
HALL, Jewell (KA: 44-72)
HANSEN, Hjalmer (NO & DN: 20-23)
HANSEN, Lydia (KA: 49-73)
*HARTING Clyde and Rowena (KA: 65-69)
HASTINGS, Raymond and Elna Mae (GC: 51-54/JM: 58-60/BG: 60-

62/MX: 62-65)
HATCH, J. D. (JA: 09-16)
HEHR, Elsie (GC: 44-47)
HEINLY, Candace (KA: 62-71)
HEINLY, Floyd and Maude (IN: 18-49)
HELSEL, Marvin and Karen (TH: 77-   )
*HENRY, W. J. (EN: 1892)
HIGH, Ellen (IN: 37-58)
HILL, Max and Neva (GC: 49-50)
HINES, Sophia (MX: 01-02)
HITTLE, Bessie (SY: 12-14)
HOFFMAN, Stanley and Marion (TZ: 59-75/KA: 75-77) (Independent 59-68)
HOLLANDER, Emil (SY: 23-24)
HOOGEVEEN, Larry and Verna (KA: 73-75)
HOOPS, Roy and Magaline (KA: 59-69/TZ: 71-   ) (Independent 59-63)
HOWLAND, Ron and Marcia (BR: 67-70)
HUBER, Merlene (KA: 55-65)
*HUMES, Mary (KA: 67-69)
HUNNEX, Charles and Annabel (CH: 10-49)
HUNNEX, William and Gloria (CH: 09-21)
HUTCHINS, Paul and Nova (PK: 59-70)
HUTTON, Howard and Mary (KA: 69-71)

IGARTA, Steve and Maxine (GU: 78-   )
IKAST, Jens and Cora (DN: 23-36, 46-49)
*IRWIN, Randy and Sandra (JA: 78-   )
ISENHART, Mae (IN: 18-21)

JANES, L. Y. (JM & CZ: 11-13)
JARVIS, Marie (IN: 05-06)
JARVIS, Robert and Laura (IN: 03-16) (Laura died 1908) (Married Lottie Theobald 1910 who died 1914)
JEFFCOAT, Ethel (GC: 50-52)
JENKINS, P. K. and Lovena (HK: 49-   ) (Independent 49-71)
JOANNIDES, Savas and Olive (GR: 63-68)
JOHNSON, Dewey and Thelma (GC: 63-70, 76-79)
JOHNSON, Donald and Betty Jo (BG: 55-56/TD 56-61)
JOHNSON, Harold and Barbara (JM: 64-66)
*JOHNSON, John and Gwen (KO: 80-   )
JOHNSON, Morris (DN: 13-15)
JOHNSON, Sidney and Jean (IN: 55-72/SA: 73-   )
JOINER, Samuel and Mrs. (KA: 22-23)
JONES, Kenneth and Elizabeth (JM: 60, 62)

KANT, Willi and Esther (BZ: 77-   )
KARDATZKE, Carl and Eva (KA: 55-56)

KERR, Aaron and Kathryn (BWI: 49-51/IN: 51-55/BG: 59-61/KA: 70-76/GU: 76-78/MX: 79-   )
KILMER, Jean and Ruth (EG: 54-56/KA: 57/EG: 57-62)
*KING, Linda (KA: 68-70)
 KINION, Warren and Devie (MX: 75-78)
 KINLEY, Philip and Phyllis (JA: 55-   )
*KINNER, Michael and Debbie (JA: 76-78)
 KIRKPATRICK, Paul and Noreda (GY: 70-71/PE: 72-74)
*KLEINHENN, Lois (JA: 72-75)
 KLINE, William and Patricia (BZ: 80-   )
 KLUGE, Arthur and Mary (GC: 54-63)
 KNUDSEN, J. G. and Anna (DN: 19-25)
 KONSTANTOPOULOS, Bill and Kay (PR: 76-78/AR: 78-   )
 KRAFT, Susie (IN: 03-11)
 KRAMER, H. C. and Gertrude (KA: 12-27)
 KRETLOW, Orlo and Carol (JA: 64-   )
 KREUTZ, Karl and Hazel (CH: 23-27)
*KRIEBEL, James (BI: 1893)

 LaFOE, Freda (JA: 60-72)
 LaFONT, Ernest and Grace (CZ: 47-51/EG: 52-71/LB: 72-76)
 LaFONT, Frauk and Margaret (KA: 46-73)
 LaFONT, Harold and Donna (KA: 60-65)
 LAMBE, Vernon and Ruth Ann (BM: 75-   )
 LATHAM, E. L. (CZ: 15-18)
 LAUGHLIN, Nellie (SY: 13-28/EG: 37-42)
 LEHMANN, Walter and Margaret (TD: 61-64)
 LEHMER, Lima (KA: 36-62, 66-70) (Married Edgar Williams 1966)
*LIMBACH, Joyce (PE: 70-78)
 LINAMEN, Janice (KA: 68-75)
 LINDEMUTH, Robert and Evelyn (KA: 74-76, 78-79)
 LINN, Otto (SW & DN: 23-25)
 LITTLE, Ralph and Helen (JM: 60-69)
 LIVINGSTON, David and Joan (KA: 56-67)
*LIVINGSTON, Nannie (JM: 09-10)
 LIVINGSTON, William and Hope (BWI & PA: 46-60)
 LUDWIG, John and Twyla (KA: 27-49)
 LUNN, Lida (DN & SW: 10)

 MAIDEN, Daisy (CH: 16-49)
 MAIDEN, Victor and Florence (IN: 06-08)
*MALONE, Edith (GC: 46-48)
*MARTIN, George and Mrs. (EN & SC: 1898)
 MARTIN, Vera (KA: 54-69)
 MARTIN, Ray and Nina (BA: 80-   )
 MASSEY, James Earl and Gwendolyn (JM: 64-66)

MATTOX, Joseph and Elva (PR: 78-)
MAURER, Ronald and Jacqueline (JA: 74-)
MAY, Edward and Anna (AU: 17-26)
McCRACKEN, Thomas and Jean (TD: 67-74/BZ: 74-)
McCRIE, Josephine (IN: 04-46) (Married George Tasker 1941)
*McCURDY, Robert (KA: 68)
McDILDA, Hazel (KA: 51-61)
MEIER, David and Lillian (BZ: 35-41/AR: 41-47/BZ: 47-76) (David died 1965) (Sponsored by York, Nebraska, 48-60)
MILLER, Adam and Grace (JA: 22-27)
MILLER, David and Barbara (BO: 80-)
MILLER, Oakley and Veryl (TD: 52-67)
*MITSCHELEN, David (JA: 72-74)
MONTAGUE, David and Margaret (KA: 70-78)
MOORS, Mona (IN: 22-55) (Married George Tasker 1955)
MORGAN, Clifton and Mary (IN: 60-70)
MORGAN, Robert and Dorothy (BR: 53-55/TD: 55-56)
MOTTINGER, William and Betty (BZ: 72-)
MURRAY, James and Ruth (KA: 21-40) (Married Ruth Fisher 1925)

NACHTIGALL, Harry and Jene (KA: 64-68/CR: 70-71/PA: 71-72/CR: 72-78)
NEFF, Thaddeus and Katrina (IN: 06-11/BWI: 12-22/EG: 23-51) (Married Katrina Burgess 1912)
*NEILS, C. G. (GR: 06)
*NELSON, Thomas (DN: 1895)
*NEVIN, Wilford and Vernie (JA: 72-73, 76-78)
NEW, Andrew and Rebecca (AU: 75-) (Independent 75-77)
*NEWBERRY, Gene and Agnes (KA: 73-74)
NICHOLS, Evalyn (IN: 04-64 (Married J. J. M. Roy 1908) (Roy died 1960)

OLDHAM, Edward and Meriam (BG: 62-65)
OLSEN, Lars and Ellen (DN: 27-40/BR: 43-46/SW: 47-49/DN: 49-57)
OLSON, George and Nellie (JM: 07-54)
OLSON, Mary (JM: 40-63)
*ORR, C. E. (TD & JM: 06-07/BI: 13-14)
*OSGOOD, Dorothy (JA: 80-)

PALMER, Ellsworth and Hilaria (CU: 50-61)
PARNELL, Charles (IN: 01-08)
PATTERSON, D. W. and Mae (MX: 08-10)
PETERSON, L. P. and Alexina (SW: 25-30)
PHELPS, Vivian (GC: 55-58/KA: 59-68)
PICKENS, Thomas and Dorothy (JM: 61-67/EN: 67-72)

PLANK, Keith and Gloria (CR: 58-64, 80-   )
PORTER, Ida (CH: 19-20)
PRUITT, Helen (TD: 53-54)
PYE, George and Mrs. (TD: 06-08)

*RAILEY, Robert (KA: 66-69)
RATHER, Archie and Rebecca (TD: 11-15/JM: 19-28/BR: 34-37/PA: 37-53) (Married Rebecca Byrum 1912)
RATZLAFF, Leslie and Nina (GC: 41-46/JM: 46-56)
*RAWLINGS, Almeda (GC: 46-48)
REAMES, David and Greta *(JA: 74-77) (KO: 79-   )
REARDON, E. A. (EG: 07-08)
*REED, Alan and Diane (JA: 80-   )
REEDY, Edward and Mrs. (TD: 11-14)
REINHOLZ, Carlton and Patricia (GC: 58-62)
RENBECK, Mary (DN: 12-15)
RENBECK, Nels and Edel (DN: 09-34)
RENZ, Russell and Velma (KA: 51-52)
RICE, Lowell and Linda *(KA: 70-72) (KA: 76-   )
RICHARDSON, Harley and Bonnie (KA: 58-60)
RICKETTS, Cova (KA: 80-   )
*RIGEL, James and Cheryl (JA: 72-74)
RIGGLE, H. M. and Minnie (SY: 21-23)
RING, Otto and Eunice (SW: 37-40)
ROARK, Warren and Alvina (BR: 26-28)
*ROBERTS, Pamela (KA: 69-71, 72-74)
ROBINSON, Simon and Mae (KA: 62-70/TZ: 70-71)
RODRIGUEZ, Joseph and Grace (CU: 43-46)
ROGERS, Sidney and Fern (KA: 34-44)
ROOT, LaVern and Darlene (BR: 64-67)
ROYSTER, James and Elizabeth (IN: 60-62/EG: 62-64/KA: 64-65)
*RUPERT, John and Mrs. (EN: 1892-93)
RYAN, Jane (KA: 52-56, 58-63) (Married Samuel Betts 1956)
RYDER, Wilma (GC: 44-45)

*SALTZMANN, Paul (KA: 66-68)
SANDERSON, Ruth (KA: 46-58)
SCHIECK, Gordon and Wilhelmina (IN: 55-67)
SCHNEIDER, Velma (KA: 52-68)
SCHWIEGER, Ruben C. and Nora (KA: 47-67)
SCHWIEGER, Ruben D. and Virginia (KA: 63-68)
SHARP, James and Dorothy (KA: 61-   )
SHAW, Frank and Susan (BWI: 11-17, 20-34)
SHIFFLER, Andrew (IN: 01-26)
*SHOFFNER, Lena (EN: 1893-95)
SHOTTON, Ronald and Ruth (MX: 63-75/PA: 76-79)

SHULTZ, Clair and Retha (TD: 45-58/JM: 58-62/KA: 62-70)
SIMPSON, James and Sibyl (EG: 61-64)
SKAGGS, Wilbur and Evelyn (EG: 45-58)
SMITH, F. G. and Birdie (SY: 12-14)
SMITH, Hermand and Lavera (TD: 43-45/KA: 46-50/ BG: 51-59)
SMITH, Nathan and Ann (JA: 51-77/KO: 78-   )
SMITH, Richard and Donna (KA: 57-62)
SPIRES, Joseph and Ramona (PK: 61-65)
SPRINGER, Robert and Mrs. (RU & SZ: 12-17)
STEERS, Bertram and Marian (IN: 65-68) (Marian died 1965)
*STEGMAN, Clara (RU: 08-09)
STEIMLA, Frank and Jennie (TD: 16-20/JM: 24-43)
STEPHENSON, Manasseh and Gretchen (CU: 46-50)
STEWART, Faith (IN: 13-26/CU: 30-58) (Independent 30-58)
STRAWN, James (IN: 07)
STRENGER, Frieda (KA: 35-46)
STRUTHERS, Charles and Florence (JM: 46-58)
*STULL, Steven and Janet (JA: 72-74)
SUSAG, S. O. (DN & SW: 11-37)
SWEENY, Naomi (KA: 55-60)

TALLEN, James and Frances (BR: 14-16)
TASKER, George and Minnie (IN: 12-46) (Minnie died 1940) (Married Josephine McCrie 1941) (Josephine died 1954) (Married Mona Moors 1955)
*TEFFT, Ruthann (KA: 69-71, 74-75)
THEOBALD, Lottie (IN: 07-14) (Married Robert Jarvis 1910)
THIMES, Edna (KA: 60-79)
TIESEL, Walter and Margaret (BR: 47-63/TD: 64-66)
*TITLEY, William (BI: 07-08)
*TUFTS, Gorham (IN: 1897, 1905)
 TURNER, Arthenia (KA: 61-66, 68-71)
 TURNER, Allen and Clovis (SK: 69-76)

*UPCHURCH, Carol (KA: 64-67)

 VAN ALSTYNE, Eugene and Barbara (KA: 77-   )
 VAN DER BREGGAN, Aletta (HO: 49-53)
 VAN DE VEUR, Nick and Nina (HA: 60-62)
 VAZQUEZ, Amelia Valdez (MX: 71-   )
 VIELGUTH, George (GM & SZ & RU: 01-13)
*VON BARGEN, Daniel (KA: 67-69)

 WALLACE, Mamie (IN: 21-27)
 WALLS, Thomas and Mary Lou (VE: 78-   )
*WARD, Sheryl (KA: 67-69)

WATSON, Belle (CH: 16-37)
WELCH, Douglas and Ruth (KA: 60-75)
*WIEBE, Roger and Fern (JA: 79-   )
WILLARD, Ethel (HK: 69-   )
WILLIAMS, Edgar and Mildred (CH: 47-49/JM: 53-58/KA: 66-70)
(Mildred died 1965) (Married Lima Lehmer 1966)
WILSON, Charles and Evelyn (KA: 80-   )
WINTERS, Pina (CH: 10-14)
WOODS, Vivian (KA: 70-75)
WOODSOME, Richard and Georgia (KA: 62-68)

*YODER, Harold and Velma (PE: 72-73)
*YODER, Lydia (TD: 06-08)
YOUNG, Edith (JM: 27-64)
YUTZY, James and Glenna (KA: 52-63)

ZAUGG, Ira (IN: 06-12)
ZAZANIS, Nicholas and Rose (EG: 28-33, 38-42/GR: 46-58)
ZORETIC, Paul and Mickey (PE: 76-79/PR: 79-   )

Apologies for any omissions or errors.

Appendix B
Church of God Missionary Publications

BOOKS AND BOOKLETS

Baker, Mabel. *Fifty Years in Kenya.* 1955.

Bolitho, Axchie A. *Bridging the Deeps in Syria.* Anderson, Indiana: Missionary Board of the Church of God, 1956.

Bolitho, Axchie A. *The Church of God in British Guiana.* Anderson, Indiana: Missionary Board of the Church of God, 1956.

Bolitho, Axchie A. *The Church of God in Japan.* Anderson, Indiana: Missionary Board of the Church of God, 1957.

Bolitho, Axchie A. *In His Glad Service.* Anderson, Indiana: Missionary Board of the Church of God.

Bolitho, Axchie A. *Arthur and Norma Eikamp, Japan.* Anderson, Indiana: Missionary Board of the Church of God, 1956.

Bolitho, Axchie A. *Introducing Calvin and Martha Lee Brallier, Kenya Colony, B.E.A.* Anderson, Indiana: Missionary Board of the Church of God, 1956.

Bolitho, Axchie A. *Introducing Herman and Lavera Smith, British Guiana.* Anderson, Indiana: Missionary Board of the Church of God, 1956.

Bolitho, Axchie A. *Introducing Wick M. and Grace Donohew.* Anderson, Indiana: Missionary Board of the Church of God, 1959.

Bolitho, Axchie A. *The Miracle of Kima.* Anderson, Indiana: Missionary Board of the Church of God, 1944.

Bolitho, Axchie A. *This Is Our Kenya.* Anderson, Indiana: Missionary Board of the Church of God.

Bolitho, Axchie A. *Making an Indian Community Christian.* Anderson, Indiana: Missionary Board of the Church of God.

Bolitho, Axchie A. *Christ Serves in Kenya.* Anderson, Indiana: Missionary Board of the Church of God, 1940.

Bolitho, Axchie A. *Introducing Lima Valera Lehmer.* Anderson, Indiana: Missionary Board of the Church of God, 1956.

Butz, Mary. *The First Ten Years.* 1968.

Byrum, E. E. *Travels and Experiences in Other Lands.* Moundsville, West Virginia: Gospel Trumpet Company, 1905.

Clark, Robert H. *In East Pakistan.* Anderson, Indiana: Missionary Board of the Church of God.

Clark, Robert H. *What Do Ye . . . More Than Others; India.* Anderson, Indiana: Missionary Board of the Church of God.

Clear, Evelyn, editor. *50th Anniversary, Missionary Board of the Church of God.* Anderson, Indiana: Missionary Board of the Church of God, 1959.

Dallas, Daniel George. *Community Development and the Organization of the Village of Mahala in Southern Greece.*

Donohew, Grace. *How Missionaries Work.* Anderson, Indiana: Missionary Board of the Church of God.

Elliott, Benjamin F. *Experiences in the Gospel Work in Lower California, Mexico,* 1906.

Firestone, Elvira. *Gathering Sheaves.* Omer F. Witt, Publisher.

268

Gaulke, David W. *Kenya Mission, Medical Department, 1955-1956.*

Gaulke, David W. *Your Hospital at Work.* Anderson, Indiana: Missionary Board of the Church of God.

Gray, Albert F. *Church of God Missions Abroad.* Anderson, Indiana: Missionary Board of the Church of God, 1929.

Greer, Hester. *Life and Work of Hester Greer,* 1974

Henry, Grace G. *Highways and Hedges, Or the Life of E. Faith Stewart.* Mentone, Indiana: Country Print Shop.

High, Ellen, *India Needs Christ.* Anderson, Indiana: Missionary Board of the Church of God, 1948.

Khan, A. D. *India's Millions.* Anderson, Indiana: Gospel Trumpet Company, 1903.

Khan, A. D. *From Darkness to Light: The Testimony of A. D. Khan.* Anderson, Indiana, Board of Christian Education, 1954.

Krenz, Willi, editor. *The Church of God in Europe 1972/73.* Essen, West Germany: Wickenburg Press, 1973.

Lehmer, Lima V. *The Ebony Stork.* Anderson, Indiana: Missionary Board of the Church of God.

Lehmer, Lima V. *Hospital Work in Kenya Colony.* Anderson, Indiana: Missionary Board of the Church of God.

Ludwig, Charles S. *Mama Was a Missionary.* Anderson, Indiana: Warner Press, 1963.

Ludwig, Twyla I. *Polished Pillars,* 1940.

Ludwig, Twyla I. *Watching the Cooking Pot,* 1948.

Ludwig, Twyla I. *What Hath God Wrought.*

Maiden, Daisy V. *From Out of China.* Anderson, Indiana: Missionary Board of the Church of God.

Marshall, Evans, editor. *Memories of Wilhelmina Fraser.* Shining Light Survey Press, 1970

Miller, Adam W. *We Build Again in Japan.* Anderson, Indiana: Missionary Board of the Church of God, 1949.

Neal & Bolitho. *Madam President.* Anderson, Indiana: Gospel Trumpet Company, 1951.

Neff, Thaddeus. *Forty Years of Missionary Service.* Anderson, Indiana, 1946.

Neff, Thaddeus. *Our Missionaries.* Anderson, Indiana: Commercial Service, 1956.

Olson, George W. *Building with Christ in Jamaica.* Anderson, Indiana: Missionary Board of the Church of God, 1942.

Philip, P. J. *Our South India Field.* Anderson, Indiana: Missionary Board of the Church of God.

Riggle, H. M. *Pioneer Evangelism.* Anderson, Indiana: Gospel Trumpet Company, 1924.

Schwieger, Ruben C. *Paths for God*. Kisumu, Kenya: National Printing Press.

Shultz, Clair W. *Faith That Moves Mountains*. Anderson, Indiana: Missionary Board of the Church of God.

Shultz, David C. *Church of God Missions: The First 100 Years*. Anderson, Indiana: Missionary Board of the Church of God, 1980.

Skaggs, Wilbur. *Advance in Egpyt*. Anderson, Indiana: Missionary Board of the Church of God.

Smith, F. G. *Look on the Fields*. Anderson, Indiana: Missionary Board of the Church of God, 1920.

Smith, F. G. *Missionary Journeys through Bible Lands*. Anderson, Indiana: Gospel Trumpet Company, 1915.

Smith, James Edgar. *The Missionary Church, What Is It?* Anderson, Indiana: Missionary Board of the Church of God.

Smith, James Edgar. *These Went before Us*. Anderson, Indiana: Missionary Board of the Church of God.

Smith, James Edgar. *You Can Be a Missionary Anywhere on Earth*. Anderson, Indiana: Mid-Century Evangelistic Advance.

Stewart, Etta Faith. *The Children of the World Are His*, 1944.

Stewart, Etta Faith. *The Children's Homes, Los Pinos: A Report of Faith Mission Work in Cuba*, 1953.

Swart, Carl and Lova. *The Boomerang of Faith*. Camrose, Alberta, Canada: Gospel Contact Press, 1975.

MAGAZINES

Missionary Herald, 1910-1913 (Merged with *Gospel Trumpet* in March 1913)
Missionary Newsletter, 1924-1930
Pioneer, 1934-1939.
Missionary Outlook, 1939-1951
Friends of Missions, 1936-1951
Church of God Missions Magazine, 1951-
Gospel Trumpet-Vital Christianity, Missionary articles & reports

THESES & DISSERTATIONS

Albrecht, James. *Development towards a Self-Reliant Church of God in Egypt through Church Growth Principles*. 1978.

Carver, E. Earl. *Showcase for God: A Study of Evangelical Church Growth in Puerto Rico*. 1972.

Carver, Robert H. *Study of Religious Customs and Practices of the Rajbanshis of North Bengal*. 1969.

Cumberbatch, Carlton. *The Role of Leadership Training in the Development of the Church of God in the English-speaking Caribbean*. 1976.

Farag, Nasser. *Pastoral Care for Families* (A Course for Ministers in the Church of God in Kenya). 1979.

Hook, Edward. *A Historical Survey of the Missionary Work of the Church of God*. 1956.

McCracken, Jean. *Development of the Church of God in Brazil: Integration of Urban Migrants into an Ethnic Church*. 1979.

Oldham, Edward. *A Manual for a Training Program for Ministers in the Church of God in Guyana.* 1977.

Pohsngap, Leaderwell. *A Study of the Administrative Structure of the Church of God in Meghalaya.* 1979.

Sharp, James. *Toward an Evaluation of Pastoral Training in the Church of God of East Africa (Kenya).* 1977.

Sohkhia, Borman Roy. *A Critical Evaluation of the Growth of the Church of God in Meghalaya.* 1979.